110
EASY-TO-MAKE
WOODWORKING
PROJECTS

Combining books *Woodworking Projects I* and *Woodworking Projects II*

WINGS BOOKS
New York • Avenel, New Jersey

This edition contains the complete and unabridged texts of the
original editions.

This omnibus was originally published in separate volumes under the
titles:

Woodworking Projects I, copyright © 1984 by Shopsmith, Inc.
Woodworking Projects II, copyright © 1985 by Shopsmith, Inc.

This 1993 edition is published by Wings Books,
distributed by Outlet Book Company, Inc., a Random House Company,
40 Engelhard Avenue, Avenel, New Jersey 07001,
by arrangement with Rodale Press, Inc.

Random House
New York · Toronto · London · Sydney · Auckland

Printed and bound in the United States of America

Library of Congress Cataloging-in-Publication Data

ISBN 0-517-09300-6

8 7 6 5 4 3 2 1

Contents

Wood Working Projects I

ACCESSORIES

KITCHEN PROJECTS

TOYS

Woodworking Projects II

FURNITURE

ACCESSORIES

HOME IMPROVEMENT

WOODWORKING PROJECTS I

60 Easy-to-Make Projects from HANDS ON Magazine

Preface

This book contains sixty woodworking project plans from back issues of *HANDS ON,* The Home Workshop Magazine published by Shopsmith, Inc. These easy-to-make wooden projects are sure to provide any woodworker, from beginner to expert, with hours of fun and enjoyment in the shop. Many of the projects are ideal gifts for friends or family, and they're suitable for most any occasion—Christmas, birthdays, weddings, etc.

These projects were designed to be completed in a short amount of time using the Shopsmith Mark V and accessories; however, most of the projects can be built using a variety of hand and power tools. An overarm pin router is required to build several of the projects, and these are designated with the symbol ▨ . Special woodworking techniques have been referred to in *Power Tool Woodworking for Everyone* by R.J. De-Cristoforo, Reston Publishing Company.

Many thanks go out to *HANDS ON* readers who have contributed their project ideas to the magazine over the years. Over a third of the projects in this book were contributed by these readers, and their projects have provided hours of enjoyment for other woodworkers.

A final note: As with all woodworking endeavors, always keep safety your top priority. And before starting any of the projects in this book (or any woodworking project for that matter), be sure to read through the entire plan first before making any cuts.

Many thanks to the following *HANDS ON* readers who contributed to this book: DANIEL AGUIAR, JEAN BUTLER, DOUG ELLIS, JACK FISHER, JIMMIE FREEMAN, KENNY GREINER, VAL HAFNER, ROGER HAVERLOCK, GARY HAVERMAN, DAVID HEMBERGER, RICHARD HOLMES, ROBERT LEE, DORIS K. LORENZ, W. C. MADDEN, ROBERT MILLER, GILBERT OLSEN, LARRY PEABODY, ED PETERSON, DALE ROESCH, PHIL ROSILE, JOHN TRAUB, BASIL WENTWORTH, KENNETH YEARWOOD, and VERNON YOUNG.

Accessories

Because wood has a natural beauty all its own, items made from wood enhance any room in any home. Woodworking projects take on even more meaning when a project is combined with a particular function, such as candle sconces that add to the decor or a chess set that provides entertainment. In this section there are over fifteen projects that are sure to bring delight to any woodworker...and provide enjoyment for the entire family.

THE QUICKEST WAY TO
MAKE GIFTS THAT PLEASE

From *HANDS ON* Nov/Dec 82

by Paul Lucas

"Ahh! Done—and with time to spare! This year's Christmas presents were a pleasure, especially since I was able to get them done early."

These were my thoughts one evening last year as I paused to turn out my shop lights. Knowing I was an amateur woodworker, each of my four aunts had wanted me to make her something out of wood.

All of my aunts are great letter writers, so I decided on a useful gift—a letter box for each aunt. Now the gifts sat in a neat row on my workbench—finished with lots of time to spare before they were to be wrapped in colorful Christmas paper.

It wasn't always this way. I used to find myself scurrying to finish my presents during those last few hours of Christmas Eve!

But throughout the years, I've discovered a few secrets. I know that gift making can be even more enjoyable if you realize one important fact—it's easier and quicker to make duplicates of a gift than it is to make several different ones.

In my small shop, I find that in addition to my woodworking tools, there are actually six techniques I use that save me time, money and make my woodworking easier.

Before making duplicate gifts, there are a couple of ground rules I follow. First, I try to keep my shop organized and uncluttered. Tools, fasteners, glue, and other shop items should all be stored in their proper place. I spend my time *using* the tools, not looking for them. Be-sides being safer, a neatly arranged shop allows me to do woodworking, rather than tool-searching.

After I've decided on my project, I make a master pattern. I take time to measure precisely and cut carefully, but I only do this step once. Making one master pattern eliminates the time-consuming steps of laying out and measuring each piece separately.

When I'm making duplicate gifts, I don't make each one individually from start to finish. Rather, I cut the parts for all gifts at the same time using the same setup and proceed in sequence. For example, I band-saw all the pieces for the gifts at the same time. Then, I sand all the pieces, and so on. Cutting down on my setup time actually gives me more productive hours in the shop. By completing one operation for all the pieces during the same set-up, I can easily make the parts to all the gifts in just a little more time than it takes me to make one.

So far, I've laid the groundwork, but what are those other secrets I use? The ones I've chosen to discuss with you here have been most helpful when making duplicate gift projects.

Most of my projects require stock less than 3/4" thick. When I need thin stock, I resaw my lumber. Resawing is a bandsaw operation that makes thin boards out of thick ones (see *Power Tool Woodworking for Everyone*). If you resaw wide boards (4" to 6"), use a wide miter gauge extension.

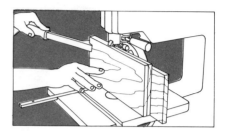

When resawing, use a miter gauge extension and remember it must be parallel to the 1/2" blade. Always use a push stick for the last few inches of the cut.

Resawing also saves me money. Creating two pieces of 5/16" stock from a 3/4" thick board gives me twice the lumber to duplicate pieces. I get two pieces of usable lumber for the price of one.

Pad sawing is another technique that increases my productivity. I stack two or more boards on top of each other. I then tape them together using masking or double-faced carpet tape. After I trace the pattern on the top board, I bandsaw all the taped pieces at once (see *Power Tool Woodworking for Everyone*). I make my cut slightly outside the pattern line so I can sand the pieces to their finished dimension. Pad sawing is much faster than bandsawing each piece separately.

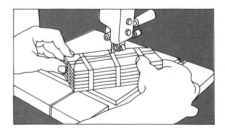

Stack several pieces of thin stock and tape them together. Then, pad saw them as one board.

Several of my small projects call for cutting tapers. To do this I use a fixed taper jig.

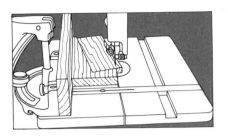

Using a taper jig, you can cut duplicate tapers without measuring each board.

This jig has one straight side for riding the rip fence and a slanted side with a heel to gauge the taper. By using this jig, I can duplicate the tapers accurately from one piece to another without measuring each piece (see *Power Tool Woodworking for Everyone*).

Belt and disc sanders are great for sanding flat surfaces or corners, but what about concave curves? My answer is to use the drum sander. But freehand drum sanding does not give me the accuracy I need. My drum sanding jig gives me this accuracy when I sand curves. The drum sanding jig works on the pin routing principle. The pin is the same diameter as the sanding drum and slightly less than my master pattern.

First, I tape the sawed workpiece to my pattern, using double-faced carpet tape. Then, I place the pattern against the drum sanding pin. The template (my pattern) rides on the drum sanding pin while the rotating drum removes exactly the correct amount of stock. Result? An exact duplicate of the pattern.

Use the drum sanding jig along with your master pattern to accurately sand curves.

Besides cutting and sanding, drilling is another operation that can be streamlined. When I need to drill a hole in exactly the same place in several pieces, I use a stop block. The stop block can be used on the fence in either the drill press or horizontal boring mode. (See *Power Tool Woodworking for Everyone*.) Using the stop block is more convenient than a C-clamp and a piece of scrap wood. This stop block rides on the fence. When properly positioned, this jig stops the workpiece. Hold the workpiece firmly against the stop block, table, and fence while drilling. Since the workpiece is stopped in exactly the same position each time, the holes are drilled in exactly the same position.

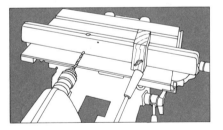

The stop block eliminates the need for you to mark each hole separately before you drill.

By using the pad sawing technique, it is possible to pad drill. Stack several workpieces on the table and against the fence; then, drill through all of them at once. Always use a backup board to avoid drilling into the fence.

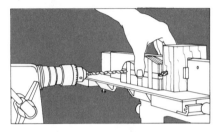

Apply the pad sawing technique to drilling so that you can pad drill.

Finally, an invaluable aid to my small shop is a router arm. I use it a lot. Pin routing eliminates tedious and time-consuming repetitive work. It takes time to make the required template, but once it is made, I can rout two or two thousand pieces—each an exact duplicate of the first.

By using these jigs and techniques, my gift making and gift giving are a real pleasure. Try these secrets the next time your aunts would like you to "make them something out of wood." You, too, will be smiling the night before Christmas.

LETTER BOX

From *HANDS ON* Nov/Dec 82

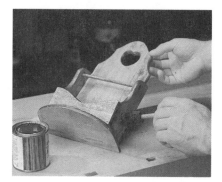

Here's a handy gift you can easily make for the holidays. Construct one or more using the techniques we discussed on pages 6-7. Hang the finished product on the wall or set it on a desk to hold all important mail.

1. Resaw stock to 5/16" thick. Sand or plane the sawn surfaces smooth.
2. Cut stock to size according to the List of Materials.
3. Cut out the heart shape in the back (A) with a router arm or a jigsaw.

4. Cut the side tapers using the fixed taper jig (see page 7).
5. Cut out all other parts on the bandsaw. Use the pad sawing technique (see page 6) to cut the curves.
6. Drill holes in the sides (B) using a stop block and the pad drilling technique (see page 7).
7. Assemble all pieces with yellow woodworker's glue and small brads. Insert dowel into sides (B) before attaching sides to back (A). Sand the project, and apply the finish of your choice.

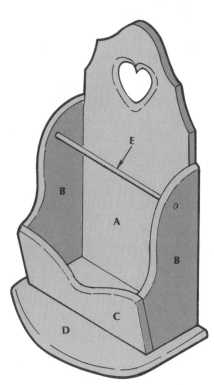

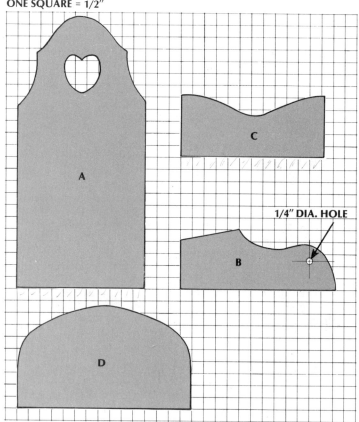

ONE SQUARE = 1/2"

1/4" DIA. HOLE

LIST OF MATERIALS

(finished dimensions in inches)

A	Back	5/16 × 5-1/2 × 11-1/4
B	Sides (2)	5/16 × 2-1/2 × 6-5/8
C	Front	5/16 × 2-1/2 × 6-1/8
D	Bottom	5/16 × 4-1/4 × 7-3/8
E	Dowel	1/4 dia. × 6-1/8

LANTERN HOLDER

From *HANDS ON* Nov/Dec 81

The age-old lantern, complete with lantern holder, still casts a warm, friendly light in the most modern home. The notched shelf of the holder cradles the lantern and the mirror reflects the lantern's soft glow throughout the room.

To construct the holder use a jigsaw, bandsaw, or pin router. Pin routing is a great way to make more than one holder, and here's how to do it.

1. Make two pin routing fixtures: one to rout out the shelf (B) and the back (A) with its design and dado, and the other to rout out the mirror recess in the back.

2. Set up for pin routing with a 1/4" pin and straight router bit.

3. Attach stock to the shelf/back fixture, and rout the outside con-tour, dado, and the inside design of the shelf (B) and back (A). Set the shelf aside.

4. Attach the back stock to the mirror recess fixture, and rout a 3/16" deep area in the back to hold the mirror.

5. Round the back and shelf edges with a 3/8" piloted rounding-over bit (with no pin). Note that edges near dado joint aren't rounded.

6. Glue the shelf (B) to the back (A) and reinforce the joint with #12 × 1-1/2" flathead wood screws.

7. Fasten the mirror in the back with push points or tiny wire brads.

Try some variations with the lantern holder—a different design in the back or even a solid back. You may substitute stained glass for the mirror. Or, even build a solid shelf to hold candles or potted plants.

LIST OF MATERIALS

(finished dimensions in inches)

A	Back	3/4 × 7 × 21-3/4
B	Shelf	3/4 × 7 × 7-1/4

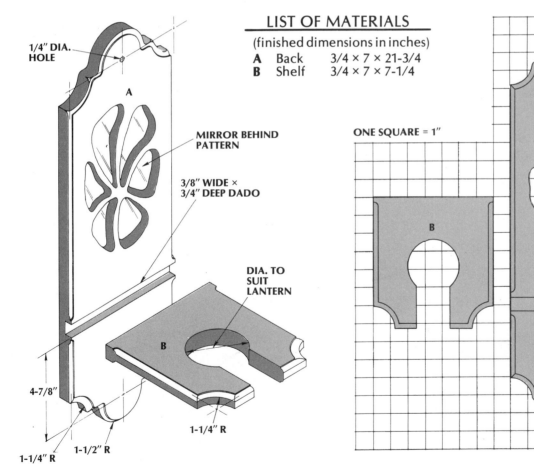

1/4" DIA. HOLE

A

MIRROR BEHIND PATTERN

3/8" WIDE × 3/4" DEEP DADO

DIA. TO SUIT LANTERN

B

4-7/8"

1-1/4" R   1-1/2" R   1-1/4" R

ONE SQUARE = 1"

A

B

From *HANDS ON* Sept/Oct 81

Organize yourself with this attractive, compact work chest. Use it to store tools, silverware, or hobby supplies. You can make fewer, deeper drawers or add more smaller drawers. Cleverly hidden dadoes and rabbets strengthen this project.

1. Cut joinery with dado blades and two stop blocks clamped to the rip fence, one block to help you start the cut and the other to end it.

2. Lower the workpiece over the dado blades *slowly;* then, feed it against the rotation of the blades. Turn off the machine before removing the workpiece from the table.

3. Dry-clamp the cabinet sides (A), and top and bottom (B).

4. Space the drawer guides (P) inside the cabinet. Check this spacing with the drawer sides (G, H, J) and temporarily tack the guides in position.

5. Adjust the table so the kerfs for the fingerholds in the drawer fronts (D, E, F) are one-third the height of the drawer fronts.

6. Glue the drawers together and check their fit in the cabinet. Adjust the guides (P), if necessary.

7. Attach the guides (P) to the cabinet sides (A) with countersunk screws. Pull out the temporary nails.

8. Glue the entire cabinet together and slide in the drawers.

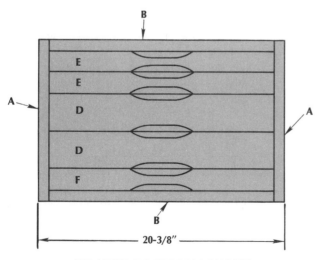

Control the stop dadoes by using an auxiliary fence with stop blocks clamped at the front and back.

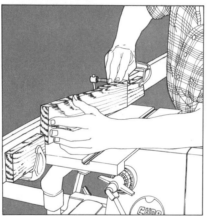

Lower drawer front between the stop blocks.

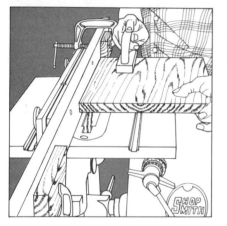

DRAWER POSITION LAYOUT

LIST OF MATERIALS

(finished dimensions in inches)

A	Cabinet sides (2)	3/4 × 9-3/4 × 13
B	Cabinet top & bottom (2)	3/4 × 9-3/4 × 19-5/8
C	Cabinet back	3/4 × 12-1/4 × 19-5/8
D	Drawer fronts (2)	3/4 × 3 × 18-3/4
E	Drawer fronts (2)	3/4 × 1-3/4 × 18-3/4
F	Drawer front	3/4 × 1-1/2 × 18-3/4
G	Drawer sides (4)	3/4 × 3 × 8-1/2
H	Drawer sides (4)*	3/4 × 1-3/4 × 8-1/2
J	Drawer sides (2)*	3/4 × 1-1/2 × 8-1/2
K	Drawer backs (2)	3/8 × 3 × 18
L	Drawer backs (2)*	3/8 × 1-3/4 × 18
M	Drawer back*	3/8 × 1-1/2 × 18
N	Drawer bottoms (5)	1/8 × 7-5/8 × 17-1/2
P	Drawer guides (10)	1/2 × 1/2 × 7-3/8

*Not shown.

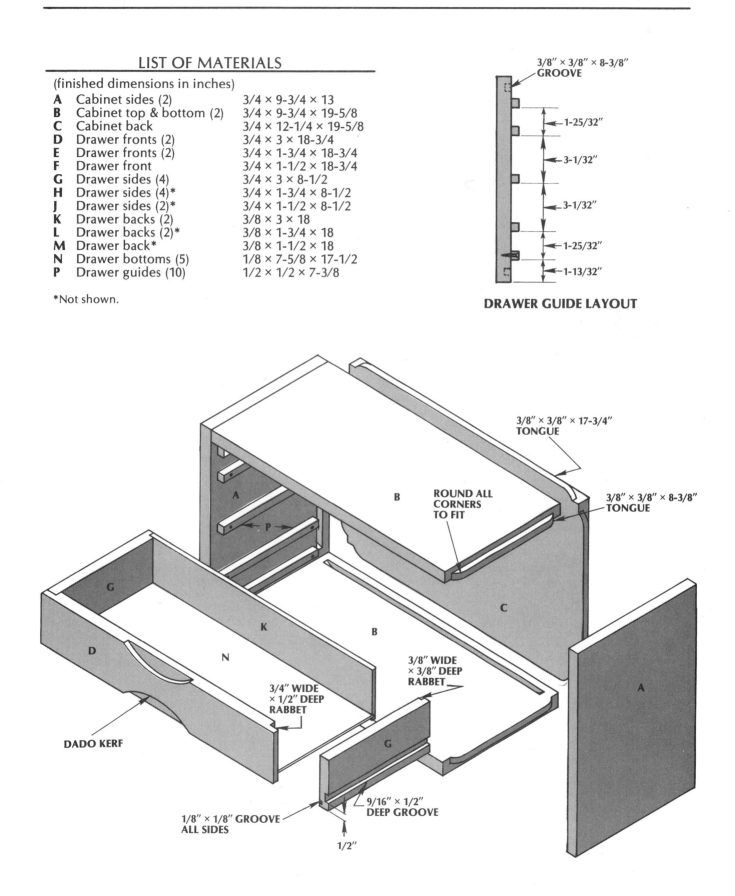

3/8″ × 3/8″ × 8-3/8″
GROOVE

1-25/32″

3-1/32″

3-1/32″

1-25/32″

1-13/32″

DRAWER GUIDE LAYOUT

3/8″ × 3/8″ × 17-3/4″
TONGUE

ROUND ALL
CORNERS
TO FIT

3/8″ × 3/8″ × 8-3/8″
TONGUE

3/8″ WIDE
× 3/8″ DEEP
RABBET

3/4″ WIDE
× 1/2″ DEEP
RABBET

DADO KERF

1/8″ × 1/8″ GROOVE
ALL SIDES

9/16″ × 1/2″
DEEP GROOVE

1/2″

From *HANDS ON* Sept/Oct 80

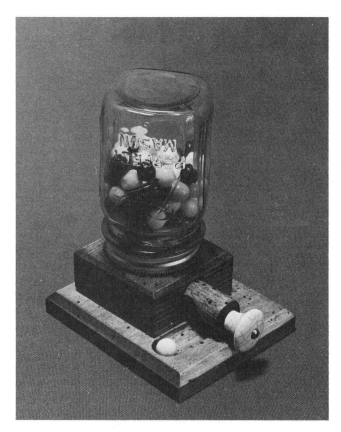

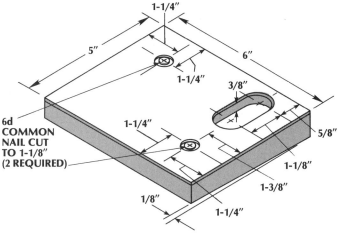

BASE FIXTURE

6d COMMON NAIL CUT TO 1-1/8" (2 REQUIRED)

This ingenious toy will fascinate children and adults. A concealed spiral groove allows the gumball to travel around the delivery shaft and into a shallow pocket to be picked up. Here's how to make one using an overarm pin router.

1. Make two fixtures—one to rout out the recess in the base and the other to aid in routing the spiral groove in the delivery shaft.

The base fixture is made from a piece of sink cutout 5" wide × 6" long. Cut out a 3/8" thick plywood template, following our pattern, and nail the template to the particleboard side of the sink cutout. Use a 3/8" table pin and a 3/8" carbide-tipped straight router bit and rout the recess in the plastic laminated side of the sink cutout. Drill two 3/32" diameter holes through the fixture for 6d nails to mount the base to the fixture. Countersink the nail heads. Use a bandsaw and taper the particleboard side of the fixture 1/8" descending from the recess. Sand smooth.

The other fixture is made from a 1' long 2 × 4. Cut a V-groove, 3/4" deep, the length of the 2 × 4 using a table saw. Attach a 3/4" × 1-1/4" × 30" strip to the 2 × 4 to clamp the fixture in place when routing the spiral groove.

2. Cut all pieces to size according to the List of Materials except the delivery shaft (D).

3. Drill holes in center block (A).

4. Insert 1" dowel rod in center block and mark delivery hole and spiral groove.

5. Rout the spiral groove in the delivery shaft with a 1/4" straight bit and V-block fixture.

6. Cut delivery shaft to length and chamfer end.

7. Insert delivery shaft in center block and drill delivery hole.

8. Attach base to base fixture and rout out the pocket using a 1/2" table pin and a 1/2" core box bit.

9. Remove base from fixture and cut chamfer around edges of base.

10. Finish all pieces.

11. Wax delivery shaft (D) and insert the delivery shaft and guide pin (C) in the center block (A). Do not glue.

12. Assemble remaining pieces.

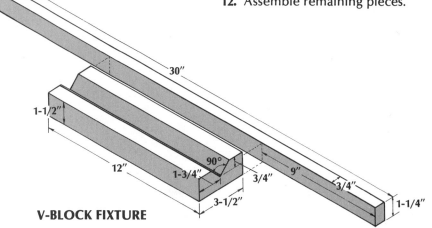

V-BLOCK FIXTURE

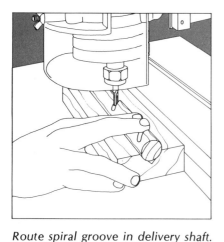

Route spiral groove in delivery shaft. Use entire 36″ dowel rod for safety.

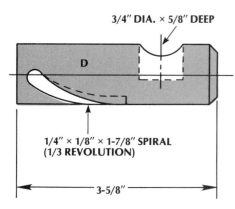

Route pocket in base using fixture.

3/4″ DIA. × 5/8″ DEEP

D

1/4″ × 1/8″ × 1-7/8″ SPIRAL (1/3 REVOLUTION)

3-5/8″

DELIVERY SHAFT DETAIL

3/16″ × 45° CHAMFER

1″ DIA. HOLE

3/4″ DIA. × 5/8″ DEEP HOLE

1/4″ DIA. × 1/4″ DEEP HOLE

3-1/2″

1-3/4″

A

5/8″

1-1/2″

1″

1-5/8″

1/4″

1/8″ SAW KERF CUT BEFORE DRILLING HOLES

3-1/4″

3-5/8″

CENTER BLOCK DETAIL

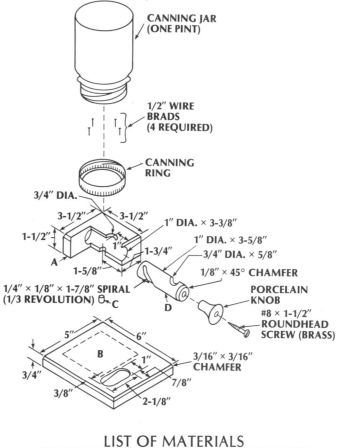

CANNING JAR (ONE PINT)

1/2″ WIRE BRADS (4 REQUIRED)

CANNING RING

3/4″ DIA.

3-1/2″

3-1/2″

1-1/2″

1″ DIA. × 3-3/8″

A

1-3/4″

1″

1″ DIA. × 3-5/8″

3/4″ DIA. × 5/8″

1-5/8″

1/8″ × 45° CHAMFER

1/4″ × 1/8″ × 1-7/8″ SPIRAL (1/3 REVOLUTION)

C

D

PORCELAIN KNOB

#8 × 1-1/2″ ROUNDHEAD SCREW (BRASS)

5″

6″

B

1″

3/16″ × 3/16″ CHAMFER

3/4″

7/8″

3/8″

2-1/8″

LIST OF MATERIALS

(finished dimensions in inches)

A	Center block	1-1/2 × 3-1/2 × 3-5/8
B	Base	3/4 × 5 × 6
C	Guide pin	1/4 dia. × 3/8
D	Delivery shaft	1 dia. × 3-5/8*

*Use entire 36″ length of dowel when routing spiral groove.

PENCIL HOLDER

From *HANDS ON* Nov/Dec 83

Whether used for pencils and odds-and-ends to better organize a desktop or in the kitchen for holding utensils, this holder makes a great practical gift.

1. Start the project by gluing up a 3" × 8" × 5" block of maple or a hardwood of your choice. You could even use a mixture of woods to create a colorful and unusual effect.

2. Square the glued-up stock, and transfer the pattern to it.

3. Mark the hole locations and drill the holes. Use Forstner bits since these leave a flat-bottomed hole.

4. Bevel the top on the table saw or bandsaw; then, cut out the contour on the bandsaw.

5. Sand the holder using the disc and drum sanders or the belt sander. Apply the finish of your choice.

ONE SQUARE = 1/2"

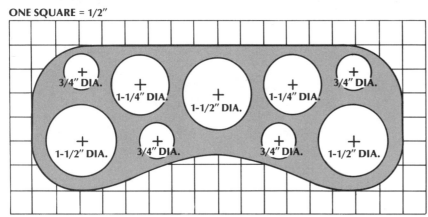

3/4" DIA. 1-1/4" DIA. 1-1/2" DIA. 1-1/4" DIA. 3/4" DIA.

1-1/2" DIA. 3/4" DIA. 3/4" DIA. 1-1/2" DIA.

TOP VIEW

SIDE VIEW

4-1/2" 3-1/2" 5" 1-1/2" 3"

From *HANDS ON* Mar/Apr 82

Keep reference books handy with this simple-to-build, adjustable book rack. It's a sturdy, useful organizer for desktop, kitchen counter, or workbench.

1. Cut all pieces to size according to the List of Materials, roughing out the curves on the bandsaw or jigsaw. Curves can be readily sanded with the 2-1/4" and 1-1/2" drum sanders. If you want to make more than one, use the pad sawing technique (see page 6).

2. Glue and clamp the stretchers (A) to the spacers (B). Then, glue and clamp the feet (C) onto the ends of this assembly.

3. Sand the top and ends with the disc or belt sander.

4. Insert the adjustable ends (D). Glue the braces (E) into place. Allow about 1/32" clearance on each side for easy operation. Stain and seal with the finish of your choice.

LIST OF MATERIALS

(finished dimensions in inches)

A	Stretchers (2)	3/4 × 3 × 18
B	Spacers (2)	3/4 × 3/4 × 2
C	Feet (2)	3/4 × 1-1/2 × 10-1/2
D	Ends (2)	3/4 × 5 × 6-1/2
E	Braces (2)	3/4 × 3/4 × 4

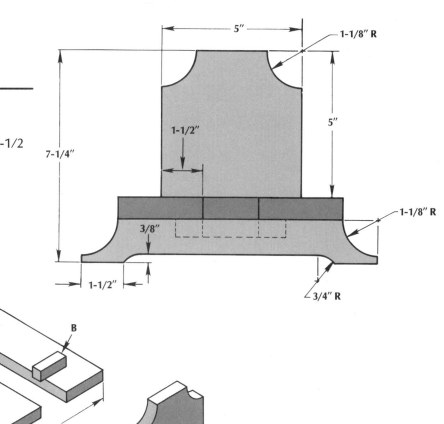

2" LONG × 3/8" DEEP DADO

BIRD FEEDER

From *HANDS ON* July/Aug 82

You'll take great pleasure in watching birds enjoy four-course meals from the separate food compartments which are unique to this feeder.

1. Select stock and materials. The front and back windows (J) and dividers (K) are plexiglass.

2. Cut all stock (except G) to size according to List of Materials, using the table saw.

3. Cut bevels. Tilt table 45° and cut bevels on deflectors (C). Tilt table 30° and cut bevels on the roof support (E). To cut the weather cap (G), tilt table 30° and cut V-groove on edge of wide board. Move the rip fence in 1/2" toward blade and repeat process to cut cap from wide stock.

4. Tilt table 7°; cut shingles (F).

5. Layout and cut contours on the ends (A, B) and dividers (K, L) with the bandsaw.

6. Rout grooves and rabbets, using a handheld router. Drill the 1/2" × 3/8" deep holes for the perches (H).

7. Nail the deflectors (C) together and attach them to the bottom (D) with brass brads.

8. Assemble the lower ends (A), front and back windows (J), and the bottom assembly with #8 × 1-1/4" brass flathead wood screws (do not insert perches until later). Assemble the upper ends (B) and the roof support (E) in the same manner and set them aside.

9. Fasten the compartment dividers (K) to the windows (J) with #4 × 1/2" brass roundhead wood screws.

10. Attach the six feed dividers (L) to the windows in the same manner. Attach the edging (M) to each side.

11. Remove one of the lower ends (A) and insert the two perches (H) and reassemble.

12. Fasten the shingles (F) to the feeder with brass brads.

13. Tack cap (G) in place and attach window sash locks to the ends (A, B).

LIST OF MATERIALS

(finished dimensions in inches)

A	Lower ends (2)	3/4 × 10-7/8 × 20-1/2
B	Upper ends (2)	3/4 × 7-1/4 × 12
C	Deflectors (2)	3/4 × 3-7/8 × 22
D	Bottom	3/4 × 10-1/2 × 22
E	Roof support	3/4 × 2-1/2 × 22
F	Shingles (18)	3/8 × 2-1/8 × 27-1/2
G	Weather cap	1/2 × 3/4 × 27-1/2
H	Perches (2)	1/2 dia. × 22-3/4
J	Windows (2)	1/4 × 7-1/2 × 22-1/2
K	Compartment dividers (3)	1/4 × 10-1/8 × 10-3/4
L	Feed dividers (6)	1/4 × 1-7/8 × 2-3/4
M	Edging (2)	1/4 × 1-1/2 × 22

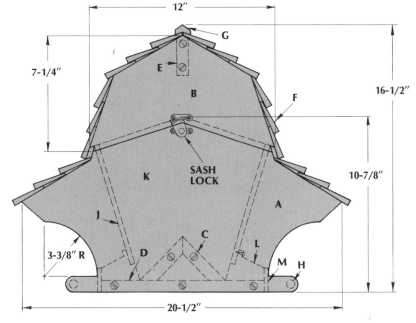

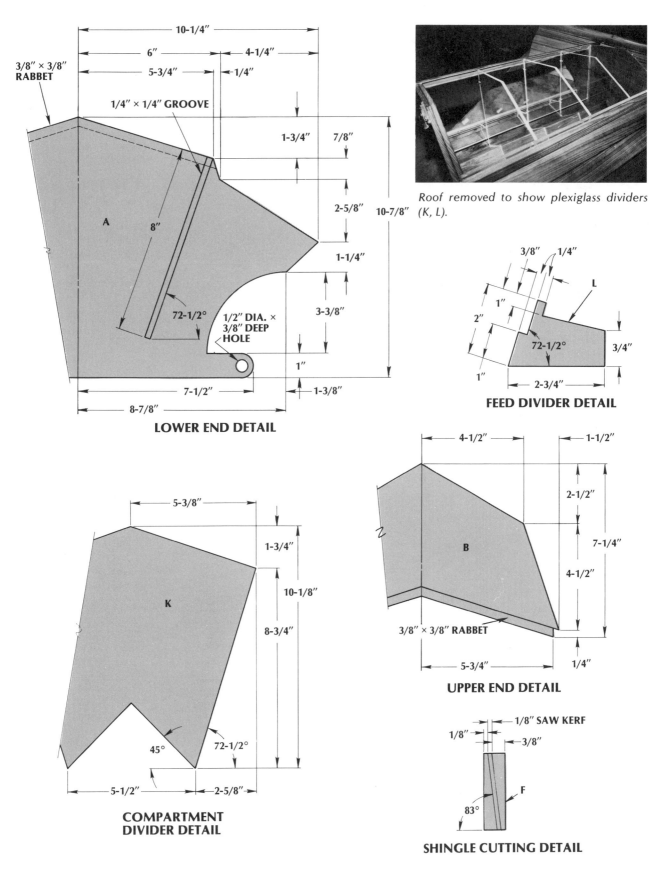

10-1/4"

6"

4-1/4"

3/8" × 3/8"
RABBET

5-3/4"

1/4"

1/4" × 1/4" GROOVE

1-3/4" 7/8"

A

8"

10-7/8"

2-5/8"

1-1/4"

72-1/2°

1/2" DIA. ×
3/8" DEEP
HOLE

3-3/8"

1"

7-1/2"

1-3/8"

8-7/8"

LOWER END DETAIL

Roof removed to show plexiglass dividers
(K, L).

3/8"   1/4"

L

1"

2"

72-1/2°

3/4"

1"

2-3/4"

FEED DIVIDER DETAIL

5-3/8"

1-3/4"

K

10-1/8"

8-3/4"

45°

72-1/2°

5-1/2"

2-5/8"

**COMPARTMENT
DIVIDER DETAIL**

4-1/2"

1-1/2"

2-1/2"

B

7-1/4"

4-1/2"

3/8" × 3/8" RABBET

5-3/4"

1/4"

UPPER END DETAIL

1/8" SAW KERF

1/8"

3/8"

F

83°

SHINGLE CUTTING DETAIL

BANDSAW SCULPTURE

From *HANDS ON* Sept/Oct 79

If you make two sets of cuts that are totally different from each other, you can end up with some fantastic sculptures—animals, people, abstract shapes.

To sculpt with your bandsaw, you have to develop two patterns. Say you want to cut out an animal: Imagine what that animal looks like from the front and draw the outline. Next, imagine what it looks like from the side (or in some cases, the top) and draw that outline. Take care to make each of your drawings exactly the same scale. Use these two outlines as patterns for making a series of compound bandsaw cuts. Once again, make your first piece out of scrap stock to see if your patterns give you what you want.

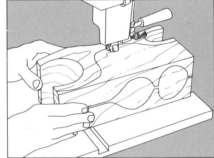

Use a bandsaw to sculpt figures from stock with the outline of the figure drawn on it.

ONE SQUARE = 1"

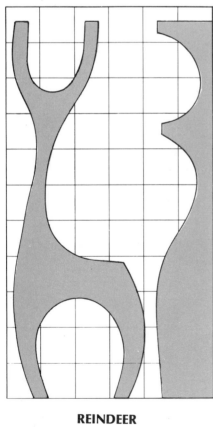

REINDEER

ONE SQUARE = 1"

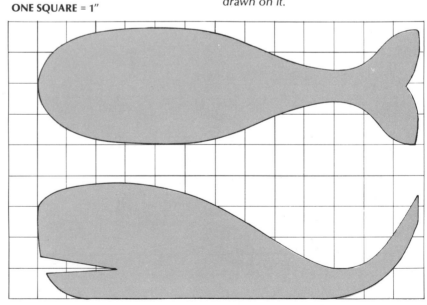

WHALE

There are some projects that you make to give as gifts that you wish you had yourself. This memo pad will be one of those projects. Follow the seven simple steps given below, but be prepared to make at least two!

1. Prepare stock by ripping and jointing a 10" long piece of wood to a 4-1/2" width. Cut a 1/16" deep × 3-1/2" wide × 3-1/2" long stop groove in one end of the piece. Use the dado attachment and a push block for this operation. Resaw the stock to 3/8" thick on the bandsaw.

2. Cut all pieces to size. The 1/16" grooves are in front (B) and back (D) only.

3. Bevel the edges of the writing surface (C) on the disc sander with the table at 45°.

4. Assemble with glue the base (A), front (B), writing surface (C), and back (D).

5. Drill holes for the supports (E).

6. Drill holes in the supports (E) for brads, using a V-block to secure the stock. Next, drill the rod (F) using the horizontal boring mode and the miter gauge for support.

7. Assemble the paper holder by putting brads into the rod (F) and clipping them to length. Press fit the assembly into the base (using no glue), then thread the paper through the slots.

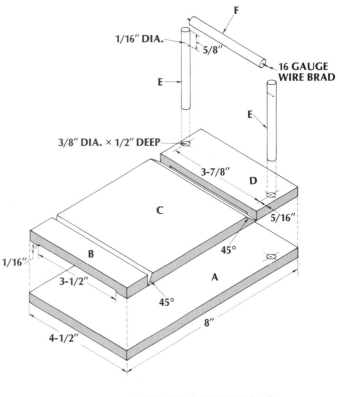

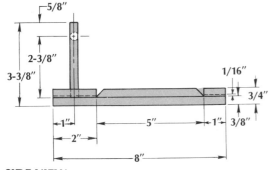

SIDE VIEW

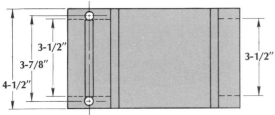

TOP VIEW

LIST OF MATERIALS

(finished dimensions in inches)

A	Base	3/8 × 4-1/2 × 8
B	Front	3/8 × 4-1/2 × 1
C	Writing surface	3/8 × 4-1/2 × 5
D	Back	3/8 × 4-1/2 × 2
E	Supports (2)	3/8 dia. × 3
F	Rod	3/8 dia. × 3-1/2

JEWELRY BOX ▣

From *HANDS ON* July/Aug 82

This simple project is one you'll want to make twice—one to keep and one to give as a sentimental gift. Making a fixture for the over-arm pin router and producing this jewelry box is a snap. Here's how.

1. Cut the stock for the fixture parts (A, B, C, D, E, F) to size according to the List of Materials.
2. Layout the plywood template (A) according to the drawing. Drill the corner curves and cut out the inside waste stock with the jigsaw. File and sand all edges smooth.

3. Drill the holes in one fixture side (C) to accept the T-nuts. Insert the T-nuts into the holes and tap them lightly to seat them in place.
4. Fasten the plywood template (A) to the fixture bottom (B) using #8 × 1" flathead wood screws. Attach the fixture sides (C) and fixture ends (D) to the fixture bottom using #8 × 1-1/4" flathead wood screws.
5. Resaw the box lid (G) from the box body (F) using the bandsaw. Set the rip fence to allow a 1/4" cut. Sand the saw marks from the box body and lid with the belt sander.
6. Clamp the jewelry box body (F) into the fixture assembly, using thumbscrews and the clamp bar (E). Make sure the box body is seated flat and secure in the fixture assembly.
7. Pin rout the box body. Use the router arm with a 3/8" bit and a 3/8" guide pin. For safer and easier handling, rout the recesses in three passes.
8. Round the edges by replacing the straight bit with a 1/4" round over bit. Adjust the depth of the bit to round off all the inside edges of the cavities.
9. Sand and finish the box. Mount the hardware and line the box with felt.

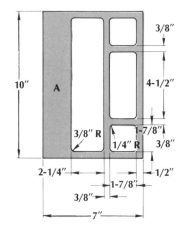

TEMPLATE LAYOUT

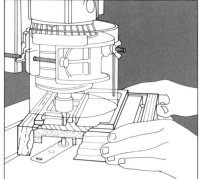

Cutaway view of the pin routing technique.

LIST OF MATERIALS

(finished dimensions in inches)

A	Plywood template	3/8 × 7 × 10
B	Fixture bottom	3/4 × 7 × 10
C	Fixture sides (2)	3/4 × 1-5/8 × 11-1/2
D	Fixture ends (2)	3/4 × 1-5/8 × 7
E	Clamp bar	3/4 × 1 × 10
F	Box body	1-1/4 × 5-1/2 × 10
G	Box lid	1/4 × 5-1/2 × 10

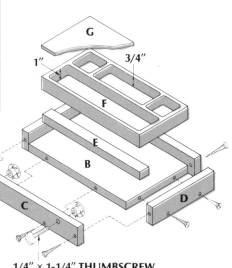

1/4" × 1-1/4" THUMBSCREW AND T-NUT

BOX AND FIXTURE ASSEMBLY

PLYWOOD PARQUET

From *HANDS ON* Sept/Oct 81

Parquet—inlaying of hardwoods in a pattern—is intricate, time-consuming, and expensive. But you can mimic the look of parquet with plywood.

Simply glue up small blocks of plywood, cut edgewise, in a geometric arrangement.

Any grade or thickness of plywood will work, although construction grade contains many voids. When voids do occur, hide them by first brushing on a varnish and sanding lightly with wet/dry sandpaper. The sawdust from sanding mixes with the varnish to form a paste that fills the cracks. For larger voids, use a wood filler or patching stick.

First construct the box; then, glue plywood parquet (E) to backing (D) of box lid. Belt sand smooth. Cut the lid from the body using a table saw, then mount hinges.

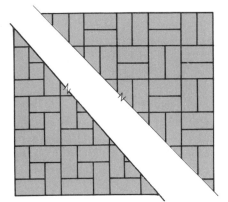

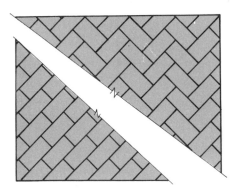

POSSIBLE PARQUET PATTERNS

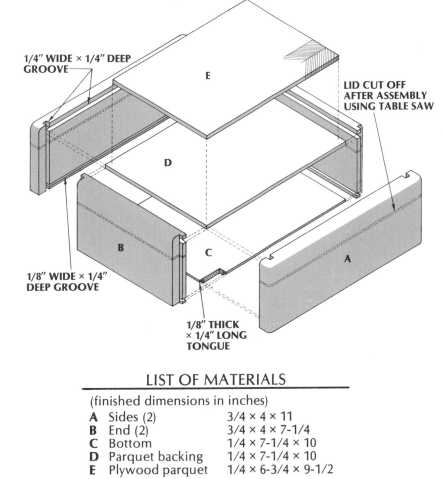

1/4" WIDE × 1/4" DEEP GROOVE

E

LID CUT OFF AFTER ASSEMBLY USING TABLE SAW

D

1/8" WIDE × 1/4" DEEP GROOVE

B

C

A

1/8" THICK × 1/4" LONG TONGUE

LIST OF MATERIALS

(finished dimensions in inches)

A	Sides (2)	3/4 × 4 × 11
B	End (2)	3/4 × 4 × 7-1/4
C	Bottom	1/4 × 7-1/4 × 10
D	Parquet backing	1/4 × 7-1/4 × 10
E	Plywood parquet	1/4 × 6-3/4 × 9-1/2

GAME TABLE

From *HANDS ON* Nov/Dec 82

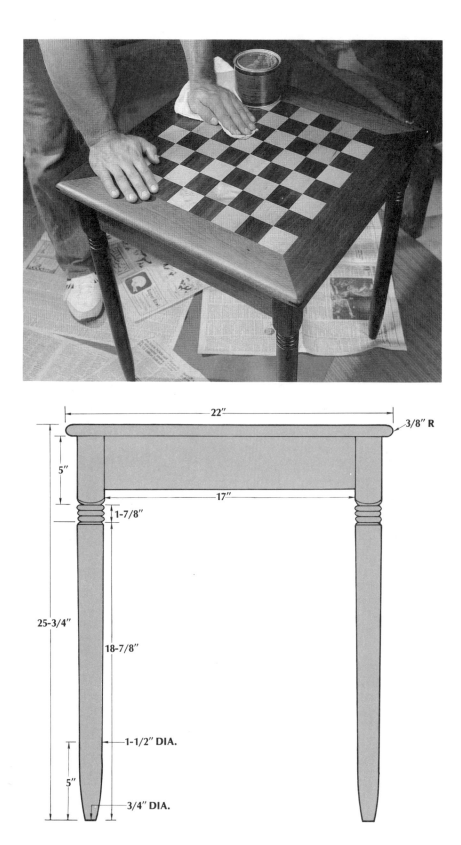

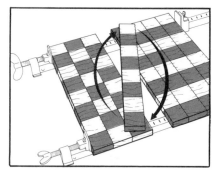

You can build this beautiful game table following the eight simple steps outlined here. We built this project out of mahogany and used maple and walnut for the checkerboard top.

1. Prepare stock for the legs (A), apron (B), and cleat strips (C) on the table saw. Make sure the stock for the legs is square and straight.

2. Drill dowel holes in the legs (A) and apron (B). Use the drill press for the legs and the horizontal boring mode for the apron pieces. After drilling the holes, be sure to mark all pieces for position.

3. Turn the legs (A) on the lathe following the drawings, or create your own style. Sand the legs while they are still on the lathe.

4. Assemble the legs (A) and apron (B) with dowels and woodworker's glue.

5. Make the checkerboard top by first setting the saw to cut 2" strips of 3/4" thick light (F) and dark (G) woods. Glue and clamp these strips together and allow to dry. Square one end and cut 2" strips across the light and dark wood. Glue and clamp these strips together alternating them to create the checkerboard pattern.

22

6. Cut the frame pieces (E) for the checkerboard. Cut each piece to approximate length and then use the disc sander to achieve a precision fit. Make the spline grooves and splines for the frame. Glue and clamp one side of the frame at a time to the checkerboard.

7. Attach the cleat strips (C) to the apron with #8 × 1" flathead wood screws. Cut the bottom (D) out of 1/4" plywood and secure it to the cleat strip with brads. Mortise the recesses for the hinges.

8. Apply the finish of your choice.

LIST OF MATERIALS

(finished dimensions in inches)

A	Legs (4)	1-3/4 × 1-3/4 × 25
B	Apron pieces (4)	3/4 × 3-1/2 × 17
C	Cleat strips (4)	1/2 × 3/4 × 17
D	Bottom	1/4 × 18-3/4 × 18-3/4
E	Frame pieces (4)	3/4 × 3 × 22
F	Light wood (4)	3/4 × 2 × 18
G	Dark wood (4)	3/4 × 2 × 18

A
1/2"
5/8"
3/8" × 2" DOWEL
MORTISE FOR HINGE AS REQUIRED
2-1/2"
2-1/4"
B
C
D
B
C

F
G
E
B
A
C
C
D
B
B
A
A
A

1/2" R
1/8" × 4" × 1" SPLINE

CORNER DETAIL

BANDSAWN CHESS AND CHECKERS

From *HANDS ON* May/June 80

1/8" cut will you need any of that scrap, and then you still don't have to tape it back on. Just set the chess piece on top to make the cut square with the blade.

This modification of the compound cuts technique works well for most small workpieces and saves a great deal of time.

MAKING THE CHESS PIECES

Select two contrasting woods to distinguish one side of the chess set from the other. We chose to make our set from walnut and maple.

Cut your wood into small blocks before starting on the compound cuts. Check the List of Materials for the number and size of blocks you'll need.

The kings, queens, rooks, and pawns (A, B, E, F) are shaped with two cuts, each exactly the same as the other. So are the bishops (C),

It's an exciting game to play, and an elegant game to watch. Chess is played with six different pieces—king, queen, bishop, knight, rook, and pawn—each piece a tiny sculpture. Most chess sets are turned on a lathe or carved by hand; however, the set pictured here is made on a bandsaw, each piece formed with a compound cut.

MAKING COMPOUND CUTS

Here's the technique of making compound cuts.
1. Make your first cut or cuts.
2. Tape the cut pieces back together.
3. Turn the workpiece 90° and cut again.
When you unwrap the tape, you'll have a three-dimensional wooden shape. It's a simple technique, but we suggest that for this project you modify step 2 to make it even simpler.

Instead of taping the pieces back together, leave about 1/8" of stock uncut underneath the head of each chess piece. This will keep the

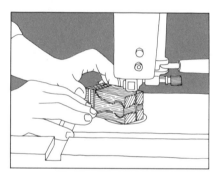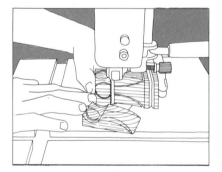

When cutting chess pieces, leave 1/8" of stock uncut underneath the head, then knock off scrap.

scrap attached with no need to tape it back on.

When you've made all your cuts, go back and saw the remaining 1/8" segments, knocking off the scrap. Only when making your last

but on the second cut put a kerf in the heads to form the bishop's miter. The knights are made with two different cuts to form the traditional horse heads. You may want to round their noses slightly to make them appear more horse-like.

LIST OF MATERIALS

(finished dimensions in inches)

A	Kings (2)	2 × 2 × 5-1/4
B	Queens (2)	2 × 2 × 4-3/4
C	Bishops (4)	1-3/4 × 1-3/4 × 4-1/8
D	Knights (4)	1-3/4 × 1-3/4 × 3-1/2
E	Rooks (4)	1-3/4 × 1-3/4 × 4
F	Pawns (16)	1-1/2 × 1-1/2 × 3-1/8

CHECKERS

If you want to add checkers to your chess set, cut or glue up two blocks 1-3/4″ × 1-3/4″ × 12″, each block made from one of your contrasting woods. Turn the blocks on a lathe to form two cylinders 1-3/4″ in diameter. Cut checkers to size with a bandsaw.

FINISHING THE PIECES

The shapes of the various chess pieces are fairly intricate and tedious to sand. However, a set of small drum sanders speeds up sanding considerably. The drums reach into most of the curves and crevices, and the chess pieces require only touch-up hand-sanding. If you decide to sand the chess set by hand, a small half-round rasp and a supply of emery boards will prove useful.

Dip the chess pieces and checkers in a can of high-gloss polyurethane wood finish. Wipe off the excess with a rag, and let dry on a sheet of wax paper. Dip the pieces again and wait for the finish to get tacky (about 10 to 15 minutes). Rub the partially dried finish into the wood with a rag. Don't worry if this rag becomes gummed up; this actually helps buff the finish. Let the pieces stand overnight to harden completely.

Rubbing the gummy polyurethane into the wood fills any mill marks and surface imperfections. The wood becomes glass smooth and takes on a soft glow. After the second coat, the polyurethane looks remarkably like a hand-rubbed oil finish, with only a fraction of the hand-rubbing.

Finally, glue felt to the underside of the chess pieces and checkers to protect the board they will rest on. And that's it, except for finding yourself a chess partner to help break the set in.

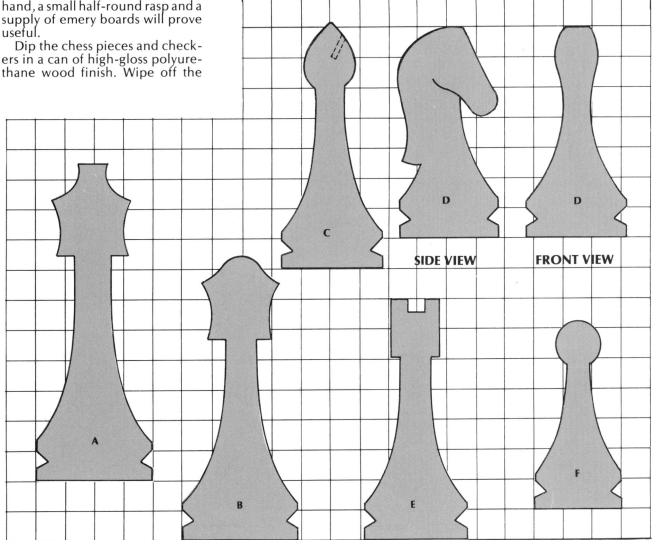

TURNED CHESS SET

From *HANDS ON* Jan/Feb 82

When you're finished with this project, you'll have a game to enjoy and a keepsake to treasure for many years. This chess set is a challenging project that can be made from a very small amount of wood.

1. Prepare about 9' of 1-3/8" stock. Cut the turning stock to size according to the List of Materials. Leave an extra 1" on all the lengths for waste stock. Select contrasting light and dark hardwoods such as maple or birch and mahogany or walnut. Mark the centers on all ends.

2. Turn all the pieces except the knights (C) according to the patterns shown. For best results, use a set of miniature woodturning chisels.

3. Turn the knights (C), forming the base and part of the head. Set the stock 3/8" off-center. Turn the neck of the knight and sand the neck smooth. Move the knight back on-center and finish turning the head, stopping just before cutting the piece free.

4. Cut the bishop's kerf with a bandsaw. The king's cross is also cut on the bandsaw. To make the rook's crown, first drill a 3/4" diameter × 1/8" deep hole in the top of the rook. Then, using the bandsaw, cut the 1/8" deep × 1/8" wide crown slots.

5. Apply the finish of your choice to the chess pieces. Finally, glue felt onto the bottoms of all pieces.

LIST OF MATERIALS

(finished dimensions in inches)

A	Kings (2)	1-3/8 dia. × 4-3/8
B	Queens (2)	1-3/8 dia. × 4-1/8
C	Knights (4)	1-3/8 dia. × 3-1/8
D	Bishops (4)	1-3/8 dia. × 3-3/8
E	Rooks (4)	1-3/8 dia. × 2-3/8
F	Pawns (16)	1-3/8 dia. × 2-1/8

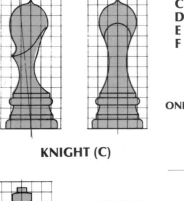

KNIGHT (C)

ONE SQUARE = 1/4"

CUT NOTCHES ON BANDSAW

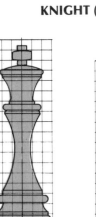

KING (A)

QUEEN (B)

3/4" DIA. × 1/8" DEEP HOLE

ROOK (E)

PAWN (F)

BANDSAW KERF

BISHOP (D)

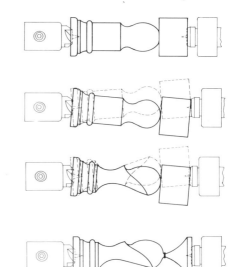

Turning a knight.

From *HANDS ON* July/Aug 80

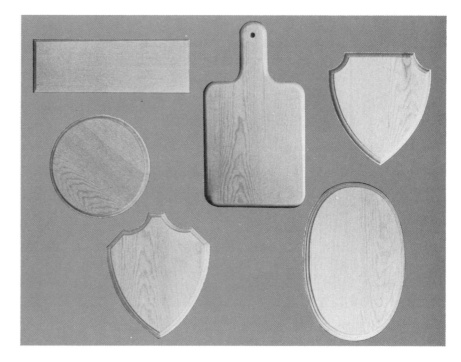

Plaques and picture frames always make a great gift and they can be made quickly and inexpensively. You can even mount pictures, decals, slogans, etc. on them. Make plaques individually by using the bandsaw or jigsaw to cut out shapes. Edges are formed using the shaper. If you want to mass produce plaques, follow the steps below.

1. Make templates of the designs you want. Trace that template and make a fixture. (Some square or rectangular plaques can be cut without fixtures.)

2. Cut blanks and attach to fixtures, using two nails or screws.

3. Cut out the shape on a bandsaw or jigsaw; then, remove the plaque or picture frame from the fixture.

4. Shape the edges, using the router or shaper. If you're making a picture frame, remember to cut a rabbet in the back.

5. Sand the face and edges of the plaques and frames with a belt sander.

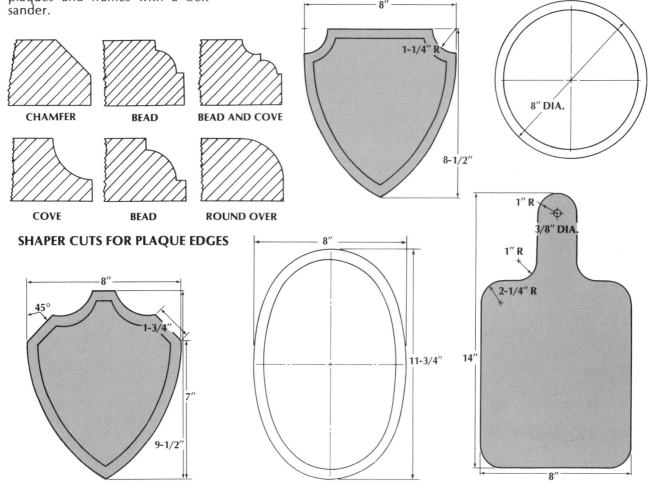

CHAMFER

BEAD

BEAD AND COVE

COVE

BEAD

ROUND OVER

SHAPER CUTS FOR PLAQUE EDGES

WHALE BOX

From *HANDS ON* July/Aug 80

Trace these whale patterns on 3-1/2″ × 3-1/2″ × 12″ blocks. Cut the top contour first on your bandsaw. Tape the pieces back together and turn the wood 90°. Cut the side contour, doing the drawer last.

Mount the drawer in the drilling fixture and drill out the compartment with a large multi-spur bit. Round the edges of the drawer and the whale with a file or flutter sheets. Sand all surfaces with a drum sander. Apply finish and glue felt in the bottom of the drawer compartment.

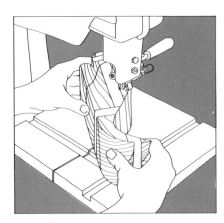

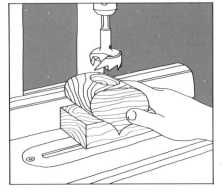

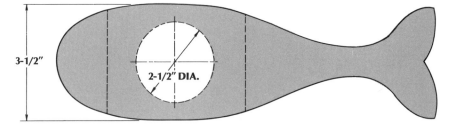

3-1/2″

2-1/2″ DIA.

TOP VIEW

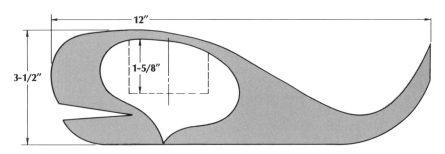

12″

3-1/2″

1-5/8″

SIDE VIEW

CANDLE SCONCE

From *HANDS ON* Nov/Dec 83

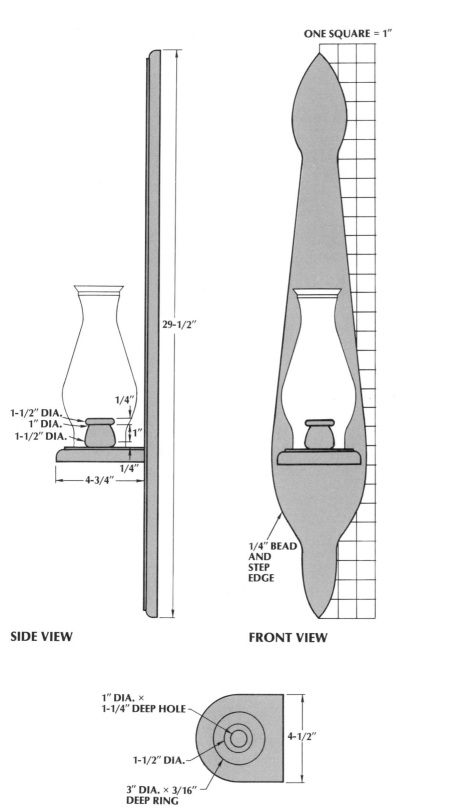

ONE SQUARE = 1"

29-1/2"

1/4"

1-1/2" DIA.
1" DIA.
1-1/2" DIA.

1"

1/4"

4-3/4"

SIDE VIEW

1/4" BEAD
AND
STEP
EDGE

FRONT VIEW

1" DIA. ×
1-1/4" DEEP HOLE

4-1/2"

1-1/2" DIA.

3" DIA. × 3/16"
DEEP RING

PLATFORM DETAIL

Make one of these beautiful sconces to hang by a door or make two pairs to grace both sides of a hall mirror.

Transfer the pattern onto 3/4" stock and cut out the basic shape for the back with the bandsaw or jigsaw. Mount the 3/4" × 4-1/2" × 5" piece of stock for the platform on the screw center and turn the 3/16" deep ring for the chimney glass (available at most department stores) in the center with the parting tool. Cut the platform to shape with the bandsaw. Next, mount a 2" length of 1-1/2" square stock to the screw center and turn the candle cup. Use the disc sander to smooth the outside contours of the sconce pieces. Shape the edges of the pieces with a 1/4" round over bit on the shaper or router. Attach the platform to the back with #10 × 1-1/2" flathead wood screws, then glue and attach the candle cup with a #8 × 1-1/4" flathead wood screw and glue.

BIRD MOBILE

From *HANDS ON* July/Aug 80

Mobiles add poetic motion to most any room. Start by making a masonite template of the bird design and trace on 3-1/2" thick blocks.

Before cutting out the design, drill a 1/8" hole where indicated on the pattern. Then, cut out the outside contour on your bandsaw and sand off the millmarks with a strip sander. Resaw the stock into 1/4" thick pieces and sand the surfaces.

Finish with oil, stain, or paint. Cut fishing line to length, and tie the lines to the birds and the crossbars (1/8" or 3/16" dowel rods). Move the lines back and forth on the crossbars until the birds are balanced.

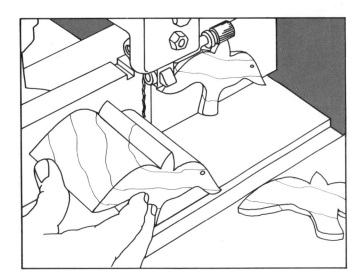

ONE SQUARE = 1/2"

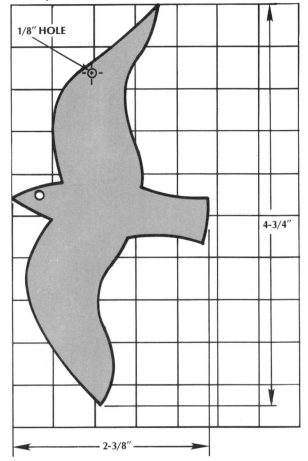

1/8" HOLE

4-3/4"

2-3/8"

From *HANDS ON* Jan/Feb 81

This candleholder can be used as a decorative accent. It conveniently holds a standard size warmer candle cup and is small enough to even slip under a fondue pot.

Just cut a 2 × 4 into blocks that are 4-1/8″ long. Glue two blocks together face-to-face to form a 3″ × 3-1/2″ × 4-1/8″ block.

Using the table saw and miter gauge set at 60°, cut the corners off the block to form the hexagon shape.

Then with the drill press and two large size drills (multi-spur bit or Forstner bit), drill 1-1/4″ diameter holes in the center of each of the six sides and the large hole 2-1/2″ diameter nearly through the top to fit the warmer cup.

Sand all flat surfaces with the disc sander. Stain and finish.

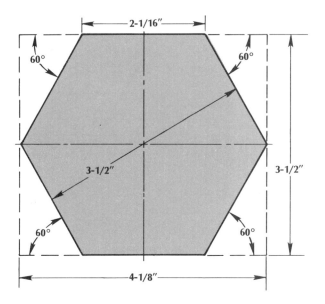

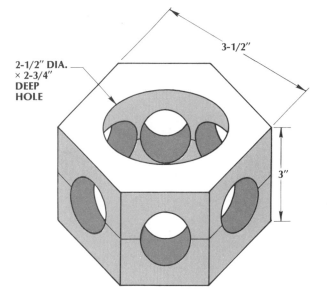

Kitchen Projects

Projects for the kitchen have always provided a source of enjoyment for the home woodworker. The beauty of wood enhances any kitchen, and the use of wooden cooking utensils adds elegance to any entertaining. Here are over twenty projects that will be sure to provide the woodworker with hours of enjoyment...and the cook with hours of use.

SPAGHETTI MEASURE

From *HANDS ON* Apr/May/June 83

ONE SQUARE = 1/2"

1-3/4" DIA.

1-1/2" DIA.

1-1/8" DIA.

7/8" DIA.

3/8" DIA.

Getting the right amount of spaghetti is easy with this simple-to-make kitchen utensil. You can measure the correct amount of spaghetti every time for one to four servings.

Resaw 3" wide × 15" long hardwood stock to 3/8" thick and lay out the pattern and hole positions. Drill the holes before you cut out the contour. Use 3/8" and 7/8" brad point bits and 1-1/8", 1-1/2", and 1-3/4" hole saws. Cut out the pattern on a jigsaw or bandsaw. Round off all the edges and the rims of the holes on both sides. Sand, then apply a nontoxic finish or leave unfinished.

To make this on a router arm, use 3/8" plywood to make the pattern. Attach the pattern to 3/8" stock and rout out the shape and holes with a 3/8" straight bit. A 3/16" round over bit shapes the edges.

From *HANDS ON* Apr/May/June 83

ONE SQUARE = 1/2"

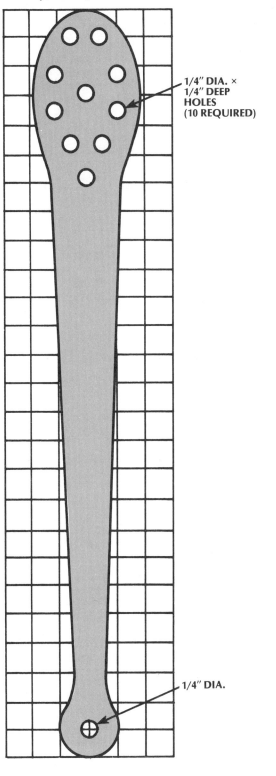

1/4" DIA. ×
1/4" DEEP
HOLES
(10 REQUIRED)

1/4" DIA.

1/4" DIA. ×
1-1/4" LONG
PEGS
(10 REQUIRED)

1/2"

This project will solve the cook's problem of how to conveniently serve pasta at dinner time. Take a 1/2" × 2" × 13" piece of hardwood stock and lay out the pattern and peg positions. Drill the peg holes 1/4" deep. Cut out the contour on the bandsaw or jigsaw. Glue in the pegs with a waterproof glue. Round the back of the fork on the disc and drum sanders. Apply a nontoxic finish or leave natural.

COOLING RACKS

From *HANDS ON* Apr/May/June 83

Few things smell as good as fresh baked bread. Bakeries, however, have made it so easy to get fresh bread that homemade bread usually appears only on a holiday. To encourage more baking at home, here are some simple and beautiful cooling racks that you can make in the time it takes to bake a loaf or two.

Cut the sides to length using hardwood from your scrap pile. Drill the 3/8" diameter × 1/4" deep holes in the sides for the dowel rods. Sand the sides and round all the edges with the belt sander or a hand sander. Next, lightly sand dowel rods, then cut them to length. Use the bandsaw or a miter box. Chamfer the ends of the rods with the disc sander. Assemble the rack with glue and clamp it with bar clamps. Apply a nontoxic finish or leave natural.

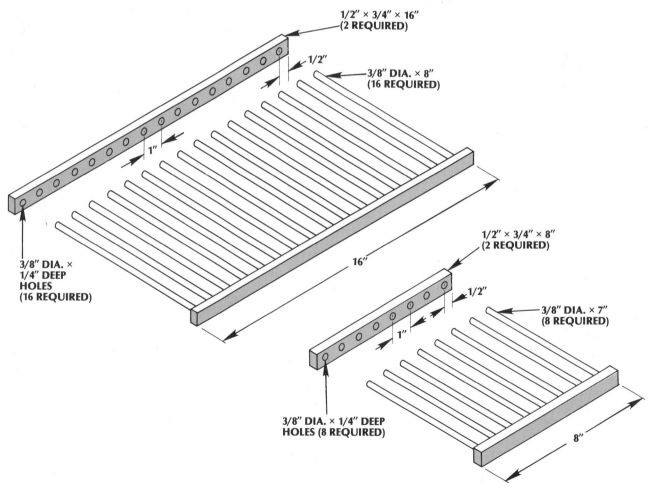

1/2" × 3/4" × 16" (2 REQUIRED)

1/2"

3/8" DIA. × 8" (16 REQUIRED)

1"

3/8" DIA. × 1/4" DEEP HOLES (16 REQUIRED)

16"

1/2" × 3/4" × 8" (2 REQUIRED)

1/2"

1"

3/8" DIA. × 7" (8 REQUIRED)

3/8" DIA. × 1/4" DEEP HOLES (8 REQUIRED)

8"

From *HANDS ON* Nov/Dec 80

Few kitchen utensils are more popular than this kitchen doofer. This ingenious device hooks on to an oven rack to push it in or pull it out, saving burned fingers and singed pot holders. Make one with a bandsaw or jigsaw or make many with a router arm. Here's how to set up for the router arm.

To make the template, first trace the doofer pattern on 3/8″ stock. Using a 3/8″ drill, drill holes for the push/pull notches. With the bandsaw, cut out template to the shape of the doofer and sand with a drum sander.

From a sink cutout, cut out the fixture and attach the template to the particleboard side using 1″ brads. Then with a 3/8″ router bit and 3/8″ pin, rout the groove in the plastic laminated side. This groove is best made in three 1/8″ cuts, each cut 1/8″ deeper than the preceding.

Cut doofer stock and attach to fixture. Alignment marks on the fixture are useful here. Rout out the doofer making two or more cuts if your stock is thicker than 1/4″. Drill the handle hole and sand with disc and drum sanders.

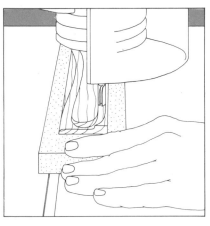

Make the doofer on a router arm.

ONE SQUARE = 1/2″

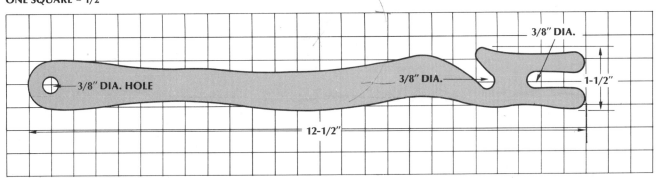

3/8″ DIA.

3/8″ DIA. HOLE

3/8″ DIA.

1-1/2″

12-1/2″

MEAT PLATTER 🄡

From *HANDS ON* Apr/May 81

This decorative meat platter looks good sitting on the table or hung on the wall. Small gutters, arranged in the shape of a tree, channel the drippings into a trough at one end of the platter and keep them from spilling over onto the tablecloth.

With a jigsaw, cut a pattern from a piece of hardboard and attach it to the unlaminated side of a sink cutout. With a 3/8" straight bit in your overarm router, pin rout a template in the cutout. On the trough end of this template, attach a 1/4" thick strip of wood. When you rout the platters, this strip will tilt the stock so that the gutters will all run downhill into the trough.

Glue up 3/4" stock for the platters using a waterproof glue. If you want, alternate dark and light colored bands of wood. When the glue sets, sand the surface smooth and attach the stock to the template. Pin rout the inside (tree-shaped) gutters with a 3/8" core box bit, and the outside gutter and trough with a 3/4" core box bit. Finally, cut the outside shape with a 3/8" straight bit.

Finish with salad bowl finish or mineral oil.

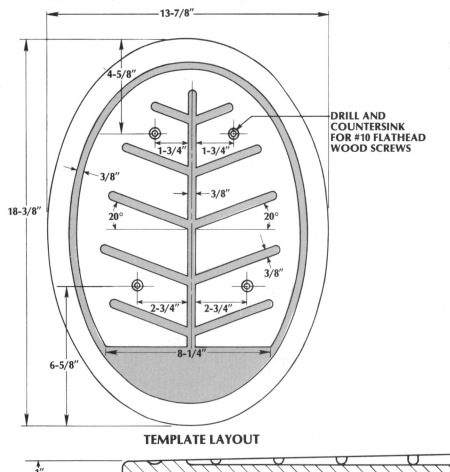

TEMPLATE LAYOUT

13-7/8"

4-5/8"

DRILL AND COUNTERSINK FOR #10 FLATHEAD WOOD SCREWS

1-3/4" 1-3/4"

3/8"

3/8"

18-3/8"

20° 20°

3/8"

6-5/8"

2-3/4" 2-3/4"

8-1/4"

SIDE VIEW

1"

3/4"

3/8"

1/4"

From *HANDS ON* Nov/Dec 83

Here is a set of salt and pepper shakers that you'll really enjoy making and using. Turn one at a time or several sets at a time out of a full 2 × 2 or glued-up stock (allow glued-up stock to remain clamped for at least 24 hours). Turn the shakers so the bases are toward the quill. If you turn more than one at a time, you'll need to leave approximately 1/2" of stock between each shaker. After you have turned the outside contour, turn off the machine and remove the tool rest and turning. Mount the saw table, then remount the turning. Raise the table level with the bottom of the stock. Set the miter gauge next to the stock and tighten the miter gauge locking screw. Release the stock from the lathe by retracting the quill, and mount the drill chuck. Using Forstner bits, counterbore and drill the inside of the shakers. If you turned more than one at a time, cut off the end shaker and repeat the boring operation for the next shaker. Sand the ends of the shakers smooth and drill the 3/32" shaker holes. Apply finish to the outside surface only. Insert cork stoppers (available at hardware stores).

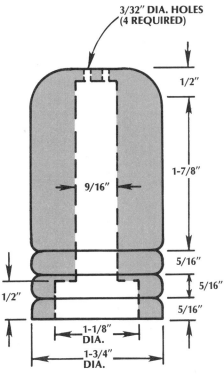

3/32" DIA. HOLES
(4 REQUIRED)

1/2"

1-7/8"

9/16"

5/16"

5/16"

1/2"

5/16"

1-1/8"
DIA.

1-3/4"
DIA.

ROOSTER TRIVET

From *HANDS ON* Nov/Dec 83

This uniquely designed trivet makes a good gift for cooks who enjoy serving casseroles hot from the oven or just need a place to set a hot skillet.

To make this trivet, prepare a 1/2" × 7-1/2" × 8-1/4" blank of hardwood—cherry, walnut, etc. Transfer the pattern to the blank. Drill holes in each of the sections to be cut out. Only one hole is necessary but a series of holes will reduce cutting time. Use a backup board to prevent chip-out on the backside. Cut the outside and inside contours on the jigsaw and file the edges smooth with pattern files. Apply a penetrating oil finish or leave plain.

ONE SQUARE = 1/2"

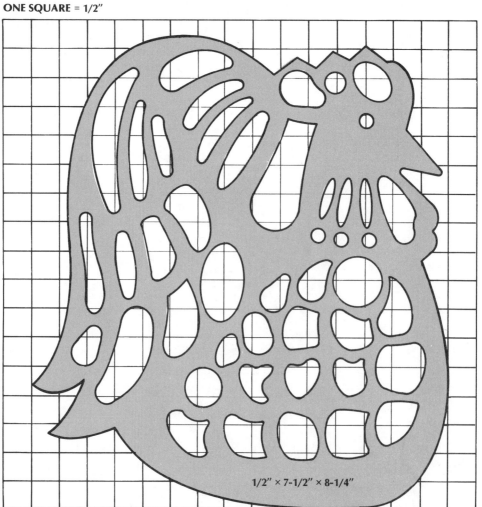

1/2" × 7-1/2" × 8-1/4"

This project will prevent countless finger burns when moving the oven rack in or out. The "kitchen fish" has a "mouth" that pushes hot oven racks in and a "gill cover" that pulls them out. And, when the fish is not in use, it makes an attractive decoration on the kitchen wall.

To make four of these fish at one time, tape together two pieces of 3/4" × 5" × 14-1/2" stock. Transfer the design from the drawing to the stock and then drill the 3/16" diameter tail hole. Next, cut out the design on the bandsaw. Resaw the stock to 3/8" and sand the surface smooth.

Make the eyes by using a round-tipped punch and hammer, or drill a small countersink with a 3/16" twist bit.

The scales are formed with a 1" wood chisel and a mallet. (It's a good idea to first practice this on scrap stock.)

Sand the project with the drum sander and round the edges by hand with fine sandpaper. Highlight the eyes and scales with stain; then, apply the finish of your choice.

ONE SQUARE = 1/2"

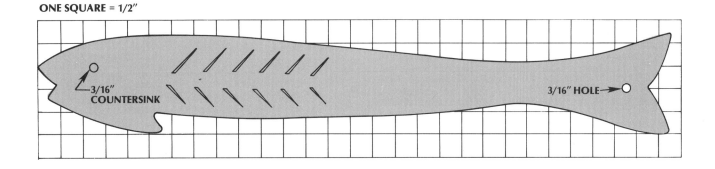

3/16"
COUNTERSINK

3/16" HOLE →

HERB CLOCK RA

From *HANDS ON* May/June 81

Here's an interesting kitchen clock filled with good things from the earth—seeds, grains, and herbs. This is a great project because of the variety, no two have to be alike. You can buy dried herbs at a natural foods store, and the clockworks are available at craft/hobby stores or by mail order.

Select a fine hardwood for the face of the clock. The body can be made from inexpensive pine. To make this on the router arm, make two pin routing fixtures; the first (Fixture 1) to cut the clock face (C) and cavities, and the second (Fixture 2) to make the rabbets for the glazing (B) and the clock face, and to cut the hole for the clock motor.

To make the face (C), attach 1/2" thick hardwood to Fixture 1. With a 3/8" pin and straight bit, rout the shapes shown. Switch to a 3/8" piloted round over bit (and no pin), and round all the edges of the clock face. Lay it aside and attach Fixture 1 to the body stock. Again working with the 3/8" pin and straight bit, cut the cavities approximately 1" deep. Remount the body on Fixture 2 and cut the rabbets and the hole.

DRILL FOR #6 FLATHEAD WOOD SCREW

15°   45°

45°

15°

11"

1/2"

5-3/4"

1/2"

1/2"   11"

CONNECT BOTH FIXTURES AND DRILL TOGETHER

FIXTURE 1

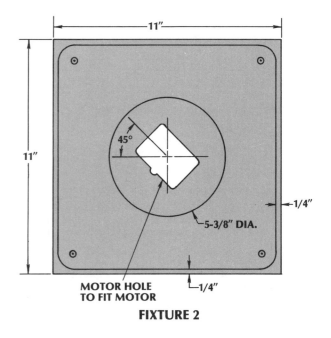

11"

11"

45°

1/4"

5-3/8" DIA.

1/4"

MOTOR HOLE TO FIT MOTOR

FIXTURE 2

Cut the glazing (B) (we used clear acrylic plastic) and drill five holes, one in the center for the clock post and four in the corners where the face (C) will attach to the body (A). Put the clock motor in place, fill the cavities with herbs, and assemble the pieces. Use #6 brass flathead wood screws to attach the face to the body.

LIST OF MATERIALS

(finished dimensions in inches)
A Body   1-1/2 × 11 × 11
B Glazing   1/8 × 10-1/2 × 10-1/2
C Face   1/2 × 11 × 11

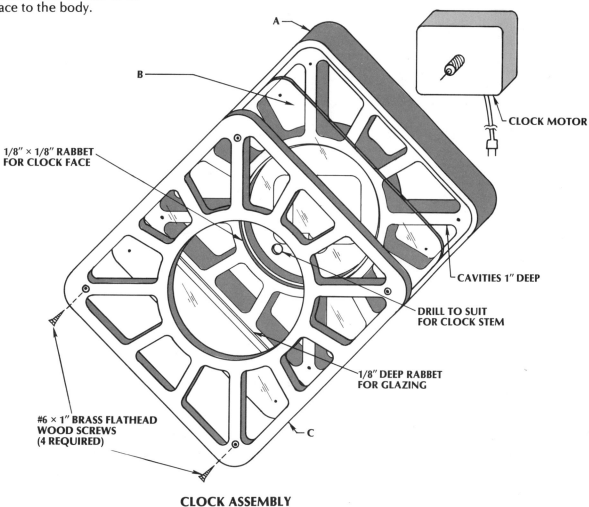

A

B

1/8″ × 1/8″ RABBET
FOR CLOCK FACE

CLOCK MOTOR

CAVITIES 1″ DEEP

DRILL TO SUIT
FOR CLOCK STEM

1/8″ DEEP RABBET
FOR GLAZING

#6 × 1″ BRASS FLATHEAD
WOOD SCREWS
(4 REQUIRED)

C

CLOCK ASSEMBLY

SALT BOX

From *HANDS ON* Nov/Dec 80

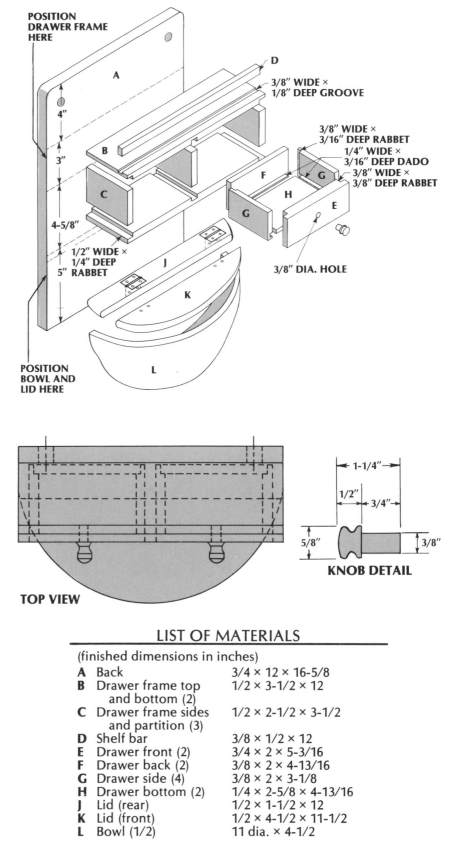

TOP VIEW

KNOB DETAIL

Not so many years ago, cooks kept a box of coarse salt near the cookstove to season soups, stews, or whatever was cooking. These antiques are still handy, but now they're used to hold matches, coupons, and many small items you have nowhere to keep.

Start this project by cutting and gluing up rings for a large bowl 11" in diameter. Allow bowl to remain clamped for 24 hours before turning. Glue up 3/4" thick stock for the back.

Resaw stock to thicknesses you need for the other parts—1/2", 3/8", and 1/4". Cut all pieces to size.

Using a dado blade or router accessory, cut joinery in drawer pieces and drawer frame. Glue up drawers and drawer frame.

Turn the wooden bowl and drawer knobs. Using a piece of masking tape, mark a straight line down the middle of the bowl. Saw the bowl in half on the bandsaw.

Glue the bowl and the drawer frame to the back and reinforce with #10 × 1-1/4" flathead wood screws. Hinge the lid pieces together and glue the rear piece to the lip of the bowl. Drill the drawer front for knobs, glue knobs in holes, and slide drawers in place. If you want, round the edges of the lid, drawers, and drawer frame with a rasp. Finish the project with oil or salad bowl finish.

What do you do with the other half of the bowl? Another Salt Box—they make unique gifts.

LIST OF MATERIALS

(finished dimensions in inches)

A	Back	3/4 × 12 × 16-5/8
B	Drawer frame top and bottom (2)	1/2 × 3-1/2 × 12
C	Drawer frame sides and partition (3)	1/2 × 2-1/2 × 3-1/2
D	Shelf bar	3/8 × 1/2 × 12
E	Drawer front (2)	3/4 × 2 × 5-3/16
F	Drawer back (2)	3/8 × 2 × 4-13/16
G	Drawer side (4)	3/8 × 2 × 3-1/8
H	Drawer bottom (2)	1/4 × 2-5/8 × 4-13/16
J	Lid (rear)	1/2 × 1-1/2 × 12
K	Lid (front)	1/2 × 4-1/2 × 11-1/2
L	Bowl (1/2)	11 dia. × 4-1/2

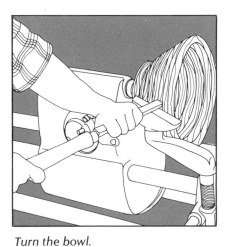

Cut the rings at a 30° angle with a jigsaw.

Turn the bowl.

Make a straight line with masking tape to aid in cutting bowl in two.

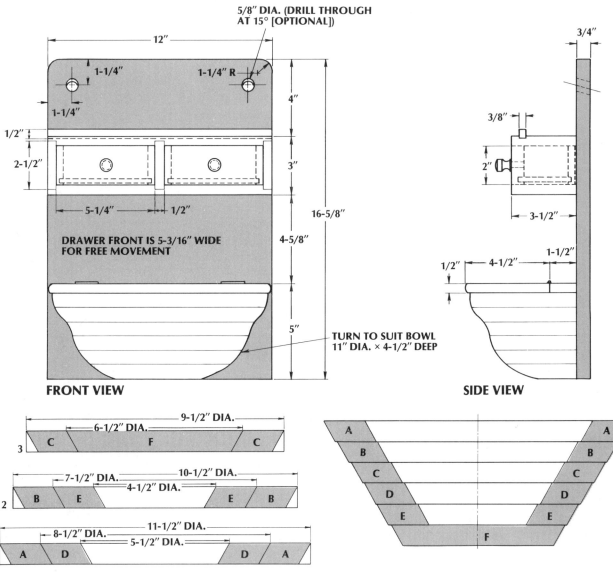

5/8" DIA. (DRILL THROUGH AT 15° [OPTIONAL])

12"

1-1/4"

1-1/4" R

1-1/4"

1/2"

2-1/2"

4"

3"

5-1/4"

1/2"

16-5/8"

DRAWER FRONT IS 5-3/16" WIDE FOR FREE MOVEMENT

4-5/8"

5"

TURN TO SUIT BOWL
11" DIA. × 4-1/2" DEEP

FRONT VIEW

3/4"

3/8"

2"

3-1/2"

1/2"

4-1/2"

1-1/2"

SIDE VIEW

9-1/2" DIA.

6-1/2" DIA.

3   C   F   C

7-1/2" DIA.

10-1/2" DIA.

4-1/2" DIA.

2   B   E   E   B

11-1/2" DIA.

8-1/2" DIA.

5-1/2" DIA.

1   A   D   D   A

Make these cuts in three pieces of stock. Note: All stock is three-quarter inches thick.

A   A
B   B
C   C
D   D
E   E
F

Detail showing ring assembly for bowl.

KNIFE BLOCK CUTTING BOARD

From *HANDS ON* Nov/Dec 80

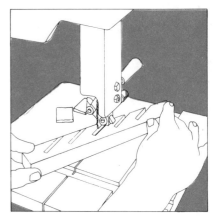

2. Resaw the knife block according to the List of Materials. Using the belt sander, sand all resawed parts smooth.

3. Cut the remaining parts to size according to the List of Materials.

4. Cut the joinery in the sides (B) and the knife block (C) using dado blades. When using the dado blade, you'll have to do some hand work where the 3/4" groove meets the 1/2" dado on the side.

5. Round the corners on the back (D), sides (B), and cutting board (A).

6. Cut knife slots in the knife block using the bandsaw.

7. Assemble parts (B, C, D, E) with resorcinol glue.

8. Rout the juice trough. On one end of the cutting board, rout a 3/4" wide × 3/8" deep trough. On the other three sides, rout a 1/2" wide by 3/8" deep trough. Use a core box router bit and a router guide for this operation.

9. Apply the finish. Use a nontoxic finish such as mineral oil or salad bowl finish.

Cut the slots in the knife block with a bandsaw.

Here's a simple project that combines two very useful kitchen accessories, a knife block and a cutting board. Not only is this project very handy, but it's also a beautiful kitchen wall decoration.

1. Prepare the stock. Resaw 3/4" stock to make the back (D) and the bottom (E). Glue up the stock to make the back (D), the knife block (C), and the cutting board (A). Use waterproof resorcinol glue. Scrub off the excess glue after clamping pressure has been applied.

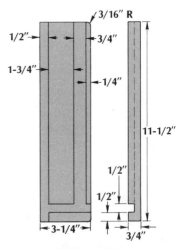

SIDE DETAIL

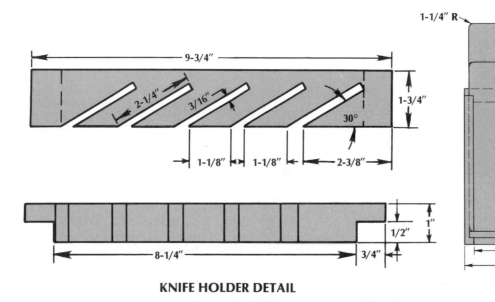

KNIFE HOLDER DETAIL

SIDE VIEW

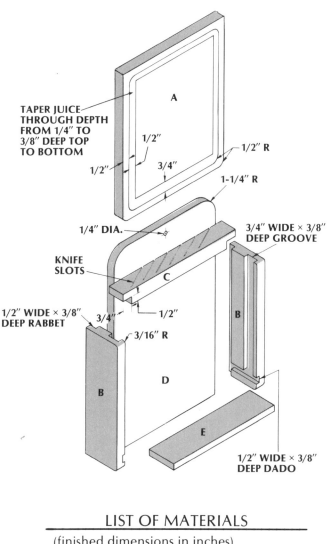

TAPER JUICE THROUGH DEPTH FROM 1/4" TO 3/8" DEEP TOP TO BOTTOM

A

1/2"

1/2" R

1/2"

3/4"

1-1/4" R

1/4" DIA.

3/4" WIDE × 3/8" DEEP GROOVE

KNIFE SLOTS

C

1/2" WIDE × 3/8" DEEP RABBET

3/4"

1/2"

3/16" R

B

B

D

B

E

1/2" WIDE × 3/8" DEEP DADO

LIST OF MATERIALS

(finished dimensions in inches)

A	Cutting board	3/4 × 9 × 13-1/4
B	Sides (2)	3/4 × 3-1/4 × 11-1/2
C	Knife block	1 × 1-3/4 × 9-3/4
D	Back	1/2 × 9 × 17
E	Bottom	1/2 × 2-1/2 × 9

CUTTING BOARDS

From HANDS ON Jan/Feb/Mar 83

Cutting boards are always quick and easy. They're even easier with a thickness planer. You need to follow only a few guidelines.

Select close-grained woods such as maple and cherry. Arrange the boards so that the grain of each is going in the same direction. Vertical annual rings, where possible, are best. Use a waterproof glue, such as resorcinol or plastic resin glue. Scrub off all excess glue with a wet shop cloth *before* it dries. Leaving any hard glue on the stock and then running it through the planer will nick and chip the knives.

You can use the router arm with a pin routing fixture to make multiples of the same shape. A core box router bit can be used to form a gutter around the edge. Select any one of a variety of bits for a decorative edge treatment.

After planing and shaping, apply a nontoxic finish such as salad bowl finish or mineral oil.

Clamp up stock for a breadboard. Scrub off all excess glue before it dries.

TOWEL/TOOL RACK ▣

From *HANDS ON* Jan/Feb 84

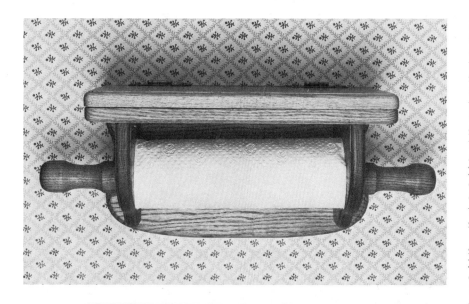

Most small repair jobs in a home don't take place in the shop; they occur on-site. Instead of making a trip to the shop for a hammer or screwdriver every time the need arises, here's an idea for a kitchen toolbox. This handy accessory doubles as a paper towel rack and tool storage area.

1. Cut all parts (A, B, C, D, F) to size according to the List of Materials.

2. Transfer the patterns from the drawings to the stock and cut out contours with the bandsaw. Sand the contours on the drum and disc sanders.

Drill the 1" diameter holes in the sides (A) for the towel bar (F).

3. Make the template for the recessed top (C) and lid (D). Draw the inside contour of the lid on a piece of 3/8" plywood. Drill 3/4" holes in the corners of the contour, then, cut the inside out with the jigsaw. Center the template on the stock and attach it with double-faced carpet tape or brads.

4. Pin rout the top (C) and lid (D) using the overarm router with a 1/2" diameter pin and a 1/2" diameter core box router bit. Make two or three passes to complete the recess.

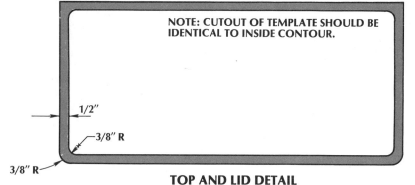

NOTE: CUTOUT OF TEMPLATE SHOULD BE IDENTICAL TO INSIDE CONTOUR.

1/2"

3/8" R

3/8" R

TOP AND LID DETAIL

ONE SQUARE = 1"

KITCHEN CABINET HINGES

D
C
A
3-1/8"
3-1/8"
1" DIA.
B

3/4"
3/4"
1/4"
8-1/2"
6-1/4"
3/4"

6-1/4"
7"
7-3/4"
3/4"

SIDE VIEW

D
C
A
B
A

11-1/4"
15-1/2"

FRONT VIEW

5. Turn both handles (E) at one time and finish sand them while they are still on the lathe. Cut the handles apart with the bandsaw and drill a 15/16" diameter × 3/4" deep hole in the end of each handle. Sand the ends of the towel bar (F) on the disc or belt sander until you achieve a snug fit with the handles.

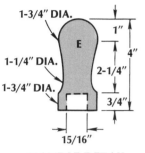

1-3/4" DIA.

1"

E

4"

1-1/4" DIA.

2-1/4"

1-3/4" DIA.

3/4"

15/16"

HANDLE DETAIL

6. Shape the edges of the sides (A), top (C), lid (D), and back (B) with the pin router or with the shaper. Use a quarter round bit on the router or select the profile that you want.

7. Assemble the towel holder by attaching the sides (A) to the back (B) with #9 × 1-1/2" flathead wood screws. Next, glue the top (C) onto the sides. The lid (D) is attached to the back with kitchen cabinet hinges.

Finish sand the project and apply the finish of your choice.

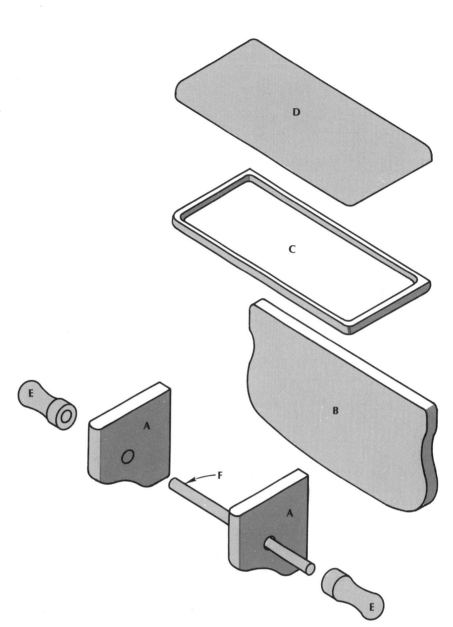

LIST OF MATERIALS

(finished dimensions in inches)

A	Sides (2)	3/4 × 6-1/4 × 6-1/4
B	Back	3/4 × 8-1/2 × 15-1/2
C	Top	3/4 × 7 × 15-1/2
D	Lid	3/4 × 7 × 15-1/2
E	Handles (2)	1-3/4 dia. × 4
F	Towel bar	1 dia. × 14-1/4

KITCHEN ORGANIZER

From *HANDS ON* Sept/Oct 80

Keep all frequently used ingredients and kitchen items within arm's reach. In this clever, compact kitchen organizer, you can store spices, paper towels, tissues, food storage bags, foil, and wrap.

1. Select stock and cut all pieces to size according to the List of Materials. Add an extra 1/2" to the width of the box top to enable you to cut away any splinters caused by edging.

2. Cut all joinery—3/4" × 2-1/2" stop dadoes are cut into the box sides for spice shelves. Cut out the lower contour of the sides (A) with a bandsaw.

3. Drill recesses in the shelves (D) for spice jars with a multi-spur bit or Forstner bit.

4. Drill a pivot hole in the top (B) to start the piercing cut for the tissue dispenser.

5. Cut out the dispenser hole with a jigsaw or sabre saw and sand the inside edge.

6. Edge around the top and inside edge of the dispenser with a router or shaper. Rip the top to width.

7. Turn a cylinder on a lathe to make the towel rod (S).

8. Cut the trough in the marker ledge (J) with a 1" flute molding bit or core box router. Switch to a V-groove cutter and make decorative grooves in the plywood back (F) of the box.

9. Make recesses for hinges in the door frame and sides (A) with a chisel or 1/4" straight router bit.

10. Drill a hole for the door knob.

11. Sand all pieces smooth and complete the assembly.

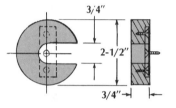

PAPER TOWEL ROD HOLDER

#8 × 1-1/4" FLATHEAD WOOD SCREW
1/4" 18 GA. × 5/8" BRAD
MARKER TROUGH
3/4"
1"
2"
1-1/4"
1/4" WIDE × 3/8" DEEP RABBET

MARKER LEDGE, STILE, AND WRITING BOARD ASSEMBLY

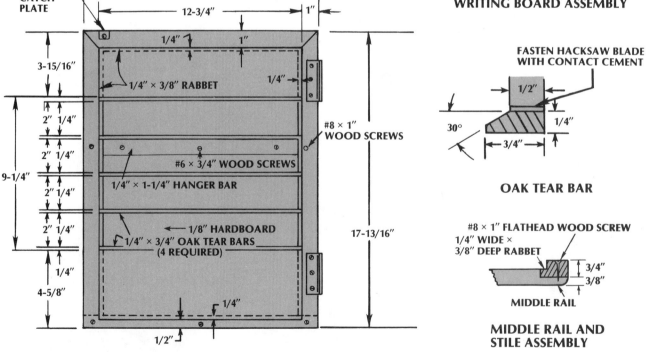

MAGNETIC CATCH PLATE
14-3/4"
12-3/4"
1"
3-15/16"
1/4"
1"
1/4" × 3/8" RABBET
1/4"
2" 1/4"
2" 1/4"
9-1/4"
2" 1/4"
2" 1/4"
1/4"
4-5/8"
#8 × 1" WOOD SCREWS
#6 × 3/4" WOOD SCREWS
1/4" × 1-1/4" HANGER BAR
1/8" HARDBOARD
1/4" × 3/4" OAK TEAR BARS (4 REQUIRED)
17-13/16"
1/4"
1/2"

DOOR (REAR VIEW)

FASTEN HACKSAW BLADE WITH CONTACT CEMENT
1/2"
30°
1/4"
3/4"

OAK TEAR BAR

#8 × 1" FLATHEAD WOOD SCREW
1/4" WIDE ×
3/8" DEEP RABBET
3/4"
3/8"
MIDDLE RAIL

MIDDLE RAIL AND STILE ASSEMBLY

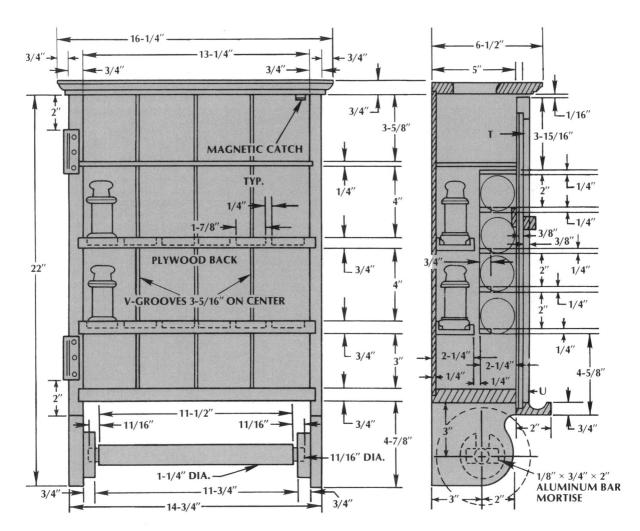

FRONT VIEW

Dimensions labeled: 16-1/4", 13-1/4", 3/4", 3/4", 3/4", 3/4", 2", 22", 2", 3/4", 11-1/2", 11/16", 11/16", 11-3/4", 14-3/4", 3/4", 3/4", 1-1/4" DIA., 11/16" DIA.

MAGNETIC CATCH

TYP.

1/4"

1-7/8"

PLYWOOD BACK

V-GROOVES 3-5/16" ON CENTER

3/4", 3-5/8", 1/4", 4", 3/4", 4", 3/4", 3", 3/4", 4-7/8"

SIDE VIEW

Dimensions labeled: 6-1/2", 5", 1/16", T, 3-15/16", 2", 1/4", 1/4", 3/8", 3/8", 2", 1/4", 3/4", 2", 1/4", 1/4", 4-5/8", 2-1/4", 2-1/4", 1/4", 1/4", U, 3", 2", 3/4"

1/8" × 3/4" × 2"
ALUMINUM BAR MORTISE

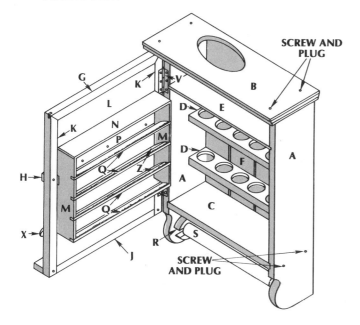

SCREW AND PLUG

SCREW AND PLUG

LIST OF MATERIALS

(finished dimensions in inches)

A	Sides (2)	3/4 × 5 × 22
B	Top	3/4 × 7 × 16-1/4
C	Shelf	3/4 × 5 × 13-3/4
D	Shelves (2)	3/4 × 2-1/4 × 13-3/4
E	Shelf	1/4 × 4-3/4 × 13-3/4
F	Back	1/4 × 13-3/4 × 17-1/8
G	Top rail	3/4 × 1-1/4 × 12-3/4
H	Middle rail	3/4 × 3/4 × 14-3/4
J	Marker ledge	3/4 × 2 × 14-3/4
K	Stiles (2)	3/4 × 1-1/4 × 17-13/16
L	Back	1/8 × 12-3/4 × 16-5/16
M	Sides (2)	1/4 × 2-1/4 × 9
N	Top	1/4 × 2-1/4 × 12-3/4
P	Hanger bar	1/4 × 1-1/4 × 12-1/4
Q	Tear bars (4)	1/4 × 3/4 × 12-3/4
R	Rod holders (2)	3/4 × 2-1/2 × 2-1/2
S	Towel rod	1-1/4 dia. × 12-7/8
T	Cork board	1/16 × 6-1/8 × 12-3/4
U	Writing board	1/8 × 10-3/16 × 12-3/4

TAMBOUR BREAD BOX

From *HANDS ON* July/Aug 82

The tambour bread box is a handsome, functional addition to any kitchen. The body is constructed of 3/4″ stock and the special tambour door is made from standard screen bead stock. This practical touch helps keep this project easy enough for the beginning woodworker.

1. Cut the stock for the base (A), sides (B), top (C), back (D), front edge (E), and door rail (F), using 3/4″ stock. Cut the false back (G) out of 1/4″ plywood.

2. Rout the edges on the base (A) and the top (C) with a 3/8″ beading bit in a hand router. With a 1/4″ router bit, cut the 1/4″ deep groove for the false back in both sides (B). Use a router guide.

3. Cut the curves on the sides (B) using the bandsaw.

4. To rout the tambour groove, make a template, according to the drawing, out of 3/8″ scrap stock.

Attach it to the side (B). Use a router with a bushing guide and a 3/8″ straight bit to rout the groove.

5. Cut the 1/4″ deep groove in the top of the tambour door rail (F) using the dado blade. Then cut the tenons on the end of the door rail.

6. Assemble the sides (B), top (C), back (D), front edge (E), and false back (G) together with glue and nails or screws. Cover the heads of the fasteners with putty or plugs.

7. Cut the screen molding (H) to the required length for the tambour door. Glue the strips one by one to the artist's canvas, square the edges, then weight the tambour door down. After the glue has been allowed to set for one hour, remove the weights and bend the door around to ensure against any tambours being stuck together. Glue the first tambour into the groove of the tambour door rail (F). Allow the door assembly to dry for 24 hours.

8. Insert the tambour door into the grooves in the bread box. Check the fit, sanding the edges if needed. Attach the base (A) with wood screws only.

9. Sand the entire project. Attach the knob and apply the finish of your choice.

LIST OF MATERIALS

(finished dimensions in inches)

A	Base	3/4 × 16-1/2 × 19-5/8
B	Sides	3/4 × 11 × 16
C	Top	3/4 × 6-1/4 × 19-1/2
D	Back	3/4 × 11 × 17
E	Front edge	3/4 × 3/4 × 17
F	Door rail	3/4 × 1-3/4 × 17-1/2
G	False back	1/4 × 8 × 17-1/2
H	Screen molding (20)	1/4 × 3/4 × 17-1/2

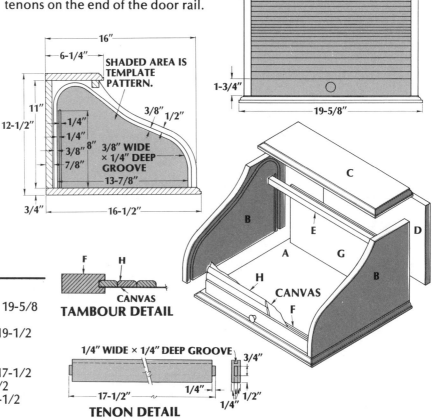

SHADED AREA IS TEMPLATE PATTERN.

3/8″ WIDE × 1/4″ DEEP GROOVE

TAMBOUR DETAIL

TENON DETAIL

1/4″ WIDE × 1/4″ DEEP GROOVE

CANVAS

GALLERY RAIL TOWEL HOLDER

From *HANDS ON* July/Aug 82

This towel holder turns a plain roll of paper towels into an attractive point of interest in any kitchen. And, it's easier to build than it might look because you make use of gallery spindles that you can buy.

1. Cut the stock for the top (A) and the two sides (B). Cut one piece 3/4" × 2-1/2" × 15" to make the rail parts (C, D).

2. Glue-up the stock for the roll pins (E) using yellow woodworker's glue. Clamp and allow to dry at least 24 hours before turning.

3. Rout or shape the edges of the top (A) and both sides of the 2-1/2" × 15" piece. Rip this 2-1/2" piece into 1-1/8" wide pieces (C, D).

4. Miter the rail parts (C, D) to size; then, cut the spline grooves. Assemble and clamp the rail together.

5. Drill the holes in sides (B) for the roll pins (E) and the bullet catches. Cut and sand the curves on the two sides (B).

6. Drill the holes in the top (A) and rails for the gallery spindles. Drill and counterbore for screws to assemble the top (A) to the sides (B).

7. Turn the roll pins (E) to shape. Remove the tool rest and sand them while they're still on the lathe.

8. Attach the sides (B) to the top (A), using glue and screws. Plug the screw holes and sand flush. Glue and assemble the gallery pins to the top and the rails.

9. Insert the bullet catches from inside the 1-3/8" hole, pressing them into place. Friction holds them secure. Apply the finish of your choice.

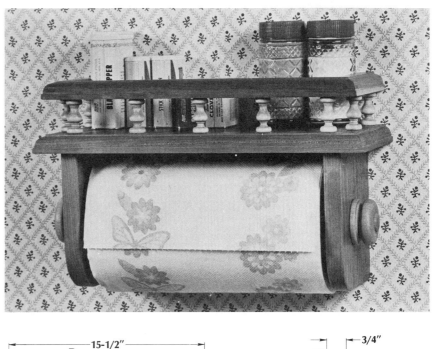

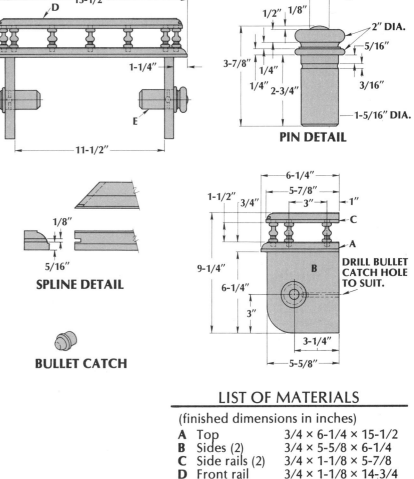

PIN DETAIL

SPLINE DETAIL

BULLET CATCH

DRILL BULLET CATCH HOLE TO SUIT.

LIST OF MATERIALS

(finished dimensions in inches)

A	Top	3/4 × 6-1/4 × 15-1/2
B	Sides (2)	3/4 × 5-5/8 × 6-1/4
C	Side rails (2)	3/4 × 1-1/8 × 5-7/8
D	Front rail	3/4 × 1-1/8 × 14-3/4
E	Roll pins (2)	2 dia. × 3-7/8

KITCHEN SLIDE RULE

From *HANDS ON* Nov/Dec 83

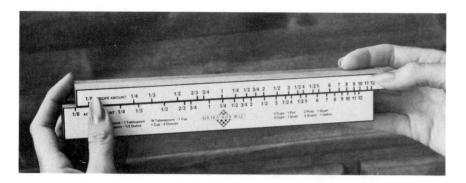

This slide rule is a handy tool that allows the cook to alter recipes for more or fewer people. It also comes in handy when you need to adjust a recipe because you have a limited supply of one ingredient on hand—two eggs instead of three, for instance.

This easy-to-make slide rule is a router attachment project. We've included the full-sized scale that you can photocopy. The slide rule is 10" long. You can easily perform the same operations on 41" long stock and make four of these calculators at one time.

Prepare enough 1" × 1-1/2" clear stock for the number of slide rules you make. Joint or sand the edges smooth. Prepare matching scrap pieces for test cuts.

Now use the drill press. Mount the router chuck with a 1/4" straight router bit and cut a 1/2" deep groove in the center of the bottom half of the stock. Use feather boards and a push stick. Switch to the dovetail router bit and rout out the dovetail slot. Next, rout the dovetail tongue. Set the machine so you are cutting with the stock between the bit and fence and feed the stock from right to left against the rotation.

Check the fit of the slide. If it's too loose, insert a bullet catch (available at most hardware stores) to provide the tension you need.

Finally, glue on the scale and apply varnish. Wax the dovetail slot with a good quality furniture paste wax.

To use the rule, set the amount the recipe calls for on the top scale over the amount you want on the bottom scale. For example, if the recipe serves eight and you need to fix enough for ten, set the eight over the ten. Now, as you read the recipe, locate the quantity your recipe calls for on the upper scale and read the actual amount you need directly below it on the lower scale.

1-1/2"

1-1/2"

10"

10"

BULLET CATCH PROVIDES TENSION (OPTIONAL)

1/4" 1/2" 1"

1/2"

1/2" 1"

5/16"

9/16"

RECIPE AMOUNT ACTUAL AMOUNT

1/8 1/8 1/8

1/4 1/4 1/4

3 TEASPOONS = 1 TABLESPOON
1 TABLESPOON = 1/2 OUNCE

1/3 1/3

1/2 1/2

16 TABLESPOONS = 1 CUP
1 CUP = 8 OUNCES

2/3 3/4 2/3 3/4

KITCHEN SLIDE RULE

1 1

1-1/4 1-1/4

1-1/2 1-3/4 1-1/2 1-3/4

2 CUPS = 1 PINT
4 CUPS = 1 QUART

2 2

2-1/2 2-1/2

3 3

3-1/2 3-1/2

4 4

4-1/2 4-1/2

5 5

2 PINTS = 1 QUART
4 QUARTS = 1 GALLON

6 6

7 7

8 8

9 9

10 10

11 11

12 12

TURNING A WOODEN PLACE SETTING

From *HANDS ON* Nov/Dec 80

For most of us, it was our first woodturning project—turning a bowl on a lathe. But afterward we went on to bigger and better things and forgot about that simple bowl that once had us basking in the glory of our own accomplishment.

However, turning wooden utensils is more than just an educational exercise. Few woodworkers have mastered it; most of us are still trying and learning. But with just a little bit of practice, you can do simple, beautiful bowls, plates, and goblets.

THE MATERIALS

Kitchen and dining utensils have to stand up under a lot of abuse. Bowls and plates are constantly banged and scraped with forks and spoons. Soup bowls and goblets have to hold both hot and cold liquids. And all utensils need to be washed again and again.

In general, close-grained hardwoods make more serviceable goblets, bowls, and plates than softwoods. They resist indentation and the density of the wood helps to repel moisture.

Oily woods do better than those with few natural oils. Teak and rosewood are permeated with oils that prevent them from absorbing moisture. With other woods, it's advisable to apply a lavish coat of waterproof finish and hope that it soaks in. But this soaking is at best an imperfect substitute for a wood's own natural, waterproofing oils.

In considering what materials to turn, you may have to make some tradeoffs. Cherry, for example, doesn't have the natural oils that rosewood has, but it's easier to find and a lot less expensive. Cedar, although it's not a hardwood, is inexpensive, loaded with oils, and will not absorb odors from the foods that come in contact with it.

LAMINATING RINGS

When you turned that first bowl, you probably used a solid laminated block of wood. And you scraped and scraped and scraped and scraped until the center was hollowed out and the sides were sloped. There is, however, an easier and more economical way to turn bowls and plates without wasting all that time and wood.

It involves stacking overlapping concentric rings. These rings are cut with either a bandsaw or jigsaw from a single piece of wood. After cutting, these rings are stacked in a cone shape. Turning is faster because the shape of the object is partially formed.

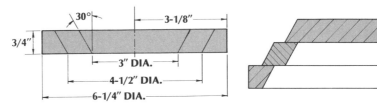

The rings needed to turn a bowl can be cut from a single board and glued and stacked.

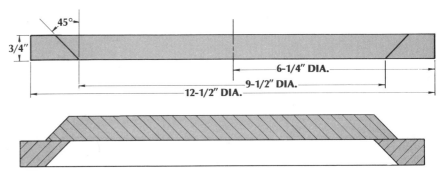

When making a bowl or plate, cuts are made, then stacked and glued to form general shape.

(continues on next page)

To cut out these concentric rings, use a compass to mark several circles on top of the board used. The circles will be cut out at an angle that is determined by the shape you want your finished turning to have and the slope of its sides.

If you use a jigsaw, you'll have to drill several 1/8" pilot holes to start the cuts. Be sure these holes are drilled at the same angle as the cuts you're about to make. Tilt the jigsaw table at the desired angle, slip a 1/8" blade through a pilot hole, and cut. Repeat until you have separated all the rings.

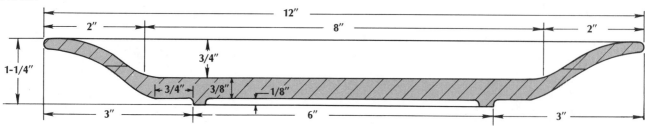

Cut the rings at a 30° angle on a jigsaw.

If you use a bandsaw, split the board down the middle instead of making pilot holes. Cut out each half-ring with the bandsaw table tilted at the proper angle. Glue these rings back together with waterproof glue.

Stack the rings one on top of the other and glue them together with waterproof resorcinol glue. If you're working with a dense, oily

wood like rosewood or teak, wipe the gluing surface with paint thinner before applying the glue to get a better bond.

Be sure, after you've stacked the rings, that all the grains run in the same direction. Laminating the

grains perpendicular to each other will in some cases increase the strength of a piece; but in this case, it will also increase the likelihood of splitting out. Wood expands up to ten times as much across the grain as with the grain when it

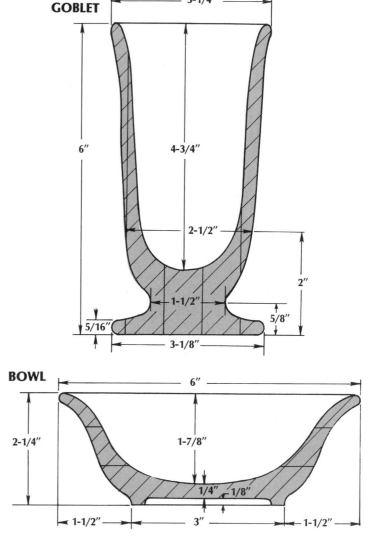

comes in contact with moisture. By running all the grains in the same direction, you insure that the laminations don't fight each other. Allow laminations to remain clamped for at least 24 hours before turning.

MOUNTING

To properly turn bowls and plates, you need to mount your stock on a faceplate twice. The first mounting allows you to turn the outside and the base of the utensil; with the second mounting, you turn the inside.

Select the proper size faceplate or screw mount and attach a mounting block to it. This block should be solid wood with no cracks or checks. Center the mounting block and glue it in place with aliphatic resin and a paper spacer between the mounting block and the turning stock. Allow the glue to dry overnight before turning. When dry, turn the outside of the bowl to the desired shape.

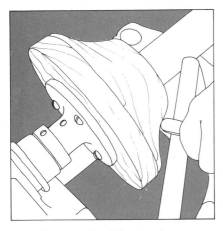

Turn the outside of the bowl.

Separate the turning from the block by carefully wedging them apart with a chisel. The paper spacer will insure that they come apart cleanly and easily, without tearing wood away from the turning stock.

Replace the mounting block with another that will fit inside the turned base, glue it to the stock as before. Turn the inside of the piece, separate it from the mount, and clean off the glue with a chisel and a little water.

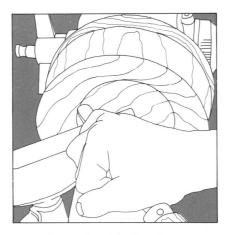

Turn the inside of the bowl.

TURNING A BOWL AND PLATE

The bowl and plate are each made from a single piece of 3/4" thick stock; the piece used to form the bowl is 6-1/2" square; and the one used to form the plate is 12-1/2" square.

To make the rings for the bowl, draw three concentric circles on the stock 3", 4-1/2", and 6-1/4" in diameter. Cut these on a 30° angle from vertical.

To make the rings for the plate, draw two concentric circles 9-1/2" and 12-1/2" in diameter, and cut on a 45° angle.

Laminate the rings, mount the turning stock, and turn the outside and inside contours.

TURNING A GOBLET

Unlike the bowl and plate, the best way to turn a goblet or utensil with nearly vertical sides is to use a solid block of wood. Cut or laminate a block 6" high and 3-3/4" on a side. Mount this using either the screw center or small faceplate.

Turn the outside of the goblet as if you were doing spindle turning, using the tailstock and dead center. After you've shaped the outside, remove the dead center from the tailstock and replace it with the chuck arbor. Mount the drill chuck on the chuck arbor, and a 1-3/4" drill bit in the chuck. With the drill

bit stationary and the workpiece turning, use the quill to drill out most of the inside contour of the goblet. Afterward, finish turning the inside as you did the bowl and plate.

PAD FINISHING

After sanding the workpiece smooth, keep it turning. Dip a #00 steel wool pad in a nontoxic finish such as mineral oil or salad bowl finish. Apply the finish evenly and liberally to the surface of the utensil as it turns. Squeeze the pad gently to achieve a uniform flow of finish onto the wood. Keep the wood wet for at least 5 minutes, giving the finish a chance to soak in.

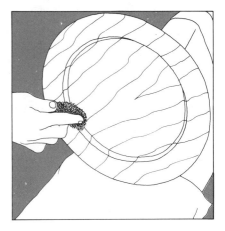

Pad finish the plate.

Apply at least two coats of finish; you can apply the second one a little more sparingly than the first. As the wood turns, the fine steel wool will buff the finish to a soft luster. Separate the piece from the mount, scrape away the glue, and apply a coat to the area where the mount mates to the utensil.

By keeping several turnings going at once, turning one while the glue on another cures and the finish on a third dries, you can turn four or more place settings in a few days. Your new place setting may not have the sentimental value of your first bowl, but you can be just as proud.

COLONIAL SPICE CABINET

From *HANDS ON* Jan/Feb/Mar 83

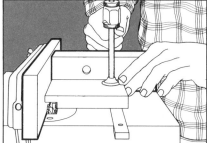

Use an auxiliary fence and a miter gauge extension to make cutting rabbets in the drawer fronts easier and safer.

This charming project is made from 1/2", 3/8", and 1/4" pine or hardwood stock that you can prepare on the bandsaw and/or thickness planer.

1. Resaw a 5' piece of 1 × 4 stock on the bandsaw for the 1/4" and 3/8" pieces. Use the miter gauge with a wooden fence extension and set up the cut so you will end up with 9/32" and 13/32" thick boards. Cutting the stock a little oversize gives you room to sand or plane it to proper thickness.

2. Prepare a 4' length of 1 × 10 and a 7' piece of 1 × 4 to 1/2" thickness.

3. Cut the back (B) from the wide stock. Then rip the 1/4" stock to 3-1/8" for the drawer backs (K, L) and bottoms (M, N). Rip the sides (A) to 4". Do not rip the back to finished width yet.

4. Cut to length all remaining parts according to the List of Materials. Tip: Cut the long stock into manageable pieces; then, use a stop block on the fence.

5. Form the rabbets in the backs of the sides (A) with the dado accessory. Use the fence shown in *Power Tool Woodworking for Everyone* for this operation. Next, cut the rabbets in the drawer fronts (G, H) using the same fence attachment and a miter gauge extension for support. Cut dadoes in the sides (A) and partitions (C, F).

6. Cut the grooves for drawer bottoms in the drawer sides (J) and the drawer fronts (G, H) with the dado accessory.

7. Cut out the contours on the sides (A). Use the bandsaw or jigsaw.

8. Dry-assemble the sides (A) and parts (C, D, E, F) with clamps and check for fit. Disassemble and then use glue and 4d finishing nails on the outside joints. Use glue only on the interior joints.

9. Rip the back (B) to width, then cut and sand the top and bottom contours. Drill the 1/4" mounting hole then attach the back with 1" brads.

10. Drill the knob mounting holes in the drawer fronts (G, H).

11. Assemble the drawers with glue and 3/4" brads. After the glue has dried, sand each drawer to fit. Use

LIST OF MATERIALS

(finished dimensions in inches)

A	Sides (2)	1/2 × 4 × 20
B	Back	1/2 × 8-1/2 × 24-3/4
C	Horizontal partitions (2)	1/2 × 3-1/2 × 8-1/4
D	Bottom	1/2 × 3-1/2 × 8-1/4
E	Drawer partitions (4)	1/2 × 3-1/2 × 4
F	Vertical partition	1/2 × 3-1/2 × 11-3/4
G	Small drawer fronts (6)	1/2 × 3-1/2 × 3-3/4
H	Large drawer front	1/2 × 3-1/2 × 8
J	Drawer sides (14)	3/8 × 3-1/2 × 3-1/4
K	Small drawer backs (6)	1/4 × 3-1/8 × 3
L	Large drawer back	1/4 × 3-1/8 × 7-1/4
M	Small drawer bottoms (6)	1/4 × 3-1/8 × 3-1/4
N	Large drawer bottom	1/4 × 3-1/8 × 7-1/2

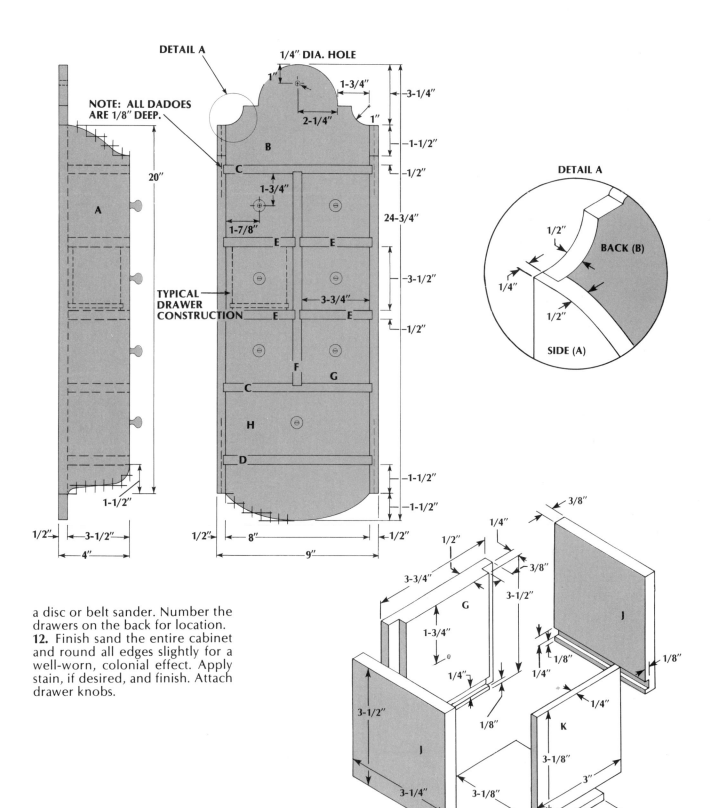

DETAIL A

1/4" DIA. HOLE

NOTE: ALL DADOES
ARE 1/8" DEEP.

TYPICAL
DRAWER
CONSTRUCTION

DETAIL A

1/2"

BACK (B)

1/4"

1/2"

SIDE (A)

a disc or belt sander. Number the drawers on the back for location. **12.** Finish sand the entire cabinet and round all edges slightly for a well-worn, colonial effect. Apply stain, if desired, and finish. Attach drawer knobs.

UTENSIL RACK

From *HANDS ON* Nov/Dec 80

Most modern kitchens are small, so space must be used efficiently. A good addition to any kitchen is a utensil rack where you can hang pots, pans, and other cooking utensils.

1. Cut all pieces to size, according to the List of Materials. Use the table saw.

2. Drill 3/4" dowel holes in the ends of the rails (A). Set up the rip fence and miter gauge to speed the process and provide accuracy.

3. Drill the 3/8" holes for the pegs (C) in two of the rails. Tilt the table 15° and determine the spacing for the holes.

4. Pad drill 3/4" dowel holes in the battens (B). Pad drilling the battens assures accurate alignment of the holes.

5. Assemble the rack by gluing the rails (A) to the battens (B) and inserting the dowels (D). After the glue has dried, sand the front of the rack flush. Next glue the pegs (C) into place.

6. Attach the plexiglass (E) to the back of the battens with #8 × 3/4" flathead wood screws. Drill countersinks in the plexiglass so the screws will be flush with the surface. The plexiglass protects the wall from hanging pots.

7. Finish the rack using polyurethane or any other water-resistant finish. Attach the rack to the wall, then make pan hooks from 1/8" diameter steel rod. Use pliers to form square corners and form the curve around 1" diameter pipe.

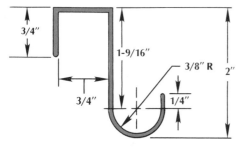

HOOK DETAIL

LIST OF MATERIALS

(finished dimensions in inches)

A	Rails (9)	3/4 × 2 × 24
B	Battens (2)	3/4 × 1-1/2 × 24
C	Pegs (10)	3/8 dia. × 3
D	Dowels (18)	3/4 dia. × 1-1/2
E	Plexiglass	1/8 × 18 × 24

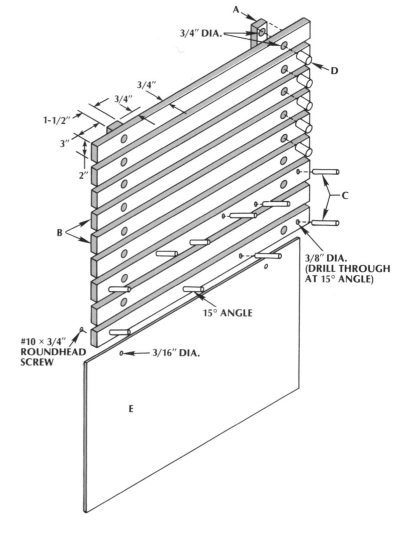

SPICE/RECIPE CABINET

From *HANDS ON* Mar/Apr/May 84

Cooks appreciate this attractive piece that organizes their recipes and spices in a neat, compact unit.

1. Prepare stock by using the bandsaw and/or thickness planer. Select good clear stock that's straight and free of defects.

2. Cut the stock to size according to the List of Materials. Rip all stock to the correct width then crosscut to correct lengths. When crosscutting, leave a little extra stock on the shelf (C), partition (F), and the drawer parts (G, H, J, K). Disc sand or cut these to final length later.

3. Cut the 45° miters on parts (A, B, D, E).

4. Cut the dadoes and rabbets in all parts. Next, cut the 1/8" groove in the drawer parts (G, H, J) for the drawer bottoms (K). Then cut the 1/8" wide × 1/4" deep groove in the top (D) of the drawer case to hold recipe cards.

5. Dry-assemble the drawer case and upper frame. Measure for the finished lengths of shelf (C) and partition (F) then cut or disc sand to length. Glue and clamp parts (A, B, C). Attach (D) to this assembly with #8 × 1-1/4" flathead wood screws and glue. Glue and clamp the remaining drawer case parts (D, E, F) to the upper frame assembly. Attach the drawer unit back (L) with brads.

6. Assemble the drawers with glue and clamps. Sand the drawers on the disc sander until they fit with the case.

Locate and drill the mounting holes for the drawer knobs.

7. Round the edges of the drawer fronts and the front edges of the case. Use a handheld router and a 1/4" quarter round bit, or use a rasp and sandpaper. Sand the project thoroughly and apply the finish of your choice.

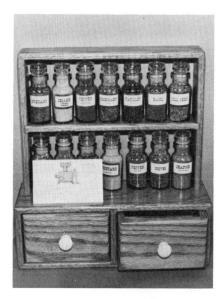

LIST OF MATERIALS

(finished dimensions in inches)

A	Shelf sides (2)	1/2 × 2-1/2 × 10
B	Top	1/2 × 2-1/2 × 13
C	Shelf	1/2 × 2-1/2 × 12-1/2
D	Drawer case top and bottom (2)	1/2 × 5 × 14
E	Drawer case sides (2)	1/2 × 5 × 4-3/4
F	Drawer case partition	1/2 × 4-3/4 × 4-1/4
G	Drawer fronts (2)	1/2 × 3-3/4 × 6-1/4
H	Drawer backs (2)	1/2 × 3-3/4 × 5-3/4
J	Drawer sides (4)	1/2 × 3-3/4 × 4-1/2
K	Drawer bottoms (2)	1/8 × 3-3/4 × 5-1/2
L	Drawer unit back	1/4 × 4-1/4 × 13-1/2

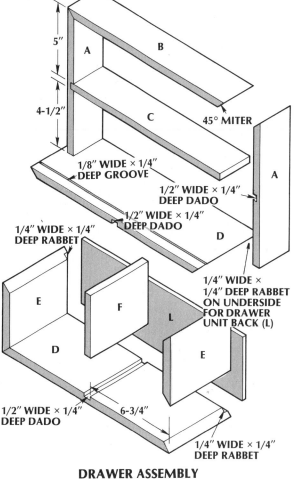

CASE ASSEMBLY

DRAWER ASSEMBLY

HOT POT TILE

From *HANDS ON* Sept/Oct 83

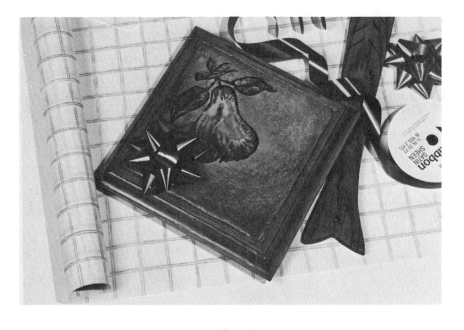

Here's a trivet that solves the problem of where to set hot dishes in the kitchen. First, select decorative tiles from a building supply or flooring outlet store. Cut 1/2" or 3/4" plywood the same size as the tile. Make the molding on the shaper or the molder and cut to size. (Thickness of the molding will depend on thickness of the plywood and the tile.)

Assemble the trivet by applying mastic to the bottom of the tile and one side of the plywood. Next, apply mastic to the edges and the molding and attach the molding. Mastic acts as a filler and an adhesive so there's no need to clamp. Set the project on a piece of waxed paper and allow to dry at least 24 hours.

Clean off excess mastic around the tile with mineral spirits and use the belt sander to remove excess mastic from the bottom of the trivet.

Finally, apply the stain or finish of your choice. Screw rubber feet on to the base as a final touch.

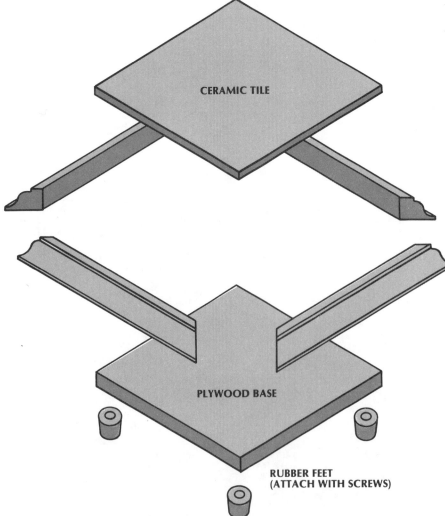

CERAMIC TILE

PLYWOOD BASE

RUBBER FEET
(ATTACH WITH SCREWS)

TOAST TONGS

From *HANDS ON* Sept/Oct 83

This project protects fingers from getting burned when removing hot items from the toaster. Select a suitable hardwood such as maple, cherry, or walnut. Cut the stock into 3/4" × 7/8" × 6-1/4" pieces. Drill the 5/8" hole in the 7/8" side of the stock. Next, cut out the excess stock with a bandsaw or jigsaw. Using the disc sander, sand off any saw marks and bevel the tips of the tongs. Finish with a non-toxic finish such as salad bowl finish or mineral oil.

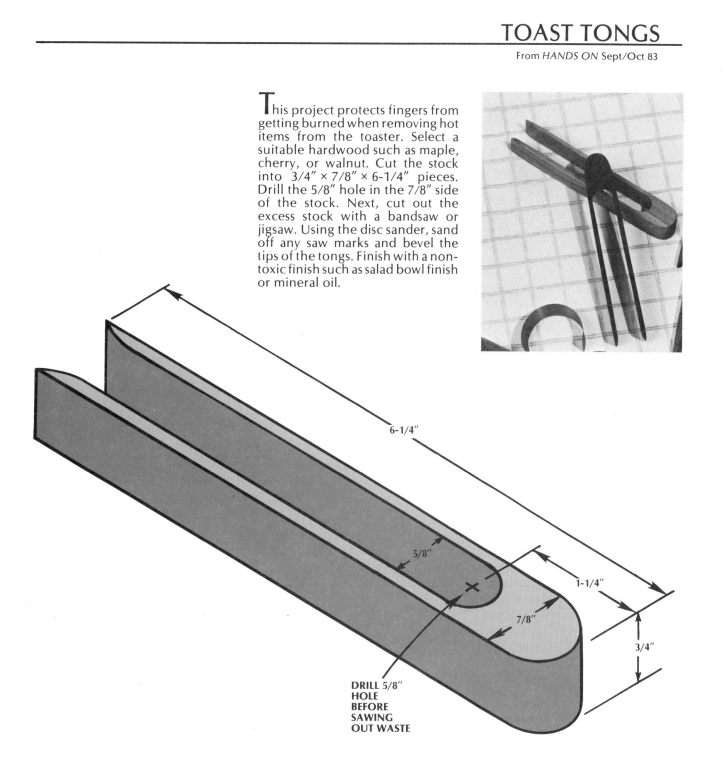

6-1/4"

5/8"

7/8"

1-1/4"

3/4"

DRILL 5/8" HOLE BEFORE SAWING OUT WASTE

Toys

Here are seventeen easy-to-build toys that will not only be a joy to make, but will also please the little ones in your life. Toys should be built with the child in mind, so there's always the need for safety. When making toys, be sure to avoid any sharp edges or corners; sand all parts of a project well to eliminate any chance of splinters; glue and clamp all parts securely and reinforce larger parts with dowels or screws; and, finally, use only nontoxic finishes.

ROCKING HORSE

From *HANDS ON* Sept/Oct 83

Design copyright © 1983 Robert Lee

Making a toy for a child is fun. Hours spent cutting, sanding, and finishing a toy are richly rewarded with the happiness shown on a child's face when he or she receives it. A very popular toy that woodworkers have made to delight children over the years is the rocking horse. Now you can make this favorite toy and please a child by using the easy-to-follow plans provided below. This simple design can be completed by the average woodworker in under 12 hours and costs less than $30 for materials.

1. Use the drawings provided to make full-scale patterns of parts (A-H). First draw a 1" grid on cardboard or hardboard; then, transfer the drawings to the grid. Next, cut out the pattern and transfer it to a 6' and 8' length of 2 × 12 stock.

Work around any knots or defects and, for maximum strength, make sure you follow the grain direction noted by arrows.

Cut the stock into manageable pieces before attempting to cut out the final shapes on the bandsaw or jigsaw. The saddle (G) can be made out of 2 × 12 stock and shaped, or made from 3/4" stock (H) and upholstered (see step 11).

Cut the braces (J) to size and chamfer the edges on the table saw (see *Power Tool Woodworking for Everyone*). Or you can use the disc sander to chamfer the ends of the braces.

2. Drill the holes for the handle, eyes, and tail where noted in the drawings. Drill the alignment holes in parts (B, C, D, E, F). Locate these holes very carefully since they are

used to align the various parts of the body during assembly. (Drill the 1" deep alignment holes for the legs [B, C] from the back without drilling through the stock.)

3. Sand all contoured parts on the disc and drum sanders. To ensure that the rockers (A) are identical, tape them together with double-faced carpet tape so they can be pad sanded.

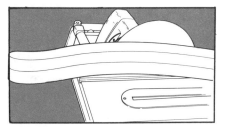

The rockers are sanded to identical contours by pad sanding.

4. Use the shaper with a groove cutter and shape a 1/4" deep groove in the back of the head (E) for the mane.

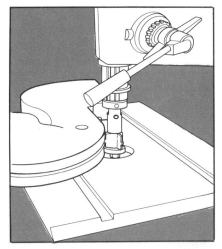

Cut the groove in the back of the head with the groove cutter.

5. Mark the outside edges of parts (B, C, D, E, G) and round them on the shaper using a 1/4" quarter round cutter or a router using a round over bit. Do not round the neck where it meets with the body since these edges must be square.

6. Assemble the main body parts (D, E, F). Use dowel rods to align the parts when gluing and clamping, but do not glue the dowels in place yet. The body can also be assembled with #10 × 2-1/2" flathead wood screws. Sand the body assembly on the disc sander so all the parts are flush.

7. Mount the legs (B, C). Align the legs with 3/8" dowel rods that extend through the body and into the legs on both sides. Disassemble and then glue and clamp the legs into place with the dowel rods.

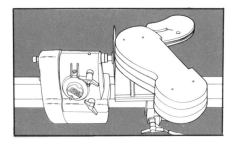

Sand the assembled body contour flush on the disc sander.

You can also assemble the legs without the glue and just use #10 × 2-1/2" flathead wood screws. This permits the final project to be disassembled for shipping or storing. The screws can be covered with stain or paint later.

8. Center the braces (J) on the feet and attach with #10 × 1-1/2" flathead wood screws. Then, place the horse with the attached braces on the rockers. Make sure the horse is sitting level on the rockers by sliding it back and forth until the body is parallel to the floor. Fasten with #10 × 1-1/2" flathead wood screws.

Attach the remaining braces (J) with #10 × 1-1/2" flathead wood screws. Round off the hard edges of the rockers at this point. (The rockers need to remain fairly square for stability.)

(continues on next page)

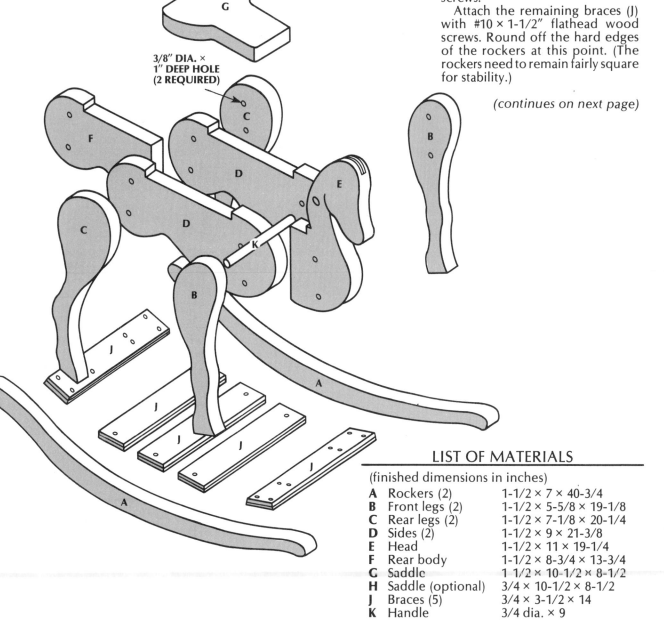

3/8" DIA. ×
1" DEEP HOLE
(2 REQUIRED)

LIST OF MATERIALS

(finished dimensions in inches)

A	Rockers (2)	1-1/2 × 7 × 40-3/4
B	Front legs (2)	1-1/2 × 5-5/8 × 19-1/8
C	Rear legs (2)	1-1/2 × 7-1/8 × 20-1/4
D	Sides (2)	1-1/2 × 9 × 21-3/8
E	Head	1-1/2 × 11 × 19-1/4
F	Rear body	1-1/2 × 8-3/4 × 13-3/4
G	Saddle	1-1/2 × 10-1/2 × 8-1/2
H	Saddle (optional)	3/4 × 10-1/2 × 8-1/2
J	Braces (5)	3/4 × 3-1/2 × 14
K	Handle	3/4 dia. × 9

9. Attach the saddle (G or H). The backup board for the upholstered saddle (H) is attached with #10 × 1-1/2″ flathead wood screws. The solid wood saddle (G) is attached with 3/8″ dowels and glue. Drill three 3/8″ dowels in the bottom of the seat and locate matching dowel holes on the body. Drill these holes with a hand drill and attach the seat with glue. Use a weight on the seat or use a web clamp for clamping.

10. Apply the stain and finish of your choice. For this project one coat of stain and two coats of polyurethane varnish were used.

11. (Optional) Upholster the saddle (H). Cut out and chamfer the top edges of 2″ thick foam rubber on the bandsaw. Then, cut the saddle covering out of cloth, vinyl, or leather. Attach the front edge of the material to the front of the backup board. Pull material back over the foam. Locate the back edge and insert an upholstery tack strip (available from upholstery shops) through the material. Fold the tack strip under the foam and pound the tacks in by hitting the seat with a rubber mallet. Tack the sides of the covering under the saddle and along the sides. Pleat the material as you go by folding it under and securing it with upholstery tacks or staples.

12. To make the horse's mane, use a skein of rug yarn and unloop it. Cut it into three equal parts (about 14″ lengths). Next, take a piece of 1/2″ wide durable tape (reinforced, duct, etc.) and lay it out on a flat surface with the sticky side up. Lay the yarn across the tape and press it down to secure it. (For additional strength, stitch the yarn onto the tape with a sewing machine.) After the yarn is secured to the tape, glue the mane into the head groove. Use a small stick to force it into the groove. (Several small pieces of wood can be used as wedges to hold the mane in place while the glue dries.)

13. The tail is made from a single skein of rug yarn, unlooped and cut. Wrap 2″ of one end of this yarn with a section of yarn and tie securely. This will help the tail stand out from the body. Glue the tail into place.

14. The eyes can be found at most craft shops. The eyes on this project have 1/4″ stems and are glued into place with aliphatic resin (yellow) glue. Or, you can simply paint the eyes on.

15. To make the ears, cut four triangles out of soft leather or vinyl. Put two triangles face-to-face and stitch where indicated in the drawing. Turn these inside out, fold the bottom corners together, and attach to the horse's head with small screws.

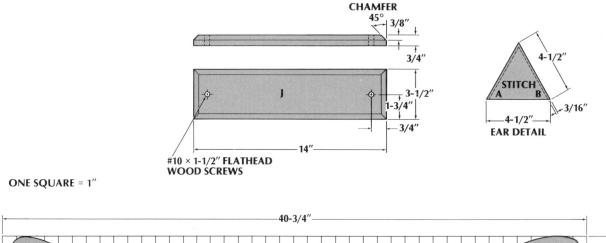

ONE SQUARE = 1″

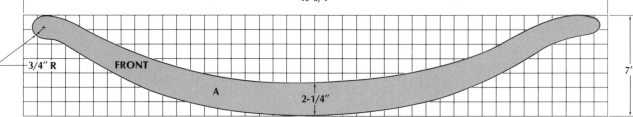

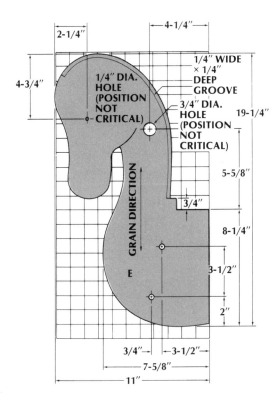

2-1/4"
4-1/4"
4-3/4"
1/4" WIDE × 1/4" DEEP GROOVE
1/4" DIA. HOLE (POSITION NOT CRITICAL)
3/4" DIA. HOLE (POSITION NOT CRITICAL)
19-1/4"
5-5/8"
GRAIN DIRECTION
3/4"
8-1/4"
E
3-1/2"
2"
3/4"
3-1/2"
7-5/8"
11"

ONE SQUARE = 1"

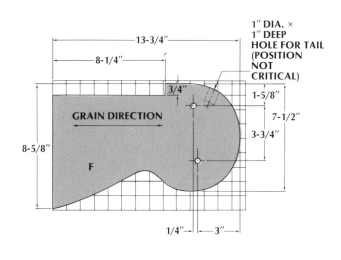

13-3/4"
8-1/4"
1" DIA. × 1" DEEP HOLE FOR TAIL (POSITION NOT CRITICAL)
3/4"
1-5/8"
GRAIN DIRECTION
7-1/2"
8-5/8"
F
3-3/4"
1/4"
3"

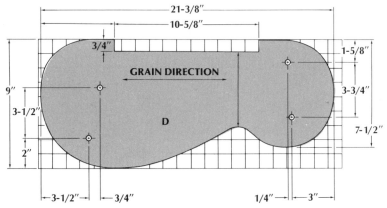

21-3/8"
10-5/8"
3/4"
1-5/8"
GRAIN DIRECTION
9"
3-3/4"
3-1/2"
D
7-1/2"
2"
3-1/2"
3/4"
1/4"
3"

TIP: MAKE PATTERN FOR PART (D) FIRST AND TRANSFER HOLE ALIGNMENT POSITIONS TO OTHER PARTS.

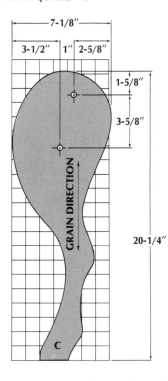

7-1/8"
3-1/2"
1"
2-5/8"
1-5/8"
3-5/8"
GRAIN DIRECTION
20-1/4"
C

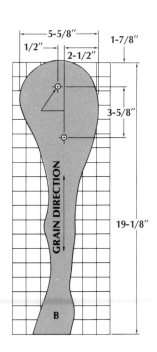

5-5/8"
1/2"
2-1/2"
1-7/8"
3-5/8"
GRAIN DIRECTION
19-1/8"
B

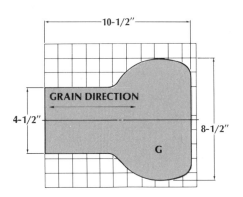

10-1/2"
GRAIN DIRECTION
4-1/2"
8-1/2"
G

TROLLEY

From *HANDS ON* Sept/Oct 81

To craft your own toy trolley, start by making the two pieces (E, F) that form the roof.

1. Cut all stock according to the List of Materials.

2. Tilt the saw to 12° and use a hollow-ground blade to cut a bevel around the outside edges of the roof (E, F).

3. Using a dado blade, rabbet the underside of both roof sections. Use a bandsaw to cut the curved undercarriage (H). Cut and shape the observation rails (B).

4. Drill holes as indicated on the patterns. Drill the axle holes in the undercarriage (H) using the horizontal boring mode. Change to the drill press mode and drill matched holes in the lower roof (E) and the trolley body (C) for roof supports.

5. Cut the wheels out using a jigsaw, bandsaw, or 1-1/2" hole saw. If you use a hole saw, you can eliminate the splintering that occurs as you pierce the wood if you stop the hole saw just as the pilot drill pierces the underside of the workpiece. Then, turn the piece over and finish the hole. Use a backup block to protect the worktable. Finish sand the wheels as round as possible. Use hardwood for the axles and wheels. As children play with toys, these pieces take a lot of abuse. Cut axles from a dowel rod and rub them with paraffin for smooth operation.

6. Assemble all pieces with aliphatic resin (yellow) glue.

7. In crafting toys, you must build safety into each piece. Sand with extra-fine sandpaper to eliminate splinters and sharp edges. Use a nontoxic product to finish your project such as mineral oil or salad bowl finish.

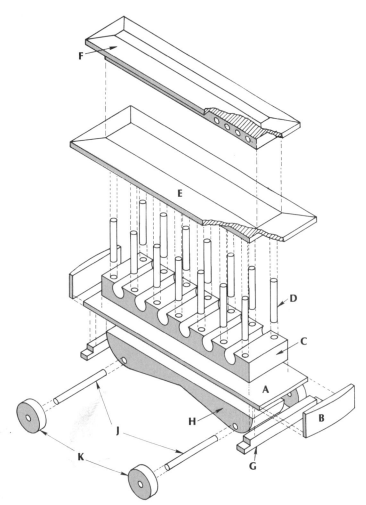

LIST OF MATERIALS

(finished dimensions in inches)

A	Base	3/16 × 2-7/8 × 10-1/2
B	Observation rails (2)	5/16 × 2-7/8 × 1-3/16
C	Body	1 × 2-1/4 × 8-3/4
D	Roof supports (14)	1/4 dia. × 2
E	Lower roof	3/4 × 3-5/8 × 11-1/8
F	Upper roof	1 × 2-1/4 × 10-1/2
G	Steps (2)	1/2 × 1/2 × 4-3/4
H	Undercarriage	1-1/8 × 1-7/8 × 8-3/4
J	Axles (2)	1/4 dia. × 2-7/8
K	Wheels (4)	1-3/8 dia. × 3/8

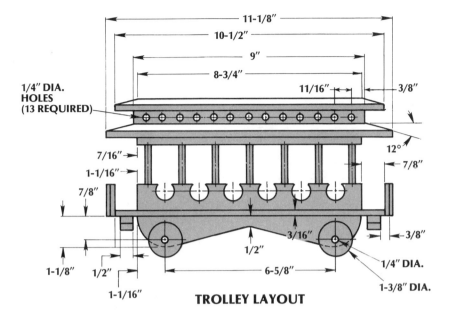

11-1/8"
10-1/2"
9"
8-3/4"
11/16"
3/8"

1/4" DIA.
HOLES
(13 REQUIRED)

12°

7/16"
1-1/16"
7/8"
7/8"

3/16"
1/2"
3/8"

1-1/8" 1/2"
1-1/16"

6-5/8"

1/4" DIA.
1-3/8" DIA.

TROLLEY LAYOUT

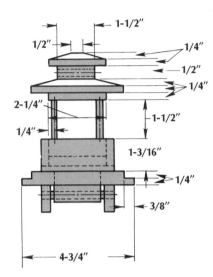

1-1/2"
1/2"
1/4"
1/2"
1/4"
2-1/4"
1-1/2"
1/4"
1-3/16"
1/4"
3/8"
4-3/4"

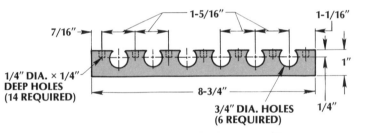

1-5/16"
1-1/16"
7/16"
1"
1/4" DIA. × 1/4"
DEEP HOLES
(14 REQUIRED)
8-3/4"
3/4" DIA. HOLES
(6 REQUIRED)
1/4"

BODY DETAIL

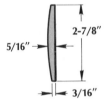

2-7/8"
5/16"
3/16"

**OBSERVATION
RAIL DETAIL**

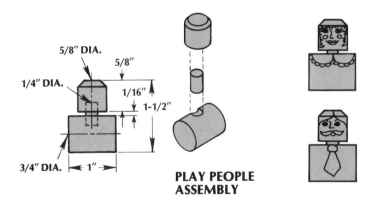

5/8" DIA.
5/8"
1/4" DIA.
1/16"
1-1/2"
3/4" DIA.   1"

**PLAY PEOPLE
ASSEMBLY**

AIRPLANE

From *HANDS ON* Nov/Dec 79

Drill holes for the wing struts (F) at a 15° angle.

Children have a particular fascination for flight. The first toy airplane was manufactured years before the first airplane had ever flown. Here's a biplane, a design that has intrigued pilots (and future pilots) since the first days of powered flight.

1. Cut all pieces to size and shape, using the patterns provided and List of Materials. Drill a 7/16" axle hole in each of the landing struts (L), with the center of the hole 1/2" from one end of the strut. Drill a 7/16" hole in the center of the propeller (H) and 3/8" holes in the center of the wheels (N) and keeper (K). Drill four 3/8" holes at a 15° angle in the top wing (D) and bottom wing (E). Centers of the wing holes should be 3" from the wing tips and 3/4" from the leading and trailing edges, as shown on the pattern. Drill two 1" holes in the bottom wing (E). The centers of these holes should be 1-1/8" from the center of the wing and 1-3/4" from either edge.

2. Glue the fuselage sides (A) to the vertical stabilizer (B). Take care

LIST OF MATERIALS

(finished dimensions in inches)

A	Fuselage sides (2)	3/4 × 3-1/2 × 12
B	Vertical stabilizer	3/4 × 7 × 13-1/2
C	Horizontal stabilizers (2)	3/4 × 4-1/8 × 4-1/2
D	Top wing	3/4 × 4 × 14
E	Bottom wing	3/4 × 3-1/2 × 14
F	Wing struts (4)	3/8 dia. × 6-1/2
G	Cowling	3-1/2 dia. × 3/4
H	Propeller	1/2 × 1-3/8 × 6
J	Pivot	3/8 dia. × 2-1/2
K	Keeper	1 dia. × 1/2
L	Landing struts (2)	1 dia. × 2-1/2
M	Axle	3/8 dia. × 4-3/4
N	Wheels (2)	1-3/4 dia. × 3/4

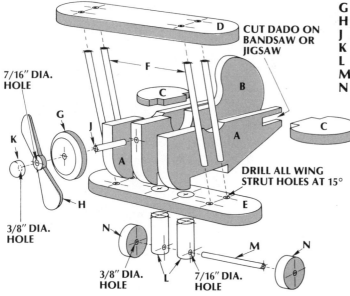

that the dadoes for the bottom wing line up exactly. Refer to pattern for position.

3. Glue the horizontal stabilizers (C) in the dadoes toward the rear of the fuselage sides (A).

4. Glue the landing struts (L) in the 1″ holes in the bottom wing (E), taking care the axle holes line up. Glue the wing struts (F) in the 3/8″ holes in the top wing (D); then, glue the other end of the struts in the 3/8″ holes in the bottom wing (E). When all is glued in place, the wing surfaces should be parallel and the wing's struts should stick out 1/8″ above and below the wings. Sand the struts flush with the wing surfaces.

5. Glue the wing assembly to the fuselage/stabilizer assembly, slipping the bottom wing (E) into the dado at the bottom of the fuselage. Reinforce the glue joint with dowels or screws.

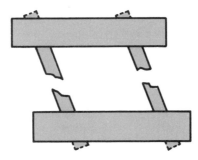

The wing surfaces should be parallel and the struts should protrude above and below just enough so that you can sand them down flush with the wings.

6. Glue the cowling (G) onto the front of the fuselage. If you wish, you can round the leading edge of the cowling with a rasp or sandpaper. Drill a 3/8″ hole through the center of the cowling, at least 3/4″ into the fuselage. Glue the pivot (J) in this hole.

7. Place the propeller (H) on the pivot (J). You can put a realistic pitch in the blades of the propeller with a rasp or sander. With the propeller in place, glue the keeper (K) on the pivot (J), leaving enough room for the propeller to turn freely.

8. Insert the axle (M) into the holes in the landing struts (L), and glue on the wheels (N).

Caution the aspiring pilot to whom you give this airplane that this is not a free-flying model. Flight plans should include a great deal of ground support.

ONE SQUARE = 1/2″

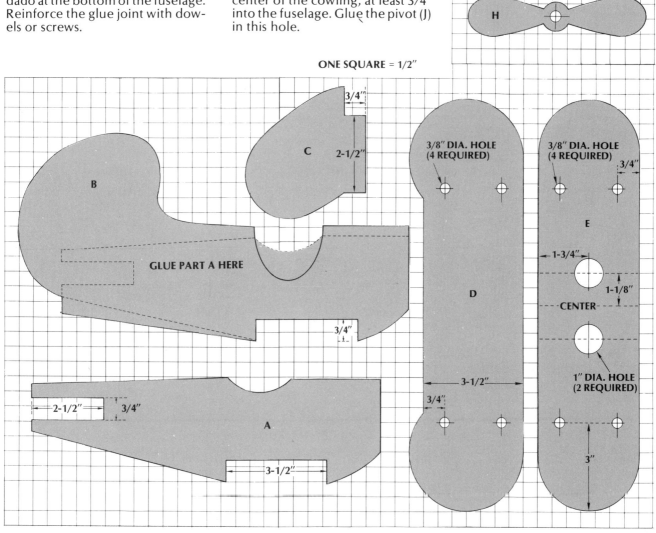

PECKING CHICKENS

From *HANDS ON* July/Aug 81

Old-fashioned toys, particularly animated ones, delight children of all ages and they are very popular at crafts fairs. You'll find yourself playing with these pecking chickens too. Swing the toy in a horizontal rotary motion and the four chickens peck, in order, at seeds in the center of the paddle.

Cut the paddle (A) out with a bandsaw or jigsaw, then round the edges. Drill all the holes in the paddle, countersinking the 1/8" diameter holes both on the top and bottom of the paddle to keep the string from snagging or wearing thin on the edges.

In the end grain of 3/4" thick stock, cut a 1/4" wide by 5/16"

deep kerf with dado blades. This kerf forms the hinge in the body of the chickens (B) for the heads (C) to pivot. Lay out and cut the chicken bodies in a way that the kerf is at an angle to cause the heads of the chickens to tilt forward slightly. Then, drill a dowel hole in the bottom of each chicken body.

From 1/4" thick stock, cut out the chicken heads (C). Drill holes in the lower neck for the hinge and the string. Attach the strings and hinge each head to the bodies (B) with finishing nails, allowing enough room for the string to slide. Mount the chickens to the paddle (A) with dowels (D).

Feed the string through the holes in the paddle and fasten the strings to a bead, using a wedge to hold the strings tight. Make sure all four strings are the same length to pull equally. Tie a weight to the bead.

Finally, glue seeds in the center of the paddle close enough for the chickens to peck at, but not actually hit.

(diagram labels:)

12"

45° 45°

7-3/4"

1-1/4" 1-5/8"

7/8" R

1/8" DIA. ON 5" DIA. CENTER
(4 HOLES EQUALLY SPACED
WITH 1/4" COUNTERSINK ON TOP
AND BOTTOM)

1/4" DIA. × 3/8" DEEP ON 6" CENTER
(4 HOLES EQUALLY SPACED)

PADDLE LAYOUT

DRILL HOLE
FOR STRING

DRILL 1/16" HOLE FOR
#18 FINISHING NAIL

1/4" DIA. HOLE 1/4" DEEP

1/4"

LIST OF MATERIALS

(finished dimensions in inches)

A	Paddle	3/4 × 7-3/4 × 12
B	Chicken bodies (4)	3/4 × 1-1/2 × 2-5/8
C	Chicken heads (4)	1/4 × 13/16 × 2
D	Large dowels (4)	1/4 dia. × 1
E	Hardwood ball	1-1/2" dia.

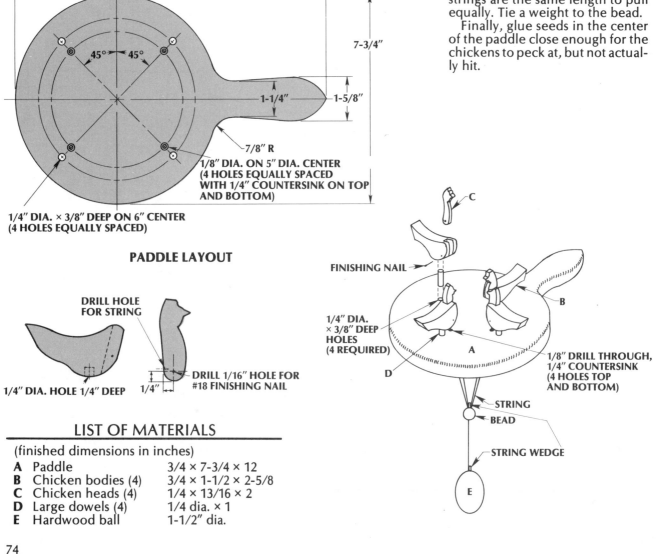

(diagram labels:)

C

FINISHING NAIL

B

1/4" DIA.
× 3/8" DEEP
HOLES
(4 REQUIRED)

A

D

1/8" DRILL THROUGH,
1/4" COUNTERSINK
(4 HOLES TOP
AND BOTTOM)

STRING

BEAD

STRING WEDGE

E

CLIMBING BEAR

From *HANDS ON* July/Aug 80

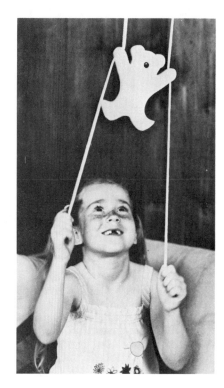

The Climbing Bear is a favorite of children and adults and it's an easy project to mass produce. Here's how.

Begin by making a hardboard template of the bear design and a support fixture to aid in drilling the bear's paws.

Cut blanks and bars to size. Stack four blanks, tape together, and trace the bear pattern on the top. Cut out the design with a bandsaw, then sand away the millmarks with a strip sander while the bears are still stacked up.

Now for the drilling: Tilt the table to 55° and, with the bears square against the support fixture, drill 3/16" holes through the paws. Reset the table to 90° and drill 3/16" holes in the bars.

Add face decoration to one or both sides of the bears. Cut jute or sash cord into pieces 50" and 8" long. To assemble, thread the 50" cords through the bears, bars, and beads, and knot the ends. Use the 8" cords as center supports, passing them through the bars and beads, and making loops.

To make the bear climb, hang the support loop from a nail or hook. First pull one cord, then the other, and the bear will shimmy up to the bar. Release both the cords and the bear will slide back down.

SASH CORD

BAR DETAIL

6-3/4"
3/16" DIA. HOLES (3 REQUIRED)
3/4"
1/2"
2-1/2"
7/8"

BEAD DETAIL

5/8"
1/2" DIA.

ONE SQUARE = 1/2"

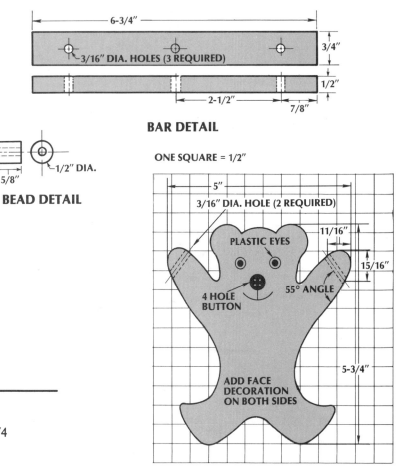

5"
3/16" DIA. HOLE (2 REQUIRED)
PLASTIC EYES
11/16"
15/16"
4 HOLE BUTTON
55° ANGLE
5-3/4"
ADD FACE DECORATION ON BOTH SIDES

LIST OF MATERIALS

(finished dimensions in inches)

A	Body	3/4 × 5 × 5-3/4
B	Bar	1/2 × 3/4 × 6-3/4
C	Beads (3)	1/2 dia.
D	Cord	5/32 dia. × 8

DOLL CRADLE

From *HANDS ON* Nov/Dec 79

Every doll needs a place to rest its head—ask any little girl. The Doll Cradle has been popular with children since the invention of dolls. And this Shaker-design cradle makes a cozy place to bed down.

The wood requirements for this project are minimal. The entire cradle can be made out of one 8' piece of 1 × 12 lumber. The curves in the rockers, headboard, footboard, and sides can be easily cut with a jigsaw, sabre saw, bandsaw, or coping saw. Simple construction techniques are followed throughout, but the results are wonderful. This project will win the heart of any little girl.

1. Cut all pieces using the patterns provided and the List of Materials. When cutting the rockers (A), take care that the grain of the wood runs horizontally for maximum strength. The bottom edge of the sideboards (C) should be cut on a 10° angle so they sit flat against the base. To cut the decoration at the top of the headboard (E), drill a 1" hole center 1-1/8" from the top edge. Then, open up the hole with your bandsaw or jigsaw.

Opening up a hole with a bandsaw to make the decoration at the top of the headboard (E).

2. Glue the sideboards (C) to the footboard (D) and headboard (E). Reinforce the glue joints with dowels or screws.
3. Shape or rout a decorative edge on the base (B). Use a quarter-round bead, or feel free to use any design you want.
4. Glue the rockers (A) to the base (B). The rockers should be positioned 2" from the head and foot of the base. Reinforce the glue joints.
5. Glue the side/foot/headboard assembly to the base/rocker assembly, centering the side, foot, and headboards on the base. Reinforce with screws.

LIST OF MATERIALS

(finished dimensions in inches)

A	Rockers (2)	3/4 × 4 × 18
B	Base	3/4 × 11 × 20
C	Sideboards (2)	3/4 × 8 × 19
D	Footboard	3/4 × 5-3/8 × 10-1/4
E	Headboard	3/4 × 10-1/4 × 11-1/4

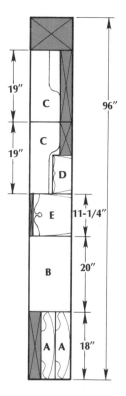

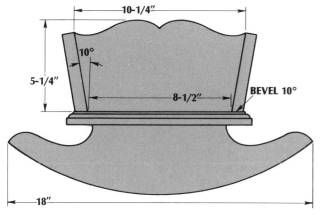

10-1/4"

10°

5-1/4"

8-1/2"

BEVEL 10°

18"

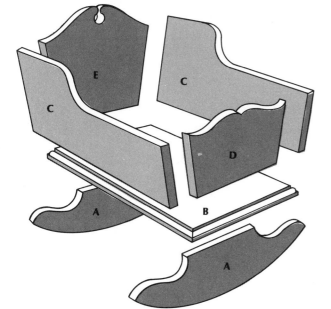

C

E

C

D

A

B

A

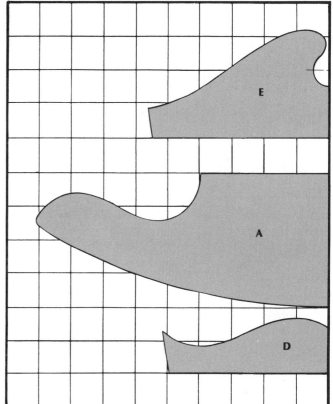

ONE SQUARE = 1"

E

A

D

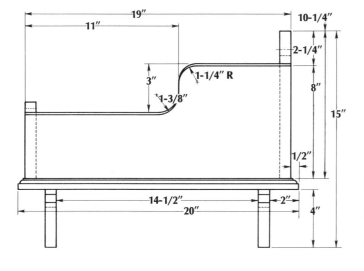

19"

11"

10-1/4"

2-1/4"

1-1/4" R

3"

1-3/8"

8"

15"

1/2"

14-1/2"

20"

2"

4"

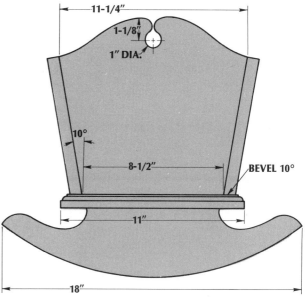

11-1/4"

1-1/8"

1" DIA.

10°

8-1/2"

BEVEL 10°

11"

18"

ROCKING PLANE

From *HANDS ON* Sept/Oct 82

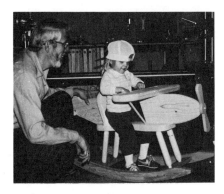

Any junior pilot will enjoy riding in this airplane. Playtime will become a new adventure. Build this rocking toy for a child and you'll feel deep satisfaction.

1. Cut all pieces to size, according to the List of Materials; then, lay out the seat (A), nose (B), wing (C), seat back (D), tail (E), stabilizer (F), rockers (G), and propeller (H). Groove the seat back for the tail, then cut the hand slots in the wing. Next, cut all contours on the bandsaw or jigsaw.

2. Turn the four legs (J) and the hub (K) on the lathe out of 2 × 2 stock. When you turn the 3/4" diameter tenons on the ends of the legs and the hub, use your calipers to check the diameters.

3. Drill the 3/4" holes required in the seat (A) by using the drill press mode with the worktable tilted

15°. Then drill 3/4" holes at 90° in the stretchers (L) for the legs (J). Also drill the 3/4" holes for the propeller hub (K) and for the struts (M). Holes for the struts are drilled at 45°. Dry-assemble the seat, legs, and stretchers to locate the position of the rockers (G). Drill 3/8" dowel holes for joining the stretchers to the rockers. Finally drill 1/2" dowel holes to join all remaining parts. Use brad point bits for clean and accurate holes.

4. Bevel the propeller (H) on the belt sander to add pitch to the blade.

5. Round off all exposed edges with the shaper, router, or a wood rasp and sand the project. Sharp corners and edges pose a danger for small children.

6. Assemble all parts with woodworker's glue, then apply a nontoxic finish.

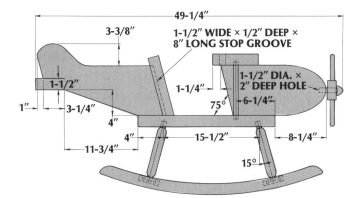

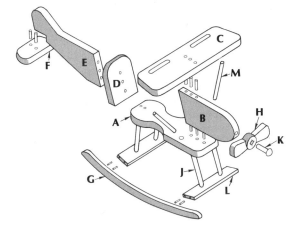

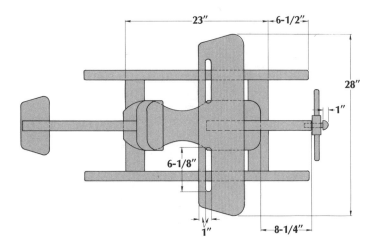

LIST OF MATERIALS

(finished dimensions in inches)

A	Seat	1-1/2 × 7-1/4 × 22
B	Nose	1-1/2 × 7-1/4 × 17
C	Wing	1-1/2 × 7-1/4 × 28
D	Seat back	1-1/2 × 7-1/4 × 9-1/2
E	Tail	1-1/2 × 11 × 16
F	Stabilizer	1-1/2 × 4-1/2 × 9
G	Rockers (2)	1-1/2 × 5 × 36
H	Propeller	1-1/2 × 3-1/2 × 10
J	Legs (4)	1-1/2 dia. × 10
K	Hub	1-1/2 dia. × 4-1/2
L	Stretchers (2)	3/4 × 3 × 14
M	Struts (2)	3/4 dia. × 12
	Dowels (13)	1/2 dia. × 3
	Dowels (8)	3/8 dia. × 1-1/2

TOY KITCHEN

From *HANDS ON* Sept/Oct 82

Children often play house, mimicking their mother and father. With their own kitchen, kids can pretend to bake and cook, without burning a finger or distracting the real cook. This toy kitchen is easily constructed from two sheets of 1/2" particleboard and a few pieces of hardware.

1. Cut all pieces to size by following the cutout diagrams provided and the List of Materials. You'll need a helper to cut the 4 × 8 sheets of particleboard safely. Cut out the sink opening in the countertop (D).

2. Assemble with nails and glue the right side of the refrigerator (B) to the bottom (A). Attach shelves (G, H), sides (B), top (E), and stove sides (C) and shelves (J), going from the right side to the left.

3. Attach the back (F) to this assembly. Bolt the stove door (N) to the kickboard (K) and attach this assembly. Then, attach the refrigerator kickboard (L).

4. Mount the refrigerator doors (P, Q) with strap hinges. First, screw the hinges to the inside of the doors; then, attach them to the side of the refrigerator. If you want the hinges mounted flush, you'll need to cut a notch in the side to recess the hinge.

5. Paint the kitchen the color of your choice, and use self-adhering vinyl shelf covering behind the stove for a finished effect. Use black paint to create spiral burners.

6. Make and attach accessories such as the faucets, knobs, and sink. The sink can be a plastic pan or tray. Make faucets as in the plans, or use discarded faucets for enhanced playability.

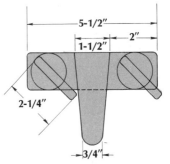

FAUCET DETAIL

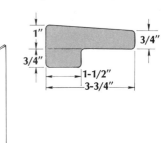

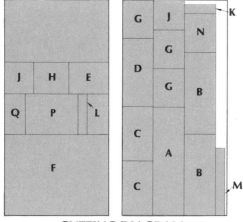

CUTTING DIAGRAM

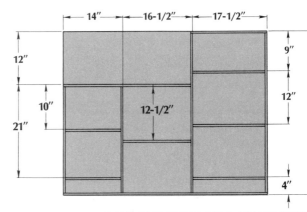

NOTE: DOORS (N, P, Q) NOT SHOWN.

LIST OF MATERIALS

(finished dimensions in inches)

A	Bottom	1/2 × 14 × 48
B	Refrigerator sides (2)	1/2 × 14 × 36
C	Stove sides (2)	1/2 × 14 × 24
D	Countertop	1/2 × 14 × 30
E	Refrigerator top	1/2 × 14 × 18
F	Back	1/2 × 37 × 48
G	Refrigerator shelves (3)	1/2 × 14 × 17
H	Shelf	1/2 × 14 × 16
J	Stove shelves (2)	1/2 × 13 × 14
K	Stove kickboard	1/2 × 4 × 14
L	Refrigerator kickboard	1/2 × 4 × 18
M	Sink front	1/2 × 4 × 30
N	Stove door	1/2 × 14 × 17
P	Refrigerator door	1/2 × 18 × 24
Q	Freezer door	1/2 × 9 × 18

NOTE: DOORS (N, P, Q) AND FACING STRIPS (K, L, M) NOT SHOWN.

SPACE SHUTTLE

From *HANDS ON* Nov/Dec 79

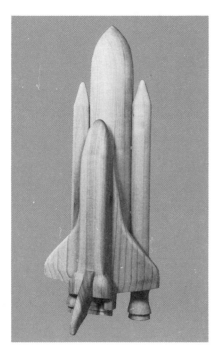

Tapering the vertical stabilizer (A) with a belt sander.

3. Glue the fuselage sides (B) to either side of the vertical stabilizer (A), taking care that the dadoes for the wings line up. Round the nose of the fuselage with a rasp or sander. Glue the wings (C) in place. Glue the rocket pods (D) to either side of the fuselage.

Round the rocket pods (D) and the nose of the Shuttle as shown.

4. Drill a 3/8" hole 1/2" deep in the narrow end of the three rockets (E). Drill three more 3/8" holes 1/2" deep in the rear of the shuttle assembly. Glue pegs (H) in the 3/8" holes in the rockets (E), then glue the other end of the pegs in the holes in the rear of the shuttle assembly. When mounted, rockets should clear the vertical stabilizer (A) and the bottom edge of the shuttle by at least 1/4".

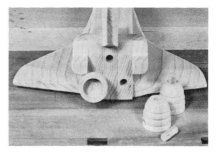

The rockets (E) are pegged to the back of the Shuttle.

5. Drill two 3/8" holes 1/2" deep, 4" and 9" from the bottom (round end) of the external fuel tank (F). Rotate the tank 90° and drill two more holes the same distance from the bottom. Rotate the tank 90° again and drill two more. Drill two 3/8" holes 1/2" deep in each of the booster rockets (G), 8" and 13" from the bottom. Glue pegs (H) in the holes in the booster rockets;

In 1981, the world's first true spaceship—the Space Shuttle—lifted off on its maiden voyage. It is planned that shuttles will ferry dozens of astronauts between earth and outer space, making spaceflight as common to our children as air travel is to us. Here is a toy Space Shuttle for those young people who will one day become part of space travel.

1. Cut all pieces to the proper size and shape. Turn the rockets (E), external fuel tank (F), and the booster rockets (G) on a lathe.

2. Round the leading edge and taper the trailing edge of the vertical stabilizer (A) and the wings (C), using a rasp or sander. Areas that join to other pieces should not be rounded or tapered. Round and taper only the areas that are shaded on the patterns. Also, round the rocket pods (D).

LIST OF MATERIALS

(finished dimensions in inches)

A	Vertical stabilizer	3/4 × 6 × 15-7/8
B	Fuselage sides (2)	3/4 × 3 × 14-1/8
C	Wings	3/4 × 10 × 10-1/2
D	Rocket pods (2)	3/4 × 1-1/2 × 2-5/8
E	Rockets (3)	1-1/4 dia. × 1-1/4
F	External fuel tank	3-1/2 dia. × 19-1/2
G	Booster rockets (2)	2 dia. × 19
H	Pegs (9)	3/8 dia. × 1

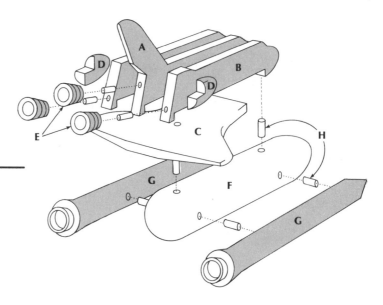

then, sand the protruding ends of these pegs until they fit snugly, but not too snugly, in the holes in the external fuel tank (F). Mount (but *don't* glue) the two booster rockets (G) on opposite sides of the external fuel tank (F), fitting the pegs in the holes.

6. Using a carpenter's square, stand the shuttle assembly on its vertical stabilizer (A), belly perpendicular to the floor. Mark the belly 8" and 13" up from the floor. Drill two 3/8" holes 1/2" deep at these marks, centered in the belly. Glue two pegs (H) in the two remaining holes

in the external fuel tank (F). These pegs should be 90° away from both the booster rockets. Sand the protruding ends of the pegs so they fit snugly into the holes of the belly of the shuttle assembly. Mount (but *don't* glue) the shuttle to the external fuel tank.

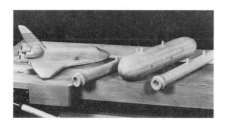

The Shuttle, the external fuel tank, and the booster rockets should all peg together and pop apart easily.

Now comes a moment of truth. In the launch position, the Space Shuttle should rest on the booster rockets (G) and vertical stabilizer (A), pointing straight at the stars. A few moments after liftoff (from your workbench), the booster rockets should separate easily and float back to earth while the shuttle and its external fuel tank continue upward. Upon reaching orbit (an arm's length above your head), the tank disengages. The Space Shuttle then completes its mission and glides back to your workbench for reassembly—and another mission.

ONE SQUARE = 1"

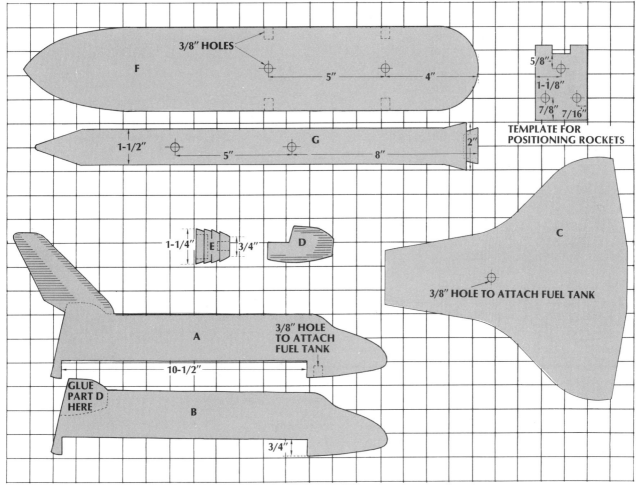

TOY TRAIN

From *HANDS ON* Nov/Dec 79

The first toy train appeared in the 1820s—only a few years after the first train. As railroads grew and locomotive designs developed and diversified, so did toy trains. But the favorite remains this classic 4-4-0 from the Golden Age of Steam.

THE LOCOMOTIVE

1. Cut all pieces to the proper size and shape, using the patterns provided and the List of Materials. Drill 7/16″ axle holes in wheel mounts (D, E) and a 7/16″ hole in engine coupler (F). Refer to patterns for position of these holes.

Drill 3/8″ holes in the center of wheels (L, M). Turn pistons (N), boiler (O), smokestack (P), and pressure dome (Q) on lathe.

2. Glue up platform sections (A, B, C). Refer to pattern for position. Cut cowcatcher with a compound miter cut—set the table at 30° and the miter gauge at 60°.

Cut the cowcatcher when the upper, mid, and lower platforms (A, B, C) have been glued up. The table is tilted at 30°; the miter gauge at 60°. **Note: Guard removed for clarity only.**

3. Glue the upper cab sides (I) to lower cab sides (J). Refer to pattern and exploded view for position—lower cab sides should protrude 3/4″ below upper cab sides. Glue cab sides to firewall (H). Glue on cab roof (K). Roof should be pitched at 15°. Reinforce glue joints with dowels or screws.

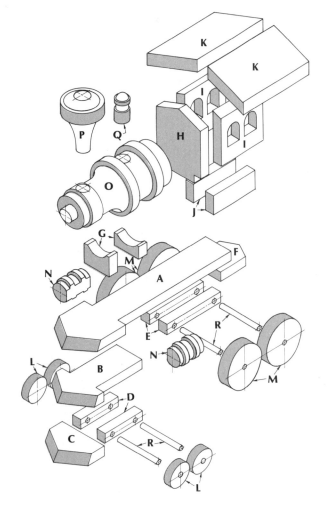

LIST OF MATERIALS

(finished dimensions in inches)

The Locomotive

A	Upper platform	3/4 × 3-3/4 × 15-1/2
B	Mid platform	3/4 × 3-3/4 × 7
C	Lower platform	3/4 × 3-3/4 × 2-3/4
D	Truck wheel mounts (2)	3/4 × 3/4 × 3-1/2
E	Drive wheel mounts (2)	3/4 × 3/4 × 5
F	Engine coupler	3/4 × 2-1/4 × 3
G	Boiler mounts (2)	3/4 × 2 × 2-1/4
H	Firewall	3/4 × 3-3/4 × 5
I	Upper cab sides (2)	3/4 × 3-7/8 × 4
J	Lower cab sides (2)	3/4 × 1-1/2 × 4
K	Cab roof (2)	3/4 × 2-3/8 × 6-1/4
L	Truck wheels (4)	1-3/4 dia. × 3/4
M	Drive wheels (4)	3-1/4 dia. × 3/4
N	Pistons (2)	1-3/8 dia. × 2-1/8
O	Boiler	3-3/4 dia. × 7-1/2
P	Smokestack	2-3/4 dia. × 4-1/4
Q	Pressure dome	1 dia. × 2
R	Axles	3/8 dia. × 3-7/8

4. Glue boiler (O) to boiler mounts (G). Reinforce glue joints. Drill 1" holes for smokestack (P) and pressure dome (Q). Refer to pattern for position.

5. Temporarily assemble wheels to mounts. Position wheel assemblies under the platform; the boiler and cab assemblies on top of the platform. Back of the drive wheels (M) should be flush with the back of the cab; the truck wheels (L) must not rub on the cowcatcher. When you have the assemblies properly lined up, mark for position and disassemble.

6. Glue on boiler and cab assemblies. Reinforce.

7. Glue truck wheel mounts (D), drive wheel mounts (E), and engine coupler (F) to platform. Take care that all axle holes line up. Refer to pattern for position of coupler. Reinforce.

8. Insert axles (R) in mounts and glue on wheels.

The underside of the engine shows the reinforcing screws before they are covered with dowels.

9. Sand a flat spot 3/4" wide on the pistons (N) and glue in position over rear truck wheels (L). Reinforce.

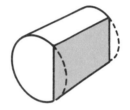

10. Glue smokestack (P) and pressure dome (Q) in holes on top of boiler (O).

THE COAL CAR

1. Cut all pieces to the proper size and shape, using patterns provided and the List of Materials. Drill 7/16" axle holes in the drive wheel mounts (E), a 7/16" hole in the car coupler (U), and 3/8" holes in the coal car platform (V) and the center of the truck wheels (L). Refer to pattern for position of holes.

2. Glue coal car sides (W) to coal car back (X). Glue coal car assembly to coal car platform (V). Reinforce.

3. Glue drive wheel mounts (E) to coal car truck mount (T), taking care that axle holes line up. Glue car coupler (U) to coal car assembly. Refer to pattern for position. Reinforce.

4. Temporarily assemble wheels to mount. Place coal car assembly on truck assembly and mark for position. Wheels must not rub on car coupler. Disassemble.

5. Glue truck assembly to coal car assembly. Reinforce. Insert axles (R) in mounts and glue on truck wheels (L). Glue coupler pin (S) in hole in coal car platform (V). Pin should extend 3/4" below platform.

THE BASIC CAR

Many different cars can be made to follow the locomotive and coal car, all mounted on a basic car assembly.

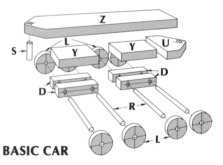

The basic car and a bottom view of a basic truck assembly.

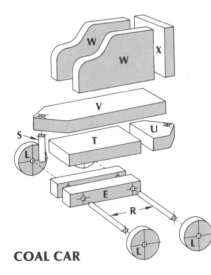

COAL CAR

BASIC CAR

LIST OF MATERIALS

(finished dimensions in inches)

The Coal Car

E	Drive wheel mounts (2)	3/4 × 3/4 × 5
L	Truck wheels (4)	1-3/4 dia. × 3/4
R	Axles (2)	3/8 dia. × 3-7/8
S	Coupler pin	3/8 dia. × 1-1/2
T	Coal car truck mount	3/4 × 2-1/4 × 5
U	Car coupler	3/4 × 3-3/4 × 3
V	Coal car platform	3/4 × 3-3/4 × 8
W	Coal car sides (2)	3/4 × 3 × 5
X	Coal car back	3/4 × 3-3/4 × 3

LIST OF MATERIALS

(finished dimensions in inches)

The Basic Car

D	Truck wheel mounts (4)	3/4 × 3/4 × 3-1/2
L	Truck wheels (8)	1-3/4 dia. × 3/4
R	Axles (4)	3/8 dia. × 3-7/8
S	Coupler pin	3/8 dia. × 1-1/2
U	Car coupler	3/4 × 3-3/4 × 3
Y	Truck mounts (2)	3/4 × 2-1/4 × 3-1/2
Z	Car platform	3/4 × 3-3/4 × 13-1/2

1. Cut all pieces to the proper size and shape. Drill 7/16" axle holes in truck wheel mounts (D), a 7/16" hole in the car coupler (U), and 3/8" holes in the car platform (Z) and the center of the truck wheels (L). Refer to pattern for position of holes.

2. Glue special car assembly (log car, box car, etc.) to car platform (Z) *before* assembling basic car.

3. Glue truck wheel mounts (D) to truck mounts (Y), taking care that axle holes line up. Glue car coupler (U) to car platform (Z). Refer to pattern for position. Reinforce.

4. Temporarily assemble wheels to mounts. Place car assembly on top of truck assemblies and mark for position. Truck mounts (Y) should be approximately 2-1/4" apart and wheels should not rub on coupler. Disassemble.

5. Glue truck assemblies in position and reinforce. Insert axles (R) in mounts and glue on wheels.

Glue coupler pin (S) in hole in car platform (Z). Pin should extend 3/4" below platform.

Design and build as many cars for the train as your child can push along. Here are three suggestions:

THE FLAT CAR

1. Cut the basic car pieces and 10 extra axles. Drill ten 3/8" holes in the car platform (Z). Holes should be spaced 2-3/16" apart in two rows 3" apart, 3/8" in from either edge of the platform.

2. Glue axles (R) in these holes, protruding above the platform.

3. Assemble basic car.

THE BOX CAR

1. Cut basic car pieces and pieces listed for box car.

2. Glue box car sides (DD) to car front and back (CC). Reinforce. Glue box car side/front/back assemblies to car platform (Z), leaving a 3" space between assemblies for doors. Reinforce.

3. Cut a 5/16" × 5/16" deep rabbet in the tops and bottoms of the box car doors (EE). Drill a 3/8" hole midway up the doors, 3/8" from one side, as shown:

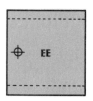

**BOX CAR
DOOR DETAIL**

LIST OF MATERIALS

(finished dimensions in inches)

The Flat Car

All materials listed for the basic car, plus:

R	Axles (10)	3/8 dia. × 3-7/8

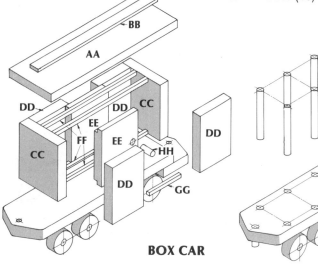

BOX CAR

FLAT CAR

PULLMAN

LIST OF MATERIALS

(finished dimensions in inches)

The Box Car

All materials listed for the basic car, plus:

AA	Car top	3/4 × 4 × 12
BB	Top rail	1/4 × 3/4 × 11-1/2
CC	Car front/back (2)	3/4 × 3-3/4 × 4-1/2
DD	Box car sides (4)	3/4 × 3 × 4-1/2
EE	Box car doors (2)	3/4 × 3-1/2 × 4-7/16
FF	Inside door slides (4)	1/4 × 1/4 × 9
GG	Outside door slides (2)	1/4 × 1/4 × 3
HH	Door pulls (2)	3/8 dia. × 1

LIST OF MATERIALS

(finished dimensions in inches)

The Pullman

All materials listed for the basic car, plus:

AA	Car top	3/4 × 4 × 12
BB	Top rail	1/4 × 3/4 × 11-1/2
CC	Car front/back (2)	3/4 × 3-3/4 × 4-1/2
II	Pullman sides (2)	3/4 × 4-1/2 × 6-3/4
JJ	Observation railings (2)	3/4 × 2 × 3-3/4

ONE SQUARE = 1"

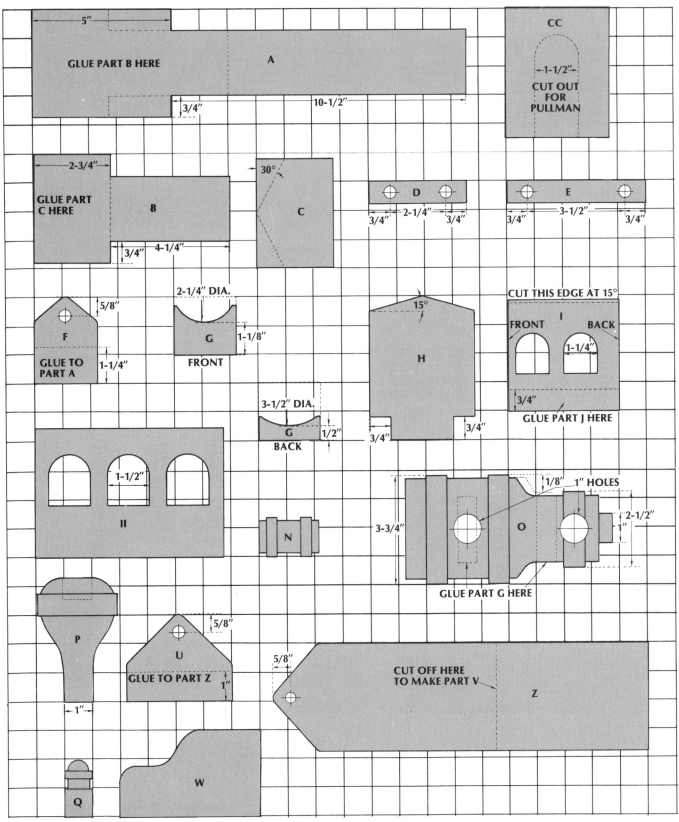

Glue door pulls (HH) in holes with end protruding from side *opposite* rabbets.

4. Glue two inside door slides (FF) to car platform (Z), 1/2" away from the box car sides (DD). Position doors in place with rabbets riding on the slides. Carefully position the two remaining inside door slides (FF) in the top rabbets, 1/2" away from the sides, and flush with the top of the box car assembly. Check to see that doors slide easily. Glue upper inside slides in place with a drop of glue at each end.

The rabbets in the box car doors (EE) ride on the inside door slides (FF).

5. Spread a liberal amount of glue on the top of the box car sides, front, back, and upper inside door slides, and glue the car top (AA) in place. Reinforce. Glue the top rail (BB) down the middle of the car top (AA). Glue the outside door slides (GG) to the car platform (Z), the inside edge flush with the inside edge of the box car sides (DD).

6. Assemble basic car.

THE PULLMAN

1. Cut the basic car pieces and pieces listed for the Pullman using the patterns provided.

The windows in the upper cab sides (I) of the Locomotive and the Pullman sides (II) can be cut with a jigsaw or coping saw, using an internal piercing cut.

2. Glue car front and back (CC) to Pullman sides (II). Glue car top (AA) to Pullman assembly. Top should stick out 1-7/8" front and back. Reinforce. Glue top rail (BB) down the middle of the car top (AA).

3. Temporarily position Pullman assembly and observation railings (JJ) on car platform (Z). Railings should be 1-1/8" away from the front and back. Mark for position; then, glue in place and reinforce.

4. Assemble basic car.

If you build a long train, a locomotive and several cars, you may find it timesaving to cut the pieces (wheels, mounts, platforms, etc.) all at once. Look over the List of Materials, add up the number and type of pieces you need, and set up for mass production.

One more tip: When you finish assembling your train, get down on the floor, hook the cars together, and play with it to your heart's content. Once you give this to a child you'll never have the chance again—unless you build one of your own.

There must be a few things more exciting to a child than a fire engine, but we can't think of any. We chose to build the most exciting of fire engines: the hook and ladder.

1. Cut all pieces to size and shape, except ladder rails, according to the List of Materials.

A quick, easy way to make perfectly round wheels is with a hole saw and then sanding them smooth on a lathe or drill press. Then, if you want, put a decorative groove in the side of each wheel on a lathe with a skew chisel.

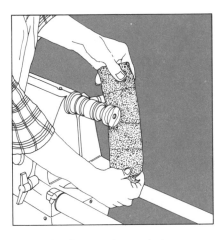

Sand wheels smooth on a lathe.

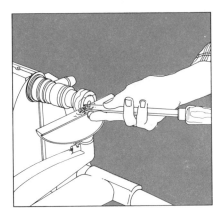

Cut decorative groove in side of wheel on a lathe.

2. Drill holes as shown on patterns, except the truck bodies and ladders. Also, drill 3/8" holes in the center of the wheels (D), a 1/4" hole through the center of the reel crank (W), and a second 1/4" hole in the reel crank, 3/8" in from the edge.

3. Glue the truck bodies (A) and drill holes as shown on patterns.

4. Insert the two axles (E) in the truck body axle holes and glue on wheels (D). Position the fenders so that the wheels don't rub in the wells and glue in place. If you wish, round the fenders with a rasp or sander. Also, round the back corners of the truck assembly as shown in the truck body exploded view. Reinforce the fender glue joints with dowels or screws.

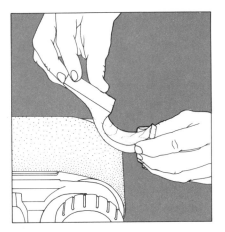

Round fenders with a belt sander.

5. Drill two 1/2" holes in the front of the truck assembly, with the centers 3/4" in from the outside edge of the fenders and 1-3/8" up from the bottom edge. Insert headlights (F) and glue in place.

6. Sand a 3/4" flat spot on the water tank (C) and glue in place in back of truck seat. Reinforce the glue joint with a dowel pin.

7. Glue the six platform supports (J) into the 3/8" holes in the lower platform (G). Then, glue the supports in the corresponding holes in the upper platform (H). The rounded ends of the platforms should face the same direction and be 1-1/2" apart.

8. The telescoping ladder slides together by means of a 5/32" groove that runs the length of the telescoping ladder rails (Q). It's easiest to cut this groove with an ordinary saw blade *before* you rip the ladder rail from the wood stock. The groove should be 5/32" deep and 1/8" from the edge of the rails.

Drill holes on the pivoting and sliding ladders. Skip a hole at one end of the two pivoting ladder rails (Q) that will attach to the pivot block (L).

9. Assemble pivoting ladder and attach to pivot block (L). Assemble sliding ladder and slide into pivoting ladder.

(continues on next page)

10. Attach a peg (M) in groove to pivoting ladder as a stop to keep the sliding ladder from scraping against the pivot block (L). Rip other ladder rails to size and drill rung holes; then, assemble.

11. Glue a wheel (D) to the lower side of the upper platform (H), lining up the hole in the wheel with the forward hole in the platform. Drill a 1/4" hole 1/4" from the end of the coupler (K). Glue a peg (M) in this hole, so that 3/16" of the peg protrudes on each side. Pass the coupler through the 7/16" hole in the pivot block (L) and insert the forward hole in the upper platform (H). When glued in place, coupler should extend 3/4" below the platform and wheel, and still allow the pivot block and telescoping ladder assembly to turn freely. The peg in the ladder will serve as a keeper for the ladder assembly.

12. Glue the ladder hooks (S) in the 3/8" × 1/2" deep holes in the edge of the upper platform (H). Glue pegs (M) into the holes, with 3/8" of the pegs protruding above the hooks. Hang assembled ladders on hooks.

13. Assemble the hose reel (T), reel supports (U), reel pivot (V), and reel crank (W) as shown in ex-

LIST OF MATERIALS

(finished dimensions in inches)

A	Truck bodies (3)	3/4 × 3 × 9-3/4
B	Fenders (2)	3/4 × 2-1/4 × 5-1/4
C	Water tank	1-1/4 dia. × 2-1/4
D	Wheels (9)	1-3/4 dia. × 3/4
E	Axles (4)	3/8 dia. × 3-7/8
F	Headlights (2)	1/2 dia. × 3/4
G	Lower platform	3/4 × 3-3/4 × 15-1/2
H	Upper platform	3/4 × 2-1/4 × 15-1/2
J	Platform supports (6)	3/8 dia. × 3
K	Coupler	3/8 dia. × 3-1/2
L	Pivot block	3/4 × 3/4 × 1
M	Pegs (9)	1/4 dia. × 3/4
N	Ladder rails (4)	1/4 × 3/4 × 12
P	Ladder rungs (33)	1/4 dia. × 1-3/4
Q	Telescoping ladder rails (4)	1/4 × 3/4 × 13
R	Telescoping ladder rungs (12)	1/4 dia. × 1-1/2
S	Ladder hooks (4)	3/8 dia. × 1-1/2
T	Hose reel	1-1/2 dia. × 2-1/8
U	Reel supports (2)	3/4 × 1-1/2 × 2
V	Reel pivot	1/4 dia. × 4-1/8
W	Reel crank	1-1/2 dia. × 3/8
X	Hose	1/4 dia. × 48 nylon rope
Y	Nozzle	3/8 dia. × 1

ploded view. Glue hose assembly on lower platform (G).

14. Pass axles (E) through 7/16" axle holes in lower platform (G) and glue on wheels (D).

15. Hook the coupler (K) into the hole in the back of the truck body, and you have a hook and ladder capable of rescuing people from burning buildings almost 2' high.

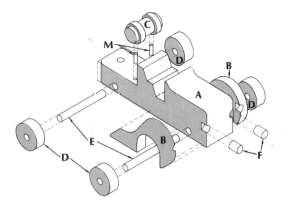

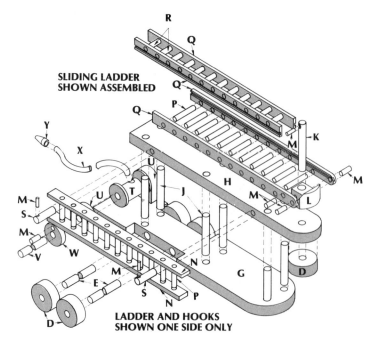

SLIDING LADDER
SHOWN ASSEMBLED

LADDER AND HOOKS
SHOWN ONE SIDE ONLY

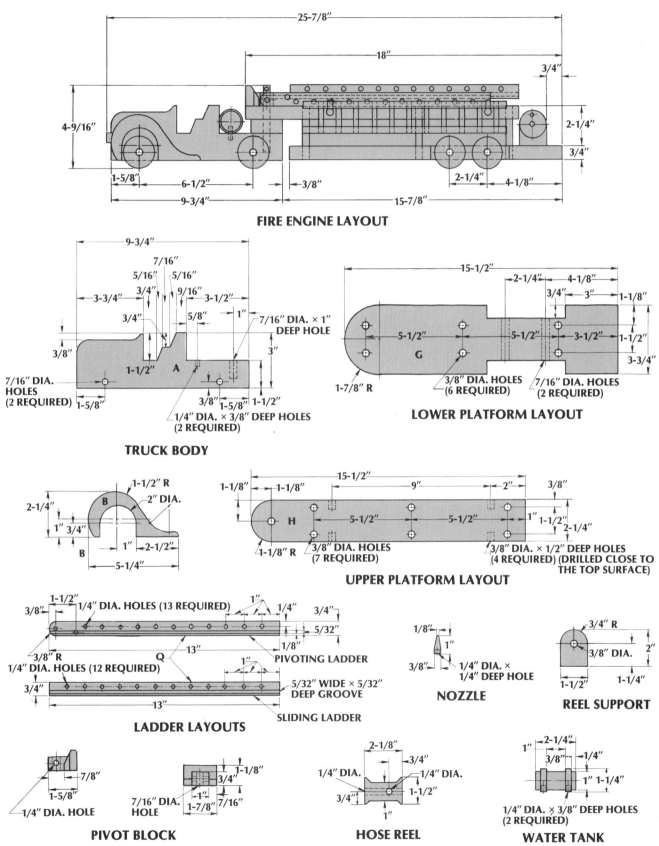

FIRE ENGINE LAYOUT

TRUCK BODY

7/16" DIA. × 1" DEEP HOLE

7/16" DIA. HOLES (2 REQUIRED)

1/4" DIA. × 3/8" DEEP HOLES (2 REQUIRED)

LOWER PLATFORM LAYOUT

1-7/8" R

3/8" DIA. HOLES (6 REQUIRED)

7/16" DIA. HOLES (2 REQUIRED)

2" DIA.

1-1/2" R

UPPER PLATFORM LAYOUT

1-1/8" R

3/8" DIA. HOLES (7 REQUIRED)

3/8" DIA. × 1/2" DEEP HOLES (4 REQUIRED) (DRILLED CLOSE TO THE TOP SURFACE)

LADDER LAYOUTS

1/4" DIA. HOLES (13 REQUIRED)

PIVOTING LADDER

3/8" R

1/4" DIA. HOLES (12 REQUIRED)

5/32" WIDE × 5/32" DEEP GROOVE

SLIDING LADDER

NOZZLE

1/4" DIA. × 1/4" DEEP HOLE

REEL SUPPORT

3/4" R

3/8" DIA.

PIVOT BLOCK

1/4" DIA. HOLE

7/16" DIA. HOLE

HOSE REEL

1/4" DIA.

1/4" DIA.

WATER TANK

1/4" DIA. × 3/8" DEEP HOLES (2 REQUIRED)

TOY TOP

From *HANDS ON* Sept/Oct 81

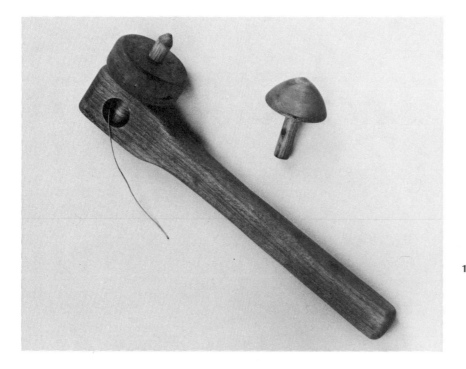

The secret to a long-spinning top is symmetry—it's got to be balanced. Never mind the geometric formula, simply drill the hole for the spindle in the exact center of the top body. Glue in the spindle and mount it in the drill chuck. Spinning the top in the drill, sand the body until it is perfectly round and balanced. Then sand a point on the lower end of the spindle.

The yoke cradles the top so you can really yank the string.

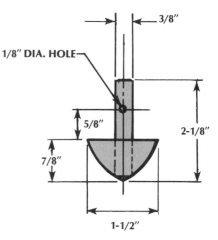

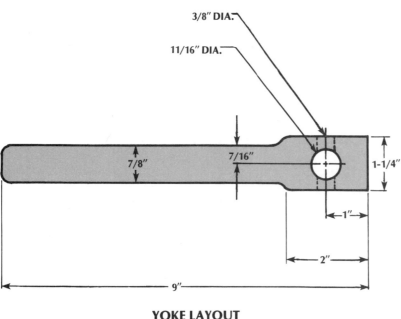

YOKE LAYOUT

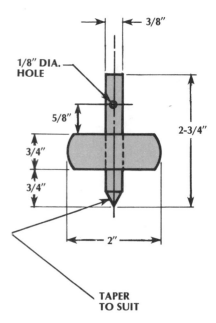

TOP LAYOUTS

POUNDING BENCH

From *HANDS ON* May/June 82

Get the children in your life hooked on woodworking early. Let them use this custom-made mallet as much as they want on their own pounding bench!

Start this child's toy with a hardwood stock such as poplar, maple, or birch.

Begin by cutting the bench and ends to size. Cut the dado in the ends that will accept the top. Lay out and cut the profile on the ends.

Lay out and drill the 1" diameter peg holes in the bench. Dry-assemble and clamp the bench together and round all edges.

Turn the pegs three at a time allowing extra stock for the lathe centers. Cut the pegs to length and chamfer the ends.

Tilt the bandsaw table 45° to form a V-block, and using the miter gauge as a fence, cut the relief slots in each end of the pegs.

Turn the mallet head and handle. If you wish to turn the handle elliptically, turn the handle round, then offset one end 1/4" in two directions.

Finish sand all pieces. Stain each piece with food coloring mixed with water (two parts food coloring to one part water). Glue top and end together, then seal with a nontoxic finish.

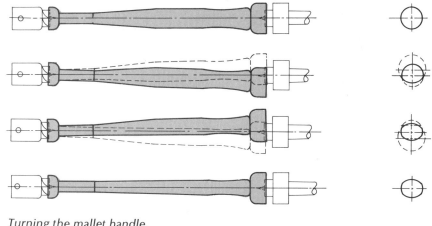

Turning the mallet handle.

3/4" DIA. HOLE

D

E

1/16" SAW KERFS AT 90°

C

1" DIA. HOLES (LOCATION NOT CRITICAL)

B

A

3/4" WIDE × 3/8" DEEP DADO

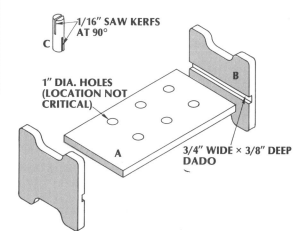

LIST OF MATERIALS

(finished dimensions in inches)

A	Top	3/4 × 8 × 15
B	End (2)	3/4 × 8 × 8
C	Peg	1 dia. × 3-1/2
D	Head	1-5/8 dia. × 3-3/8
E	Handle	3/4 × 1 × 9

PUZZLES

From *HANDS ON* Nov/Dec 79

Puzzles have always been popular with children and are one of the few toys that come apart without breaking. The puzzles we have included here have one added attraction—they stand up on their own when a child pieces them together.

1. Glue up stock 1-1/2" thick or thicker. If you're making the Tortoise, your stock needs to be 6" × 11-1/2"; the Hare, 10" × 11-1/4"; the Partridge in a Pear Tree, 8-3/4" × 11-1/2". When making the partridge, consider using a contrasting color of wood. We have made a walnut partridge to roost in a poplar pear tree.

2. Cut out the contour of the puzzle.

3. Using a saw with a thin blade, cut out the separate pieces of the puzzle. A bandsaw with a 3/16" or 1/8" blade works well; so does a coping saw or sabre saw with a scroll blade. If you use a jigsaw, use soft wood and a slow speed. Otherwise, the blade will warp in the wood and the pieces of the puzzle will not slide together smoothly.

Using our puzzles as examples, you can design your own around your child's favorite animal or object. When cutting the pieces, take care that you use enough reverse curves, or heads and necks, so that they all interlock.

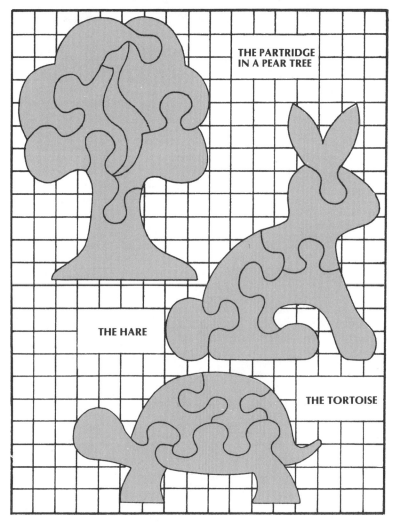

THE PARTRIDGE IN A PEAR TREE

THE HARE

THE TORTOISE

Each piece of a stand-up puzzle should interlock with the adjoining pieces.

From *HANDS ON* Sept/Oct 82

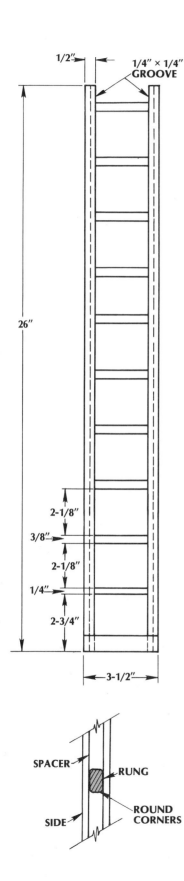

Young and old alike are amused by this clever toy. The bottom rung of the ladder is the trick that keeps the firemen on the ladder at the bottom.

1. Cut all pieces for the ladder and base. Precision is important. Plans show a 1/4" × 1/4" groove to accept rungs and spacers. You can make this with the table saw and dado accessory. An alternative method is to form the ladder by using a 1/4" mortising attachment to form squared holes for each of the rungs.

2. Assemble all parts using woodworker's glue. Then round all sharp edges. Too large a flat on rungs (D) will slow or stop the action of the toy.

3. Make the racers (F) following the pattern provided. Drill the holes in each racer; then, cut them on the bandsaw or jigsaw. Sand and fit them to the ladder. Apply a nontoxic finish. A little paraffin helps to lubricate the racers on their journey; furthermore, you may choose to make them of hardwood.

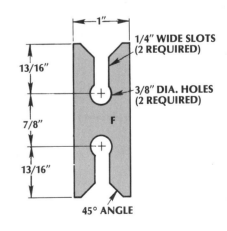

LIST OF MATERIALS

(finished dimensions in inches)

A	Base	3/4 × 3-1/2 × 5
B	Sides (2)	1/2 × 3/4 × 26
C	Spacers (20)	1/4 × 1/4 × 2-1/8
D	Rungs (9)	1/4 × 3/8 × 3
E	Rung	1/4 dia. × 3
F	Racers (2)	3/4 × 1 × 2-1/2

KITE STRING WINDER

From *HANDS ON* Mar/Apr 81

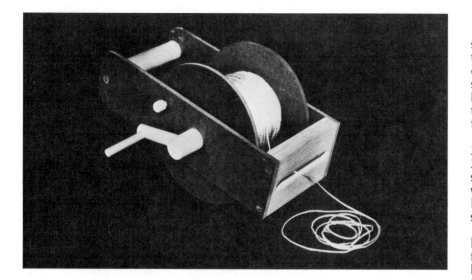

Look up in the sky on a blustery spring afternoon and you're likely to find it dotted with kites. And down on the ground, plenty of kids struggling with the kite strings. Here's a simple kite string winder that takes the frustration out of kite flying.

Turn a large dowel on the lathe 3-1/2" in diameter. Cut this into a 3-1/2" long section and make this section into a spool by gluing a washer (D) on each end. Drill a 1" hole through the center of the spool.

Assemble winder frame with the handle (E) at one end and the string feeder (A) at the other. This feeder has a slot routed in it to help feed the string onto the spool evenly.

Make the crank (G, H) and axle (F) out of dowel stock. Pass the axle through the side (B) with the spool (C) in place and fix the spool to the axle with a dowel. Wooden or hardboard washers (D) will keep the spool from rubbing on the sides (B).

Drill one of the sides for a locking pin (J). If you wish, this pin can be attached to the frame with string to prevent youngsters from losing it.

LIST OF MATERIALS

(finished dimensions in inches)

A	String feeder	3/4 × 3 × 4-1/2
B	Sides (2)	1/4 × 3 × 11
C	Spool	3-1/2 dia. × 3-1/2
D	Washers	2 dia. × 1/4
E	Handle	1 dia. × 4-1/2
F	Axle	1 dia. × 6-3/8
G	Crank handle support	3/8 dia. × 3-1/2
H	Crank handle	3/8 dia. × 2-5/8
J	Locking pin	1/4 (I.D.) × 1/2 (O.D.) × 1-1/4
K	#6 × 3/4 Flathead wood screws (6)	
L	1" I.D. Washers (2)	

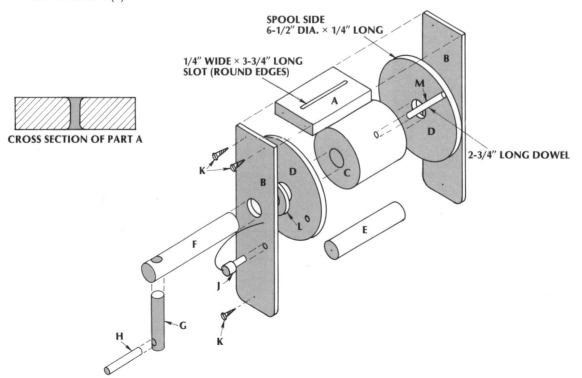

CROSS SECTION OF PART A

SPOOL SIDE
6-1/2" DIA. × 1/4" LONG

1/4" WIDE × 3-3/4" LONG
SLOT (ROUND EDGES)

2-3/4" LONG DOWEL

PULL DOG

From *HANDS ON* Nov/Dec 83

Delight the toddler in your life with this cute little puppy. He loves to chase and nip at the heels of children who squeal with joy. Here's how to make it.

Transfer the pattern to 1/2″ stock. Note that there are three pieces and they overlap at the finger joints. Cut out the dog body on the bandsaw or jigsaw. Next, put the pieces together and drill a 1/8″ hole for the 1/8″ dowel hinge pin. Sand the body of the dog, rounding off all edges, and round the joints. Glue the hinge pins in place. Cut the 3/4″ × 3/4″ × 3-1/4″ wheel holders and form the 1/2″ wide × 3/8″ deep dadoes in them. Glue and clamp the dog body to the axle holders. After the glue has dried, clamp the dog to the worktable and use the horizontal boring mode to drill the 5/16″ axle holes. You can make your own wheels with a hole saw, turn them on the lathe, or buy wheels at a craft store. Attach them to the axle with glue. Paint the dog with nontoxic paints. Cut ears out of vinyl or leather and attach with glue. Finally, mount a screw eye in the front for the pull string.

ONE SQUARE = 1/2″

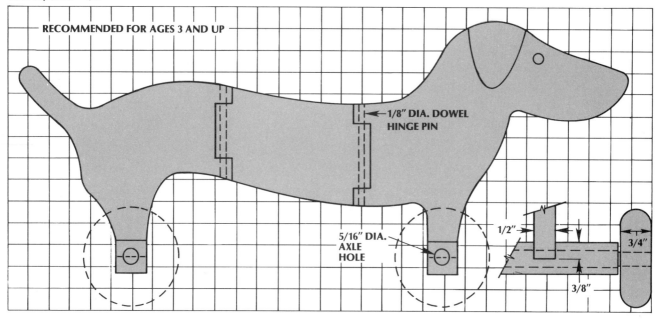

RECOMMENDED FOR AGES 3 AND UP

←— 1/8″ DIA. DOWEL HINGE PIN

5/16″ DIA. AXLE HOLE

1/2″

3/4″

3/8″

WOODWORKING PROJECTS II

50 Easy-to-Make Projects from HANDS ON Magazine

Preface

This book contains fifty woodworking project plans from back issues of *HANDS ON*, The Home Workshop Magazine published by Shopsmith, Inc. These easy-to-make wooden projects are sure to provide any woodworker, from beginner to expert, with hours of fun and enjoyment in the shop. The projects are ideal gifts for friends or family, and they're suitable for many occasions—Christmas, birthdays, weddings, etc.

A word of appreciation is addressed to the dozens of *HANDS ON* readers who have contributed their project ideas to the magazine over the years. Their ideas continue to provide success and enjoyment for many other woodworkers.

A final note: As you undertake these (and any other) woodworking projects, keep safety your top priority. Use the recommended tools and procedures. Also, remember to plan your work before you begin. Be sure to study every project plan thoroughly, including the diagrams and list of materials, before making any cuts.

Many thanks to the following *HANDS ON* readers who contributed to this book: SVEN ABRAHAMSEN, CHERYL BARNETT, JAMES CURTIS, MARK DI SALVO, DALE EBY, JAMES FILLENWARTH, JACK FISHER, PAUL HERMON, R. M. HOUSELY, BILL HOWELL, OREON KEESLAR, CLARK PATTON, RUDE OSOLNIK, PAUL RASANEN, DAVE STRUBLE, YOSH SUGIYAMA, BOB THOMPSON, TOM THOMPSON, STEVE WILSON, and ROGER ZIEGLER.

Furniture

Not only will you gain a sense of accomplishment after completing these projects, but you'll also end up with very practical, beautiful furniture pieces. This section contains fourteen projects from which to choose. Select the one that fits your needs or fancy most, and get started. Once you see the results of your work, you'll probably be back to start in on your next choice.

One of the simplest pieces of furniture you can make is a table. Basically there are only nine parts—four legs, four rails, and a top. And, if you know how to rip, crosscut, dowel, and glue—you can make any table, any size.

But, simple doesn't mean plain. By using woodworking techniques such as shaping, molding, and turning, you'll easily add elegance to a simple project.

Four simple end tables illustrate this point. You can make the table you want using the various techniques illustrated.

The basic end table measures 18" wide × 24" long × 22" high. Here's how to make one in ten easy steps.

1. Select your stock. To save time and frustration, first select stock that's properly dried, straight, and free of knots and defects.

Alternate the end grain on the boards for the top. This will reduce the effects of any warping that may take place.

2. Prepare the stock. First, rip stock to the proper width, then crosscut it to approximate length. Allow an extra 8" on the legs (A) and rails (B,C) and 2" for the top (D) pieces.

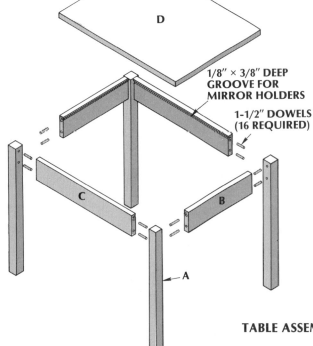

1/8" × 3/8" **DEEP GROOVE FOR MIRROR HOLDERS**

1-1/2" **DOWELS (16 REQUIRED)**

D

C

B

A

TABLE ASSEMBLY

LIST OF MATERIALS

(finished dimensions in inches)

A	Legs (4)	1-1/2 × 1-1/2 × 21-1/4
B	End rails (2)	3/4 × 3-1/2 × 13-1/2
C	Side rails (2)	3/4 × 3-1/2 × 19-1/2
D	Top	3/4 × 18 × 24
	Dowel pins (16)	3/8 dia. × 1-1/2
	Mirror holders (6)	

3. Prepare legs (A) and rails (B,C). Use a disc sander to get the finished length on the legs and rails. With a good combination square, check the ends of these pieces for squareness as you go. Arrange the legs and rails, and then mark them for their location on the finished project.

4. Assemble the top. Arrange the boards for the top so end grain alternates, then mark the boards in order to keep track of this arrangement. To glue up, joint the edges of each board. For added strength and easier alignment, dowel the edges by using horizontal boring. Apply an aliphatic resin (yellow) glue evenly to facing edges and clamp using bar clamps.

After the glue has dried, remove the clamps and scrape off any excess glue with a cabinet scraper.

Cut the top to size by first jointing one edge. Then, clamp a straight guide board perpendicular to the jointed edge and trim one end of the top. You now have two square edges as guides to obtain final width and length.

5. Mounting the top. There are many effective ways to secure the top to the frame, one of which is to use at least two screw pockets per side. Using mirror holders is another good method for mounting tabletops. Screwed to the underside of the top, these holders project into a saw kerf on the rail. Use six holders for this table—one for each end and two for each side. Whichever method is chosen, it is necessary to perform the operations on the rails before proceeding further.

6. Joinery. Among the several different ways to join legs to rails, one of the most common methods is by using dowel joints. They're simple to make and very strong when properly glued and clamped. Using a square, carefully mark the location of dowel holes on the legs. Allow an extra 1/16" depth on each dowel hole for glue. From the location of the dowel holes on the legs, mark the location of the matching

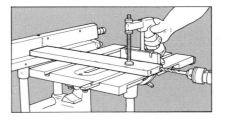

Boring dowel pin holes in the end of a rail with horizontal boring. The rip fence and miter gauge are used to position the stock.

holes on the rails. (Dowel center finders make this easy.) Bore the holes in the rails using horizontal boring.

7. Customize the table. At this point, special operations should be used on the table components. Check out the variations provided or use your own to create a really unique piece of furniture.

At this stage, finish-sand all the components.

8. Assemble the frame. Glue and clamp the side rails and legs together. Check for squareness as you proceed. Scrub off any excess glue. (This will raise the grain around the joints slightly but a little touch-up sanding will remedy that.)

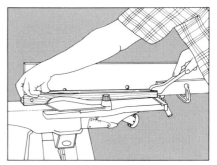

Set jointer at 3/16" depth-of-cut and make two passes on each side. Note use of stop block and safety push stick.

After these two assemblies have dried, glue them to the end rails and clamp.

9. Attach the top. Flip the top upside down and center the frame on it. If you use the mirror holders, locate and drill holes for the mounting screws and secure the top in place. If you made screw pockets, drill pilot holes into the tabletop and secure the top with #8 × 1" roundhead wood screws.

10. Finishing touches: Before applying any finish, go over the entire project with a tack rag to remove dust. Select the stain and/or finish of your choice and apply.

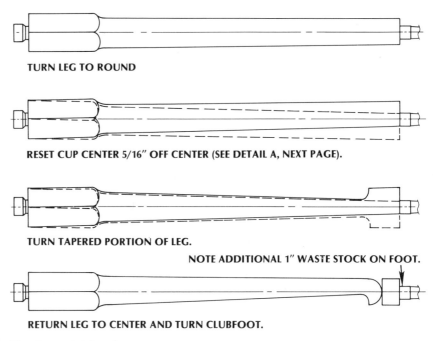

TURN LEG TO ROUND

RESET CUP CENTER 5/16" OFF CENTER (SEE DETAIL A, NEXT PAGE).

TURN TAPERED PORTION OF LEG.

NOTE ADDITIONAL 1" WASTE STOCK ON FOOT.

RETURN LEG TO CENTER AND TURN CLUBFOOT.

Turning a clubfoot leg.

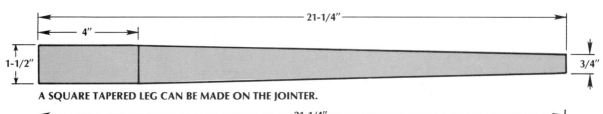

A SQUARE TAPERED LEG CAN BE MADE ON THE JOINTER.

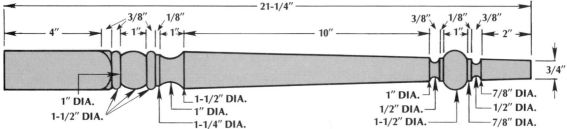

FOR AN ORNATE TURNING, MAKE A STORYSTICK WITH ALL THE DIMENSIONS MARKED ON IT AND TRANSFER THESE DIMENSIONS TO EACH LEG AFTER IT HAS BEEN TURNED TO ROUND.

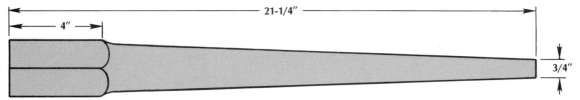

A TAPERED LEG SUCH AS THIS CAN ALSO BE MADE.

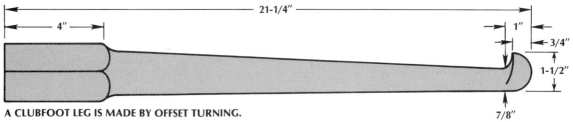

A CLUBFOOT LEG IS MADE BY OFFSET TURNING.

LEG VARIATIONS

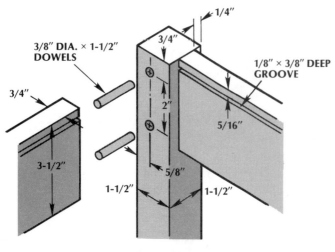

LEG TO RAIL CONSTRUCTION DETAIL

DETAIL A

The square tapered legs of this Mission-style oak table were all done on the jointer. The shaper with the V-cutter was used to chamfer the top.

Simple, turned tapered legs, a rounded table edge, and partial shaping of the rails combine to give this walnut table a warm look.

This Early American-type table made of cherry features turned legs with a series of beads and coves. The rails were formed on the bandsaw. The ogee edge on the top was done on the shaper.

This mahogany Dutch Colonial-type table has clubfoot legs turned on the lathe. The rails have molded bead on the bottom edge. The bead-and-step edge on the tabletop was done on the shaper.

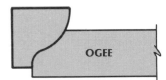

OGEE

BEAD-AND-STEP

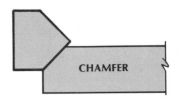

CHAMFER

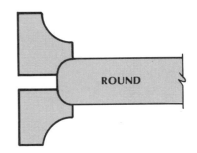

ROUND

TABLETOP EDGE VARIATIONS

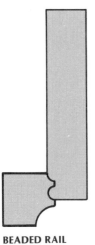

BEADED RAIL

3-1/2"
3-3/8"
2-3/4"
ONE SQUARE = 1/2"
DECORATIVE BANDSAWN RAIL

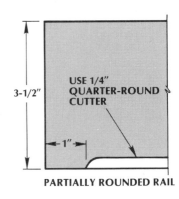

3-1/2"
USE 1/4" QUARTER-ROUND CUTTER
1"
PARTIALLY ROUNDED RAIL

RAIL VARIATIONS

THE QUILT RACK

From *HANDS ON* Jan/Feb 82

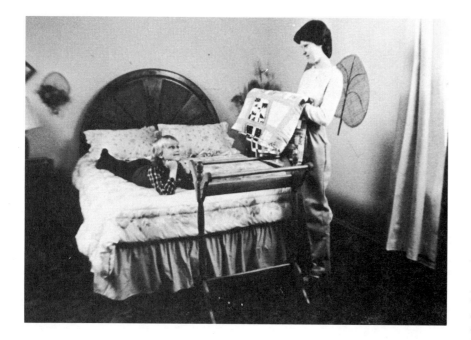

To save on your heating bill it makes sense to crank down the furnace thermostat each night; then, to help you stay cozy and warm in bed it makes sense to add a nice thick quilt or a colorful wool blanket.

When you're making up the bed, it's nice to have just the right place—like this quilt rack—to store those extra blankets and quilts.

Choose the stock you wish to use. We used mahogany. Keep in mind that stock for the spindles must be as straight and true as possible.

You'll make two spindles, and they don't have to be absolutely identical. You'll form one spindle, and then before sanding it, you'll form the other. Use calipers or a cardboard template to help duplicate the design. Then you can sand and finish both spindles.

No one is going to be disappointed if you don't follow the dimensioned drawing for the spindles right down to the smallest detail. The joy of lathe work is that it allows you the freedom to craft what *you* think looks good.

Whatever your design, mark out its pattern with a pencil on the stock *before* you begin to turn it.

Sand on the lathe carefully. Sandpaper acts as hundreds of tiny little scraping tools, and you can take off more stock than you might think. A neat little trick is to tear out a half-moon in the edge of the sandpaper to make it easier to use in the coves and over the large beads.

To assemble, you can clamp it by attaching hand clamps to the legs, drawing a cord tightly around them, and wedging them tightly.

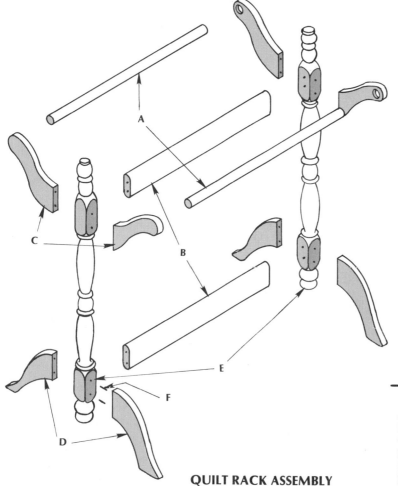

QUILT RACK ASSEMBLY

LIST OF MATERIALS

(finished dimensions in inches)

A	Rods (2)	7/8 dia. × 24-1/4
B	Spreaders (2)	3/4 × 3 × 22-1/4
C	Supports (4)	3/4 × 3-1/2 × 9-1/2
D	Legs (4)	3/4 × 3-1/2 × 10-3/4
E	Spindles (2)	2 × 2 × 33-1/4
F	Dowels (24)	3/8 dia. × 2

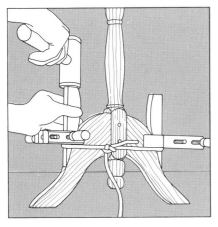

Clamping legs to spindles. Scrap wood wedges draw rope tight. Clamps keep rope in place.

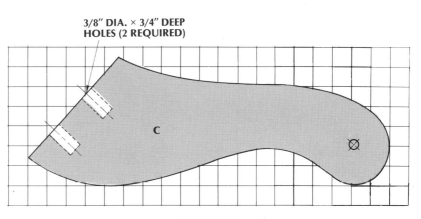

3/8" DIA. × 3/4" DEEP HOLES (2 REQUIRED)

SUPPORT

ONE SQUARE = 1/2"

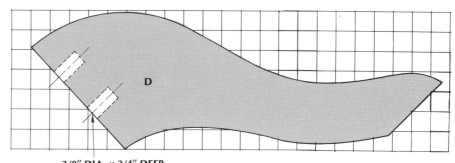

3/8" DIA. × 3/4" DEEP HOLES (2 REQUIRED)

LEG

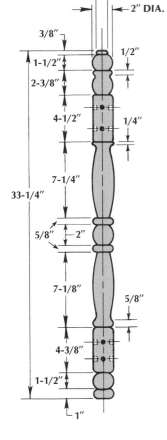

1-1/4" DIA.

2" DIA.

3/8"

1/2"

1-1/2"

2-3/8"

4-1/2"

1/4"

33-1/4"

7-1/4"

5/8" 2"

7-1/8"

5/8"

4-3/8"

1-1/2"

1"

SPINDLE PROFILE

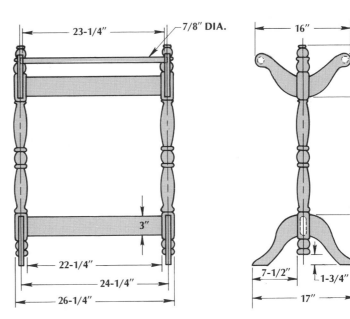

23-1/4"

7/8" DIA.

3"

22-1/4"

24-1/4"

26-1/4"

16"

7"

35"

18-3/4"

8"

7-1/2"

1-3/4"

17"

QUILT RACK LAYOUT

From *HANDS ON* Jan/Feb/Mar 83

The plans for this gateleg table are based on those from a small antique shop in London, England. The table there was of mahogany; this one is from walnut. You can build your own version by following the steps outlined below.

1. Prepare turning stock by cutting wood to 1-1/4″ square and 1″ longer than finished length. To obtain square finished turning stock, joint one side of each turning blank

on the jointer. Then, place the jointed side against the fence and joint the second side square to the first. Mark these two sides. You can plane the two remaining sides to proper thickness on the thickness planer—1-1/8″ for parts (A,B,C) and 1″ for part (D). Or, rip stock to 1/16″ oversize and joint to square final dimension on the jointer. All stock must be true and straight.

2. Prepare remaining stock. You will need 3/4″ stock for the main stretcher (E) and 5/8″ stock for the remaining pieces (see List of Materials).

3. Glue up tabletop (L) and set aside. In this version, the adjacent edges are simply prepared on the jointer and then glued together. The battens (K) provide added strength.

4. Cut mortises in parts (A,B,D,G) for stretchers. Mark off the square sections then the mortises on the turning stock. (Remember: The turning stock has 1/2″ waste on each end.) Use a mortising accessory, a router accessory, or a drill. All mortises are 1/16″ deeper than the lengths of the tenons to allow for glue. You can then chisel the mortises square or round off the tenons.

5. Cut stretchers (F,G,H,J) to size. Cut the tenons on these parts using the dado accessory. *Note:* All tenons are 1/8″ smaller in width and height than the stock except for the tenons on the upper stretchers (F,H). Take an extra 1/4″ off the tops of these tenons (3/8″ total). This will prevent the tenon from splitting the tops of the turned legs since they are so close to the end.

6. Turn parts (A,B,C,D). Accurately mark the centers on the ends of each piece. Seat the lathe centers with a soft mallet.

Turn a 2″ section in the middle of the tapered section and mount a steady rest to prevent whip.

Start turning by roughing to round a 2″ long section at the center of what will be the long tapered section. Sand lightly and then install a steady rest.

Cut the shoulders, then round the turned sections. Form the design by turning next to the squares and work your way toward the center. Turn the feet as required on parts (A,B). Remove the steady rest and complete the turning making light passes to reduce chatter. Sand turning while still on lathe.

7. Cut off excess at top end of each turning and sand square on the disc sander. See drawings for accuracy.

8. Cut and sand to length the opposite ends using the disc sander, quill feed, and the extension table with the fence.

9. Mark and cut the notches in the main stretcher (E) for the legs (A). Use the bandsaw or jigsaw to cut the notches for the gatelegs (B).

10. Drill 1/4″ diameter × 1/2″ deep dowel holes in the ends of the main stretcher (E) and legs (A). Drill countersunk holes for #8 × 1-1/2″ flathead screws in (E) and (C) for the gateleg pivots (D).

11. Dry-assemble all leg assemblies and check for fit and squareness. Disassemble, then assemble with glue.

12. Cut tabletop (L) into the three parts. Joint the adjacent edges of the leaves, then clamp all three parts back together. Mark and cut the mortises for the hinges with a hand chisel or hand-held router. Mount the hinges.

13. Draw an ellipse on the bottom of the tabletop. Secure a temporary batten on the underside to hold the table rigid, then cut the ellipse on the bandsaw or jigsaw. Sand the sawn edges.

14. Shape the tabletop edge with the shaper. Use a 1″ collar and the bead and cove cutter. Cut from below in at least two passes. Make sure that at least 1/8″ of the top is riding on the collar during the final pass. Put a prop under the table for added support. Remove the temporary batten after you have formed the edge.

15. Install the battens (K) on the underside of the leaves with #6 × 1″ flathead screws. Be sure that the battens are a minimum of 1″ from the inside edge so that they will clear the main stretcher (E) when the leaves are down.

16. Finish-sand and apply the finish of your choice. Assemble the gatelegs and tabletop to the frame with screws.

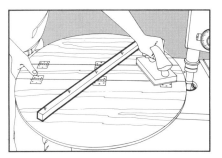

Cutting the decorative edge of the tabletop on the shaper. Use starter pin for this operation.

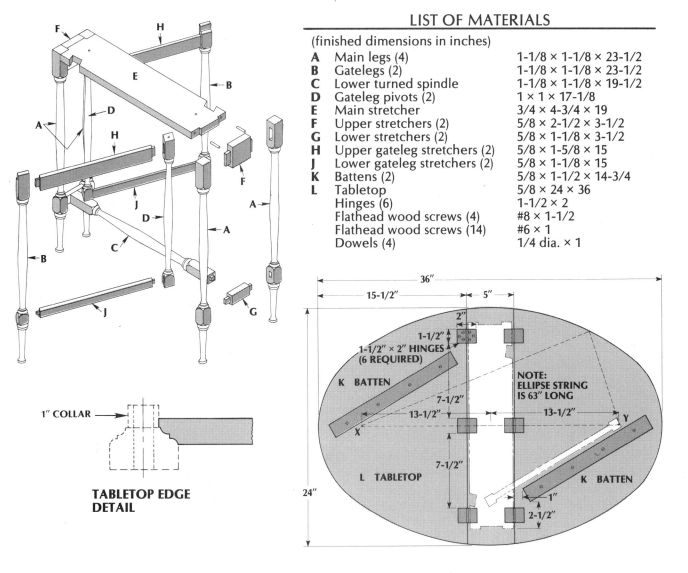

LIST OF MATERIALS

(finished dimensions in inches)

A	Main legs (4)	1-1/8 × 1-1/8 × 23-1/2
B	Gatelegs (2)	1-1/8 × 1-1/8 × 23-1/2
C	Lower turned spindle	1-1/8 × 1-1/8 × 19-1/2
D	Gateleg pivots (2)	1 × 1 × 17-1/8
E	Main stretcher	3/4 × 4-3/4 × 19
F	Upper stretchers (2)	5/8 × 2-1/2 × 3-1/2
G	Lower stretchers (2)	5/8 × 1-1/8 × 3-1/2
H	Upper gateleg stretchers (2)	5/8 × 1-5/8 × 15
J	Lower gateleg stretchers (2)	5/8 × 1-1/8 × 15
K	Battens (2)	5/8 × 1-1/2 × 14-3/4
L	Tabletop	5/8 × 24 × 36
	Hinges (6)	1-1/2 × 2
	Flathead wood screws (4)	#8 × 1-1/2
	Flathead wood screws (14)	#6 × 1
	Dowels (4)	1/4 dia. × 1

TABLETOP EDGE DETAIL

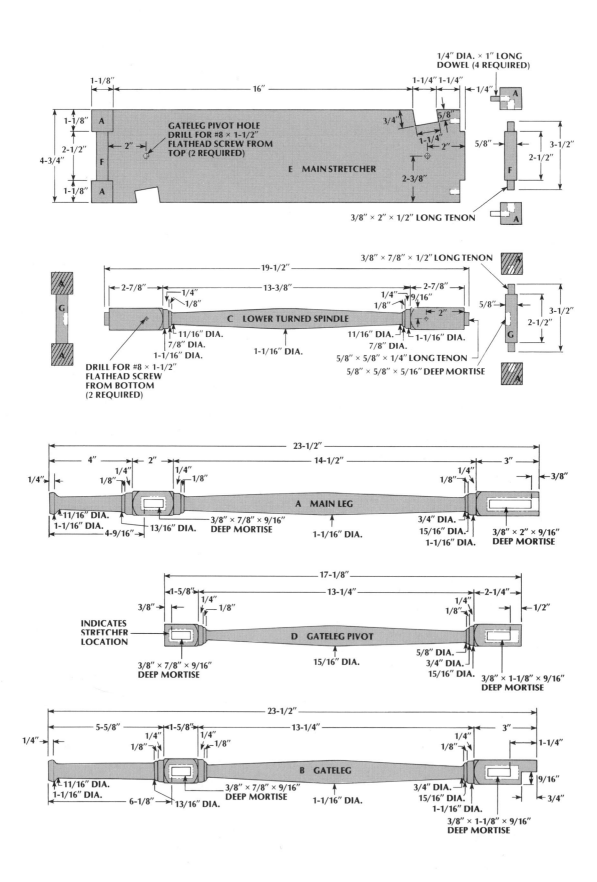

1/4" DIA. × 1" LONG
DOWEL (4 REQUIRED)

1-1/8" 16" 1-1/4" 1-1/4" 1/4"

1-1/8" 3/4" 5/8"

2-1/2" A

4-3/4" F GATELEG PIVOT HOLE
DRILL FOR #8 × 1-1/2"
FLATHEAD SCREW FROM
TOP (2 REQUIRED) 2" 1-1/4" 2"

1-1/8" A E MAIN STRETCHER 2-3/8"

5/8" 3-1/2" 2-1/2" F

3/8" × 2" × 1/2" LONG TENON

3/8" × 7/8" × 1/2" LONG TENON

19-1/2"

2-7/8" 1/4" 13-3/8" 1/4" 9/16" 2-7/8"

1/8" 1/8"

G C LOWER TURNED SPINDLE 2" 5/8" 3-1/2" 2-1/2" G

A 11/16" DIA. 11/16" DIA. 1-1/16" DIA.

7/8" DIA. 7/8" DIA.

1-1/16" DIA. 5/8" × 5/8" × 1/4" LONG TENON

DRILL FOR #8 × 1-1/2" 1-1/16" DIA. 5/8" × 5/8" × 5/16" DEEP MORTISE

FLATHEAD SCREW
FROM BOTTOM
(2 REQUIRED) A

23-1/2"

4" 2" 1/4" 14-1/2" 3"

1/4" 1/4" 1/8" 1/4" 3/8"

1/8" 1/8"

A MAIN LEG

11/16" DIA. 3/4" DIA.

1-1/16" DIA. 13/16" DIA. 3/8" × 7/8" × 9/16" 15/16" DIA. 3/8" × 2" × 9/16"

4-9/16" DEEP MORTISE 1-1/16" DIA. DEEP MORTISE

1-1/16" DIA.

17-1/8"

1-5/8" 1/4" 13-1/4" 2-1/4"

3/8" 1/8" 1/4" 1/2"

1/8"

INDICATES
STRETCHER
LOCATION D GATELEG PIVOT

3/8" × 7/8" × 9/16" 15/16" DIA. 5/8" DIA.

DEEP MORTISE 3/4" DIA.

15/16" DIA. 3/8" × 1-1/8" × 9/16"

DEEP MORTISE

23-1/2"

5-5/8" 1-5/8" 1/4" 13-1/4" 3"

1/4" 1/4" 1/4" 1-1/4"

1/8" 1/8" 1/8"

B GATELEG 9/16"

11/16" DIA. 3/4" DIA.

1-1/16" DIA. 13/16" DIA. 3/8" × 7/8" × 9/16" 15/16" DIA. 3/4"

6-1/8" DEEP MORTISE 1-1/16" DIA. 1-1/16" DIA.

3/8" × 1-1/8" × 9/16"

DEEP MORTISE

From *HANDS ON* Jan/Feb 84

Why is it that some projects take only a few hours and others take many hours to complete? Part of the answer is found in the care with which a project is approached. Think of each board as an individual project; then the hours spent on one piece of furniture represent the putting together of many projects. While you could dedicate an evening to producing a cutting board or a trivet, you may balk at giving that much time to one side of a cabinet or a piece of molding.

This wall-mounted curio cabinet is a project that will take more than one evening or one day if properly approached. Slow down, enjoy the wood, measure carefully, and take your time; then reap the rewards of your efforts.

1. Take the time necessary to select good, properly cured, straight stock. Good stock results in fewer problems throughout the entire project. Select the best pieces for the sides, face frame, and doors. Make your selection based not only on the quality of the wood but also the grain configuration.

2. Rip all stock to the proper width according to the List of Materials. Remember to joint one edge first, rip to width plus 1/32", then joint the other edge, removing that extra 1/32".

3. Crosscut all the stock to length except for the door parts (G,H) and the molding (J,K). Allow an extra 1/8" of length on each board for careful trimming later.

4. Crosscut the sides to final length and mark the locations of the rabbets and dadoes. Transfer the bottom contour from the drawing to the sides.

5. To form the rabbets for the back, set up the dado attachment and attach a wooden auxiliary fence to the rip fence. Cut the 3/8" × 3/8" rabbets on the sides (A) and top (B). Be sure to use push blocks and a feather board.

Remove the fence and cut the dadoes in the sides (A) for the bottom and shelves (C). Then form the rabbets on the ends of the sides for the top.

6. Cut the contours on the bottom of the sides with the bandsaw or jigsaw. When cutting, leave the line. Next, sand the contours with the drum sander.

7. Assemble the cabinet case (sides, top, bottom, and shelves) with aliphatic resin glue and #8 × 1" flathead wood screws or 6d finishing nails. Countersink the screws (or nails).

8. The face frame pieces (D,E,F) are cut to fit. Starting with the stiles (D), mark the correct length and cut on the bandsaw leaving the line. Disc sand the stiles to exact length. Measure the width of the assembled case and subtract the widths of the stiles to obtain the length of the rails. Cut and sand the rails to length. Transfer the contour for the bottom rail, then cut it out with the bandsaw or jigsaw and sand.

Locate the dowel holes 5/8" from the edges then drill the dowel holes by utilizing horizontal boring. Glue and assemble the face frame. After the glue has dried, attach the frame to the case with #8 × 1-1/2" screws or 6d nails.

9. The door frames for this cabinet can be made by selecting the desired design of shaper molding knives. The actual length of the rails will depend on the cutter you use. Whichever cutter is used, form the ends of the rails first then mold or shape the edges of the stiles and rails. Use scrap pieces for testing. Assemble the frames with glue and check for squareness.

10. Sand the entire project. Start with #80 grit paper and work your way up through #220 grit paper. Slightly round off all edges to prevent any splintering.

11. Cut the 3/8″ plywood back to exact size and apply a stain or matching hardwood veneer. Attach the back with 4d nails.

12. Form the molding for the top on one piece of stock. Since this molding projects 45° from the cabinet surface, it can be mitered by setting the miter gauge at 56-1/2° and the table at 30°. Hold the trim flat to the table and cut all three pieces to length. Take the actual measurements from the cabinet.

13. Mark the locations of the hinges and mortise the face frame and door frames with a chisel.

14. Apply the finish of your choice. After the final coat has dried, install the glass in the doors and then mount the doors on the cabinet.

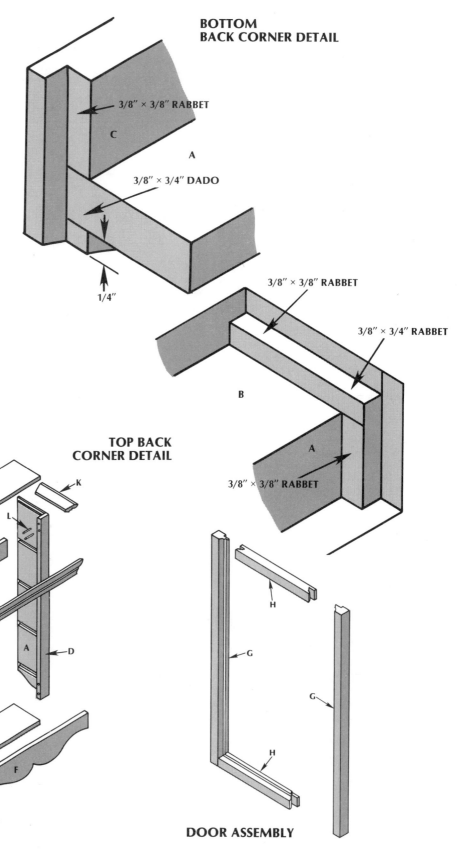

BOTTOM BACK CORNER DETAIL

3/8″ × 3/8″ RABBET

C

A

3/8″ × 3/4″ DADO

1/4″

3/8″ × 3/8″ RABBET

3/8″ × 3/4″ RABBET

B

A

3/8″ × 3/8″ RABBET

TOP BACK CORNER DETAIL

K

B

L

M

E

J

A

D

K

D

C

F

A

D

CASE ASSEMBLY

H

G

G

H

DOOR ASSEMBLY

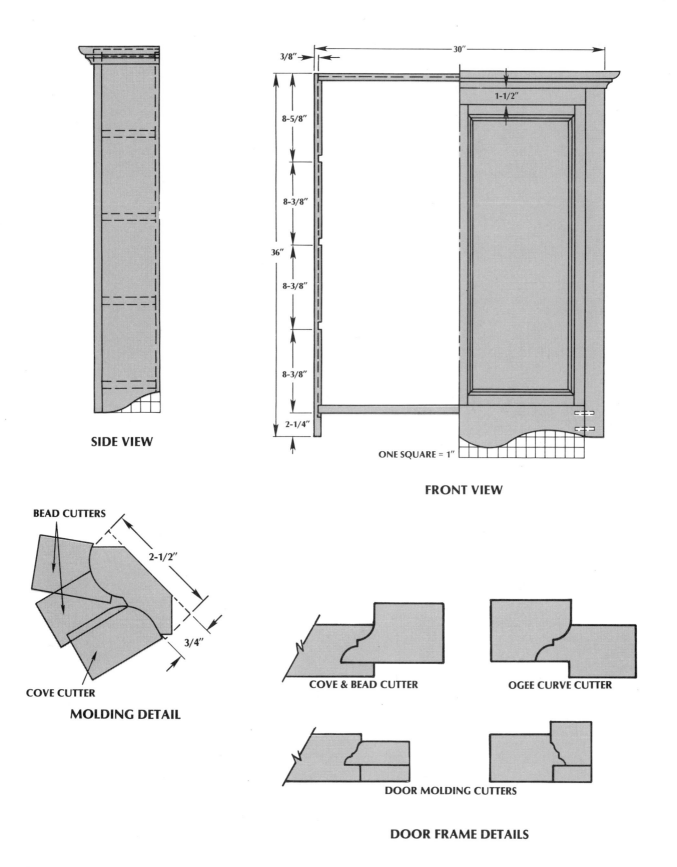

SIDE VIEW

3/8"

30"

1-1/2"

8-5/8"

8-3/8"

36"

8-3/8"

8-3/8"

2-1/4"

ONE SQUARE = 1"

FRONT VIEW

BEAD CUTTERS

2-1/2"

3/4"

COVE CUTTER

MOLDING DETAIL

COVE & BEAD CUTTER

OGEE CURVE CUTTER

DOOR MOLDING CUTTERS

DOOR FRAME DETAILS

BOOKSHELVES

From *HANDS ON* Apr/May/June 83

LIST OF MATERIALS

(finished dimensions in inches)

A	Sides (2)	3/4 × 11 × 60
B	Shelves (5)	3/4 × 10-1/2 × 34-1/2
C	Top	3/4 × 10-3/4 × 34-1/2
D	Top rail	3/4 × 2 × 34-1/2
E	Bottom rail	3/4 × 3 × 34-1/2
F	Back	1/4 × 35-1/4 × 59-1/2
G	Dowel pins (16)	1/4 dia. × 1-1/4

Here's a project that you can put together in a few hours. The cost for materials is little more than a tank of gas in the family sedan. The woodworking on these basic adjustable bookshelves is simple—just a matter of crosscutting, ripping, forming a rabbet in the back, and drilling some holes up the sides.

We selected two 6' and two 8' pieces of #2 common 1 × 12 shelving stock at the local lumberyard for this project. A piece of scrap stock was used for the rails and a leftover piece of 1/4" plywood for the back. The boards were as straight as we could find and the knots were tight. The only problem we encountered was that the edges were a little nicked up. We couldn't complain since the price was reduced. To solve the problem we ripped all the stock twice—once to shave off one edge and then the second time to cut to width.

BOOKSHELF ASSEMBLY

1. Prepare your stock. Use the saw or jointer to clean up the edges of the boards. Crosscut the boards to length according to the List of Materials. Rip the boards to finished width. Don't cut out the plywood back yet.

2. Cut the rabbets. Cut a 3/8" wide × 1/4" deep rabbet in the back inside edges of the sides (A) and in the top (C).

3. Drill the shelf adjustment holes. Mark off the adjustment holes on the insides of the two sides (A). Use a storystick (a board with marks every inch or two depending on your spacing) to ensure all the holes are evenly spaced. Set the rip fence 2" from the center of your drill bit and drill the holes 1/2" deep. Skip this step if you want to permanently mount the shelves.

Sand the faces of all the boards before you start the next step.

4. Assemble the case. Attach the rails (D,E) to the top (C) and bottom shelf (B). Then, attach these assemblies to one side and then the other. Check for squareness as you progress. Measure the back and cut it out. Attach this with 4d finish nails or #6 × 1" flathead wood screws and no glue.

5. Cut the dowel pins (G). The shelves are supported by 1-1/4" lengths of 1/4" dowel pins. Cut these pins on the bandsaw if you have one but, if you don't, use a miter box and a handsaw. Hold them with pliers and chamfer the ends with the disc sander.

6. Finishing touches: Countersink the nails and fill the holes with putty. If you used wood screws, you will need to fill these holes with plugs.

Apply the stain and finish of your choice.

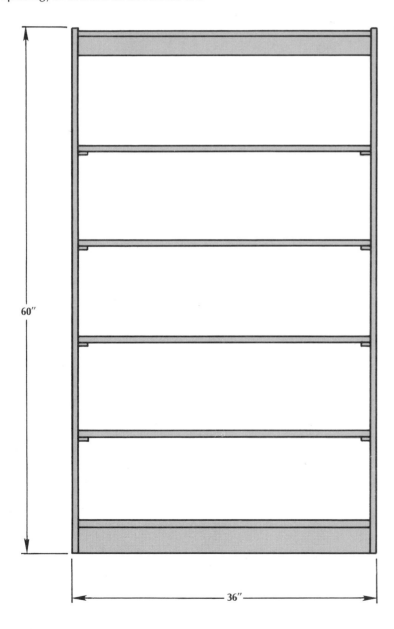

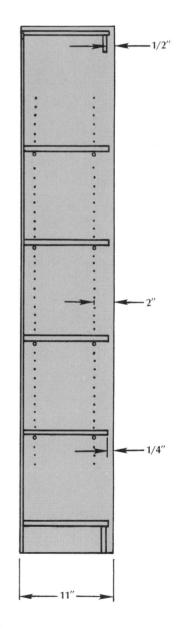

CANDLE STAND

From *HANDS ON* Jan/Feb 82

Simple and functional—those are the hallmarks of Shaker furniture. This graceful pedestal table is a faithful copy of an original Shaker design, and it's a perfect project for the lathe.

Start with gluing up stock for the top, using 1/4" dowels to strengthen the edge joints. Allow this to set up and dry for at least 24 hours. Locate the center, then cut the stock to a rough circle with the bandsaw or jigsaw.

Make the tabletop brace. You'll want to mount it so that its grain runs perpendicular to the grain of the top. The Shakers used this method to prevent the top from cupping and warping.

Now mount the brace temporarily to the top. Attach them both to the large faceplate. Use slow speed to turn the edge first, then scrape the recessed top surface. Finish-sand before you remove it from the lathe.

Next, glue up the stock for the spindle, again allowing plenty of time for the glue to dry. Turn the spindle and final-sand it on the lathe.

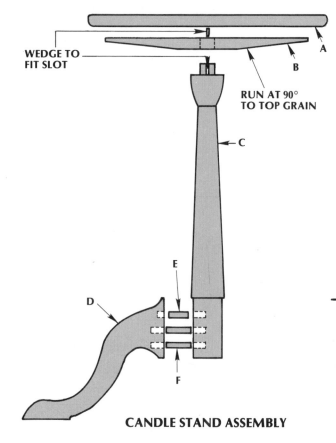

WEDGE TO FIT SLOT

RUN AT 90° TO TOP GRAIN

CANDLE STAND ASSEMBLY

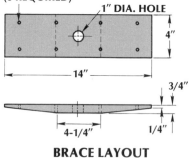

1/4" DIA. HOLES WITH 3/8" DIA. COUNTERSINK (8 REQUIRED)

1" DIA. HOLE

4"

14"

3/4"

4-1/4"

1/4"

BRACE LAYOUT

LIST OF MATERIALS

(finished dimensions in inches)

A	Top	16-3/8 dia. × 3/4
B	Brace	3/4 × 4 × 14
C	Spindle	2-1/4 dia. × 19-1/2
D	Legs (3)	3/4 × 4 × 12-1/2
E	Dowels (3)	3/8 dia. × 7/8
F	Dowels (6)	3/8 dia. × 1-1/2
	Flathead wood screws (4)	#6 × 1
	Flathead wood screws (4)	#6 × 1-1/4

Make a pattern for the legs (see drawing). Lay out the pattern on the stock so that the grain runs lengthwise from the top to the bottom. This is a necessity for strength. Use the bandsaw or jigsaw to cut them, then sand the contours with the drum sander. To round the top edges, use the shaper or router, or do it by hand. To finish the concave radii on the legs where they join the pedestal/spindle, use a 1-1/2″ × 1-1/2″ drum sander.

Drill the dowel holes in the pedestal for mounting the legs. Use dowel center finders to locate the holes you'll drill in the legs. Use care not to drill through the legs!

Saw a kerf in the top of the spindle; remove the brace from the tabletop and mount it to the spindle, tapping in a small wedge to lock the pieces together.

Attach the legs with dowels and glue. Cut up an old rubber inner tube and wrap it tightly around the pieces to clamp them all equally.

Screw on the top and apply the finish of your choice.

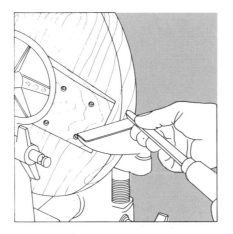

Slow speed turning of tabletop. Note position of toolrest.

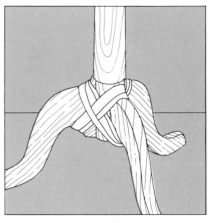

Rubber from old inner tube interwoven around legs to grip and clamp equally.

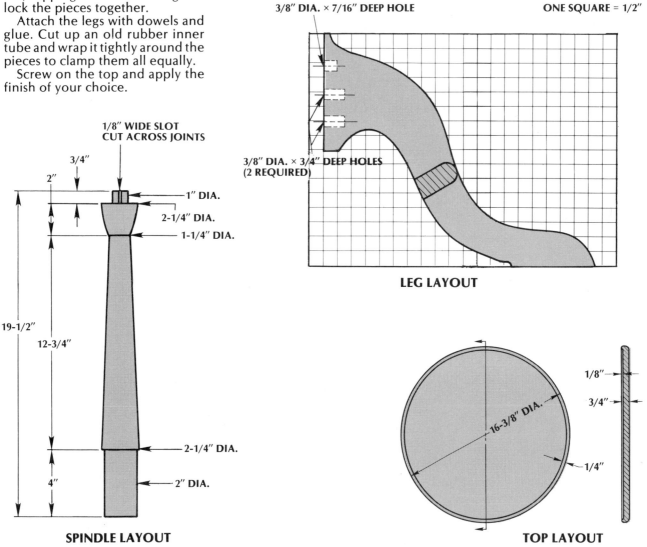

3/8″ DIA. × 7/16″ DEEP HOLE

ONE SQUARE = 1/2″

3/8″ DIA. × 3/4″ DEEP HOLES (2 REQUIRED)

LEG LAYOUT

1/8″ WIDE SLOT CUT ACROSS JOINTS

3/4″

2″

1″ DIA.

2-1/4″ DIA.

1-1/4″ DIA.

19-1/2″

12-3/4″

2-1/4″ DIA.

4″

2″ DIA.

SPINDLE LAYOUT

16-3/8″ DIA.

1/8″

3/4″

1/4″

TOP LAYOUT

ENTERTAINMENT CENTER

From *HANDS ON* Mar/Apr 82

Your living room is the new frontier for all sorts of electronic audio-visual gadgetry, and you can organize it in this beautiful, simple project.

Use two sheets of 1/2" plywood, double-faced birch veneer. Check the size of your components and television. Dimensions given here are only suggestions, based partly on the standard 19" wide stereo component.

Build the project on its back. First dry-assemble the parts, using utility or flathead wood screws with a pilot hole and countersink.

To assemble, attach face strips (D) to shelves (B). Next, attach bottom partition (E) to the two bottom shelves (B), then attach this assembly to the right-hand side (A).

In the middle section, attach shelves (G,L) to the center partition (F) and then fasten this assembly to

LIST OF MATERIALS

(finished dimensions in inches)

A	Sides (2)	18 × 56
B	Shelves (3)	17-1/2 × 40
C	Shelf	18 × 40
D	Face strip	2-1/2 × 40
E	Bottom partition	14-1/2 × 18
F	Middle partition	18 × 27-1/2
G	Shelf	15-1/2 × 18
H	Upper partition	9 × 18
J	Door	5-1/2 × 15-1/2
K	Door	12-1/2 × 13
L	Shelf	15-1/2 × 17-1/2
	Hinges (2)	1" × 2"
	Magnetic catches (2 pr.)	
	Knobs (2)	
	Screw plugs (64)	3/8" dia.
	Light chain	20" (approx.)
	Flathead pivot screws (2)	#6 × 1"
	Utility screws (64)	#8 × 1"
	Edge stripping	480" (40')

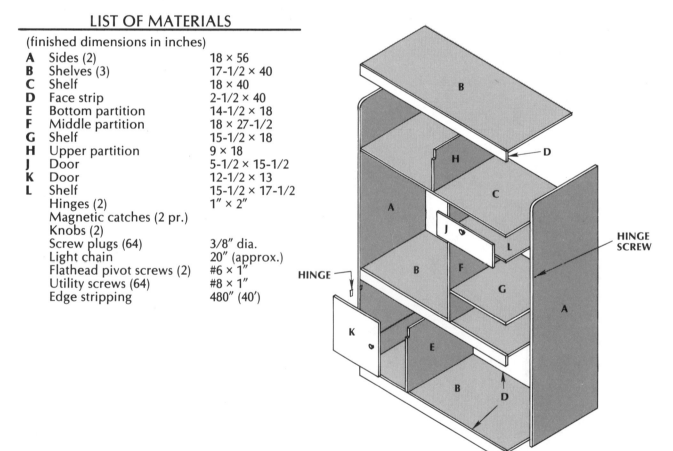

the right-hand side assembly. Attach part (H) to shelf (C) and fasten this to the rest of the assembly. Finally, add top shelf (B) and the left-hand side (A).

The next step is to disassemble the entire project and apply veneer strips to all exposed edges. Once applied, reassemble the project with screws and glue. Use dowels to plug the countersunk screws.

Mount the hinges to the lower door (K) and pivot screws for the small door (J). Round over the lower inside edge of this door to allow for movement. Using screw pivots instead of hinges on this small door eliminates a "step" between the door and the shelf. Lightweight chain keeps the door from folding down too far. Apply the finish of your choice, and start organizing all that fancy equipment.

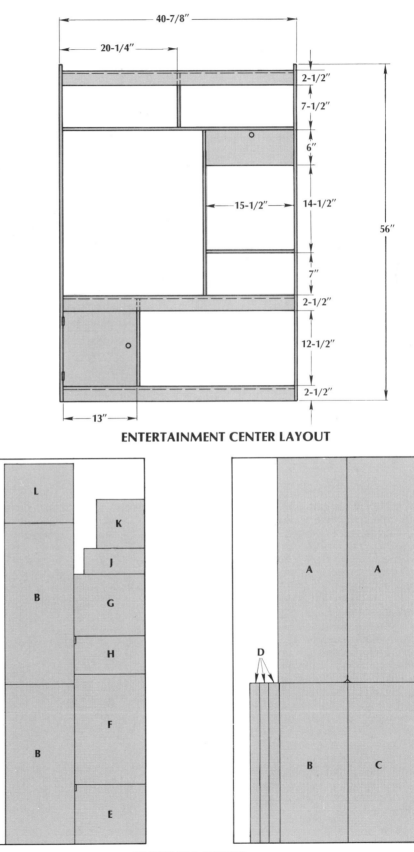

ENTERTAINMENT CENTER LAYOUT

NOTCH DETAIL

CUTTING LAYOUT

STACKABLE DRESSER DRAWERS

From *HANDS ON* Nov/Dec 81

Set up the saw table at 90°; set the miter gauge with extension and stop block clamped onto it at 15° to the saw blade and cut the first side of the pin. Using stop blocks assures that each spreader pin will be identical to all others.

For the opposite side of the pin, move the miter gauge to cut 15° in the other direction.

To finish the pin, set the table and miter gauge to cut at 90°. Adjust the height of the blade to cut no more than 7/16" deep. This cut removes 80% of the waste stock and opens the face of each pin's shoulder. Finish the pin with your hand chisel.

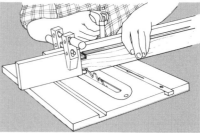

Making rough cut of dovetail pin shoulder.

The idea of traditional joinery was partly to encourage the illusion that furniture looked like it was carved from a single, thick slab of wood. The better the joinery was hidden, the better the piece.

In contemporary design, however, the joinery isn't at all bashful. In fact, modern craftsmen flaunt perfectly fitted, exquisite joints.

Once assembled, this contemporary, stackable chest of drawers shows locking dovetails on the sides that align to look like the units are held together with butterfly joints. It goes beyond beauty though; its interchangeable units lock together and you can make as many as you want or as few as you need.

In choosing the wood for this project, go ahead and revel in the unique compatibility of different woods joined together. We built the chest of contrasting poplar and walnut.

When gluing up stock for the sides and drawer fronts, the specialty glue joint helps align each piece.

The secret to making these joints identical to one another is to mark off the dovetail pins on both ends of one spreader, then use this master spreader to mark all the others.

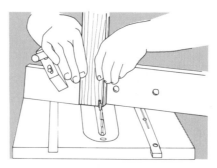

Cut for dovetail pin. Miter gauge set at 15°.

Use the existing dovetail pins on the master spreader to trace onto the sides for positioning the dovetail slots. Tilt the table 15° to the right with the fence on the left side of the blade. Cut one side of the slot on the front, back, top, and bottom of all sides.

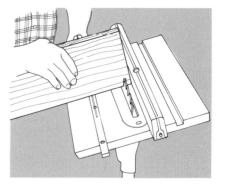

First cut: dovetail slot. Fence on left side.

Now set the fence on the right side of the blade for cutting the second side of the slot in all sides, front, top and bottom. Finish the slot on a bandsaw or jigsaw.

Use a chisel or knife to gain final fit of the pin into the slot. Number each joint for final assembly, but don't assemble them yet.

Make the 1/4" rabbet in the back pieces with a dado blade.

Locate and drill the aligning holes through each spreader for the 3/8" dowels that lock the units together.

The drawers rest within a three-element, self-aligning assembly: the blind dado, the guide, and the dovetailed slot in the drawer side. This allows for easy sliding.

Cut the blind dado in the carcase side. For correct distance, experiment with scrap, then clamp a stop block onto the fence extension. To position this slot accurately on each piece, measure from the top of the side and cut with the top against the fence.

Cut the plywood backs; glue the carcase together. Check the squareness of each carcase as you clamp it.

Glue the wood to make the drawer stock, then cut the pieces to size, allowing 1/16" on each side for total drawer clearance.

Cut the lock joints into the pieces. Rout or dado the 1/4" groove for the drawer bottom.

Cut the dovetail slot in the drawer sides that will accept the guide. Mark the sides according to the drawer guide blind dado already cut into the carcase side. Dado the main portion of this, and finish forming it with a dovetail cutter router bit.

From straight stock at least 3" wide, cut dovetails on the edges of both sides. A wider board makes this easier to control and then it's a simple matter to rip the portion you need from this stock.

Use the disc sander to fit the guide to the blind dado. Then glue and screw these guides into the slot.

Cut the plywood bottom and glue up the drawers.

LIST OF MATERIALS

(finished dimensions in inches)

10" Unit

A	Sides (2)	3/4 × 10 × 16-3/4
B	Spreaders (4)	3/4 × 2-1/4 × 36
C	Back	1/4 × 9-1/4 × 35-1/4
D	Drawer front	3/4 × 9-1/4 × 35-1/4
E	Drawer sides (2)	3/4 × 8-3/8 × 16-1/4
F	Drawer back	3/4 × 7-7/8 × 33-5/8
G	Drawer bottom	1/4 × 16-1/8 × 33-3/8
H	Drawer guides (2)	3/4 × 3/4 × 15-1/4

6" Unit
(not shown in dimensioned plans)

	Sides (2)	3/4 × 6 × 16-3/4
	Spreaders (4)	3/4 × 2-1/4 × 36
	Back	1/4 × 5-1/4 × 35-1/4
	Drawer front	3/4 × 5-1/4 × 35-1/4
	Drawer sides (2)	3/4 × 4-3/8 × 16-1/4
	Drawer back	3/4 × 3-7/8 × 33-5/8
	Drawer bottom	1/4 × 16-1/8 × 33-3/8
	Drawer guides (2)	3/4 × 3/4 × 15-1/4

Top Unit

B	Spreaders (2)	3/4 × 2-1/4 × 36
J	Top	3/4 × 17-3/4 × 38
K	Sides (2)	3/4 × 1 × 16-3/4

Base Unit

B	Spreaders (2)	3/4 × 2-1/4 × 36
L	Front	3/4 × 3-1/4 × 34-1/2
M	Sides	3/4 × 4 × 16-3/4

Miscellaneous

N	Dowels (4 per unit)	3/8 dia. × 1-1/2
	Drawer pulls	3/4 × 1-1/2 × 5-3/4
	Flathead wood screws (4 per unit)	#9 × 1-1/4
	Flathead wood screws (4 per unit)	#6 × 1

3/4" × 1/4" DEEP BLIND DADO
SEE DETAIL A
1"
17-3/4"
1"
K
B
J
K

TOP UNIT ASSEMBLY

Cut the wood to make the top. Into the bottom of the top, cut a blind dado which will lock in the small side pieces (use a chisel to square up the end of the dado). Then glue in the top's sides and spreaders. Cut the pieces for the bottom unit, then glue and screw them together.

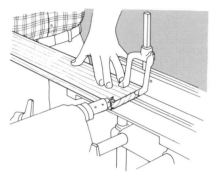

Forming dovetail guides.

Place dowels in the spreaders and assemble the units on top of one another. Finish-sand.

Lay out and cut parts for the drawer pulls (see Drawer Pull Layout) using the bandsaw set at 20°. Disc sand the outside of the pulls with a sander set at approximately 20°. Glue the halves of the pulls together, sand the inside surface on the drum sander, and mount them with wood screws from the inside of the drawer front.

Stain and seal the project inside and out, wax the drawer guides, then move it into your bedroom—and breathe a sigh of relief that you finally have all the drawer space you need!

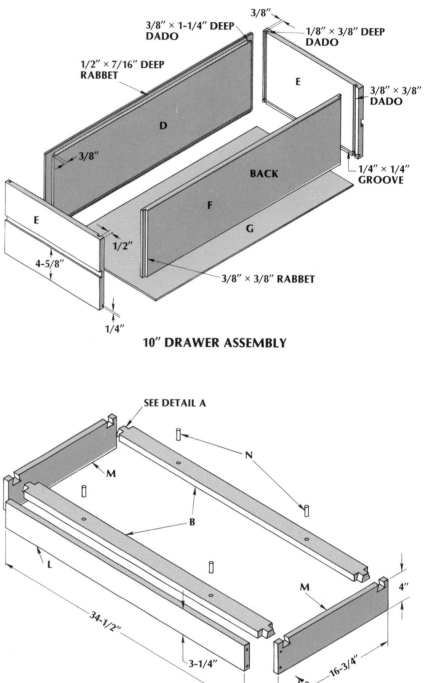

3/8" × 1-1/4" DEEP DADO

3/8"

1/8" × 3/8" DEEP DADO

1/2" × 7/16" DEEP RABBET

E

3/8" × 3/8" DADO

D

3/8"

BACK

1/4" × 1/4" GROOVE

F

E

G

1/2"

4-5/8"

3/8" × 3/8" RABBET

1/4"

10" DRAWER ASSEMBLY

SEE DETAIL A

N

M

B

L

M

4"

34-1/2"

3-1/4"

16-3/4"

#9 × 1-1/4" FLATHEAD WOOD SCREWS

BASE UNIT ASSEMBLY

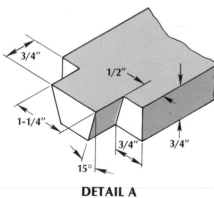

3/4"

1/2"

1-1/4"

3/4"

3/4"

15°

DETAIL A

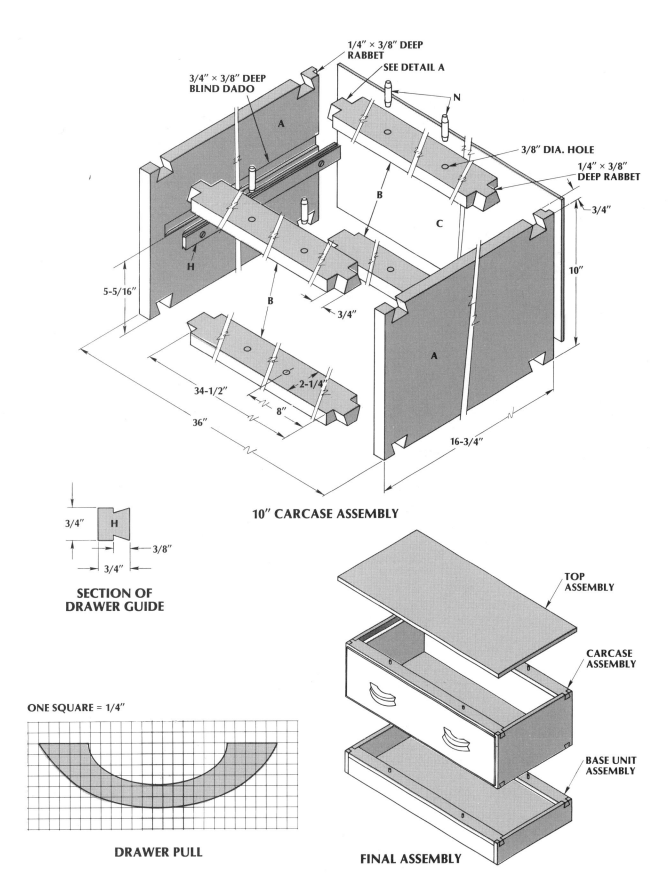

1/4″ × 3/8″ DEEP RABBET

SEE DETAIL A

3/4″ × 3/8″ DEEP BLIND DADO

N

A

3/8″ DIA. HOLE

1/4″ × 3/8″ DEEP RABBET

3/4″

B

C

H

10″

5-5/16″

B

3/4″

A

34-1/2″

8″

2-1/4″

36″

16-3/4″

10″ CARCASE ASSEMBLY

3/4″

H

3/8″

3/4″

SECTION OF DRAWER GUIDE

ONE SQUARE = 1/4″

DRAWER PULL

TOP ASSEMBLY

CARCASE ASSEMBLY

BASE UNIT ASSEMBLY

FINAL ASSEMBLY

CHILD'S DESK & CHAIRS

From *HANDS ON* Mar/Apr 82

Every child deserves a desk of their very own to store their favorite coloring books and crayons, paints and paper, and their own small library of books. Here's a project that uses only one piece of 4 × 8 plywood (we found 1/2" worked well). You get a full 4' desk top and storage shelf plus two chairs just right for that special little person in your life and his or her little friend.

Carefully follow the cutout diagram in marking all the pieces on a sheet of plywood. You can use fir plywood, interior or exterior glue, good one side (A/D) or good two sides (A/B) or special order a sheet of Medium Density Overlay plywood that's specifically made for painting. Make all straight cuts first, then drill holes on the inside of the lines for cutting out the curved pieces. These can be cut on the jigsaw or a hand-held saber saw.

Sharp exposed plywood edges pose a splinter hazard for young hands, so round over these edges with sandpaper or a carbide-tipped 3/8" rounding over router bit.

Dry-assemble all pieces. It helps to drill pilot holes and to use some of those new drywall/particleboard utility screws with a variable speed drill. After positioning all pieces, disassemble and glue. Put it all back together using the screws to clamp the project together.

Fill edge voids with wood putty and apply a primer coat before final painting with a *lead-free* paint. Then bring it out of the shop and watch as the kids create their projects on it!

CHAIR LAYOUT

23-15/16"
2"
12"
2"
2"
12-7/8"

NOTE: 1-1/4" RADIUS TYPICAL EXCEPT WHERE NOTED

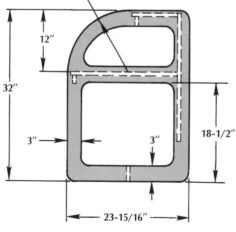

12" R
12"
32"
3"
3"
18-1/2"
23-15/16"

DESK LAYOUT

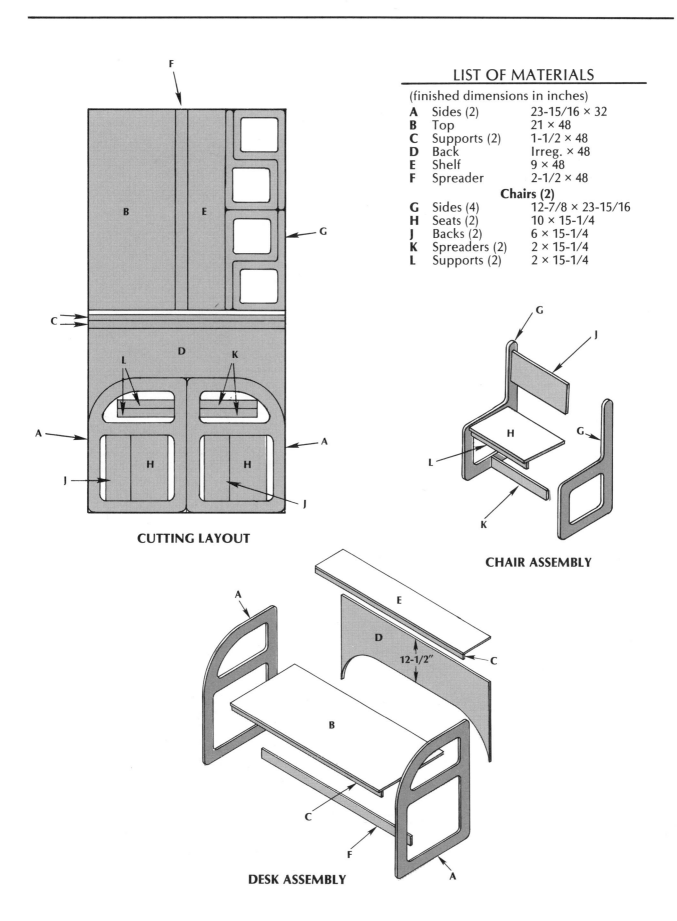

CUTTING LAYOUT

CHAIR ASSEMBLY

12-1/2"

DESK ASSEMBLY

HEIRLOOM CRADLE

From *HANDS ON* Apr/May/June 83

One of the greatest joys in woodworking is to see the project you've made used and appreciated. This cradle will not only succeed at this, but will continue to be used and appreciated for generations to come. Because of this, the cradle will be an heirloom—a part of you that will be around well into the 21st century.

Designed with simple classic lines, the construction of this cradle is basic and the joinery rugged. Features include wide feet to prevent tipping, a locking pin on the basket, and wedges that knock out so the whole cradle can break down and store easily.

1. Glue-up stock where necessary according to the List of Materials. Use a hand-held belt sander to smooth the glued-up sections.

2. Transfer the patterns onto all the contoured parts (A,B,C,D,E,F). Mark the location of the holes in the headboard (E) and footboard (F). Do not cut any of the contours yet.

3. Cut the mortises in the feet (A), posts (B), and stretcher (C) with the mortising attachment. If you do not have a mortising attachment, drill several holes and chisel out the waste. We used the drilling method and left the mortises round on the posts so that we could have rounded tenons.

4. Cut the tenons on the bottoms of the posts (B) and ends of the stretcher (C) using a dado attachment. Round the tenons of the stretcher with a rasp.

5. Drill holes. First drill the 1/2" diameter holes in the feet through the post for the pegged mortise and tenon joint with the two parts assembled. Then, drill the 3/4" diameter pivot holes in the posts (B), headboard (E), and footboard (F). Finally, line-up a post with the headboard and drill the locking pin hole through the post into the headboard.

6. Cut the contours on the posts (B), stretcher (C), sides (D), headboard (E), and footboard (F) using the bandsaw. Sand all of these edges using the drum and disc sanders.

7. Assemble the feet to the posts with glue and 1/2" diameter dowels (P). Sand the ends of the dowels flush with the outside surfaces. Tip: Scrub off the excess glue with a wet rag. This works better than chiseling or sanding it off later.

8. Assemble the basket by attaching the sides (D) to the headboard (E) and footboard (F) with glue and #10 × 1-1/2" flathead wood screws. Countersink the screws 3/16" below the surface, and then plug these holes. Use a hand-held belt sander to sand the outside of the cradle smooth and the plugs flush.

The stretcher is joined to the post with classic wedged-through mortise-and-tenon construction.

Cradle pivot pin is a 3/4" diameter hardwood dowel capped with a button.

The post is joined to the foot with a pinned mortise-and-tenon. Pins are hardwood dowels.

Locking pin slips out when you want to rock baby to sleep. The pin is turned from one piece with grain running lengthwise.

9. Cut the cleat strips (G,H) to size, and mount them to the inside of the cradle with #8 × 1-1/4" flat-head wood screws.

10. Cut the bottom (Q) to size and bevel the two sides edges. Sand all the edges.

11. Make the spacers (M) by first resawing 3/4" stock to 3/8" thick. Draw 2" circles on the stock, and drill the 3/4" holes. Cut the washers on the bandsaw or jigsaw and sand the edges. Set aside.

12. Make the pivot pins (J) and the pivot lock pin (L). The pivot pins (J) are made of 3" lengths of 3/4" hardwood dowel. The caps to these are turned on the lathe using the screw center. After they are turned, use a jig to hold them while you drill the 3/4" × 1/2" deep holes for the pin. If you are using a good durable hardwood like cherry or maple, you can turn these pins out of one piece of stock.

Turn the locking pin as one piece from a 4" length of 3/4" stock.

13. Make the wedges (N) for the post and stretcher joint. These wedges are cut-to-fit and should be centered and fit snugly with a tap from a mallet.

14. Finish sand all the subassemblies with a fine grit sandpaper. Then apply a nontoxic finish of your choice.

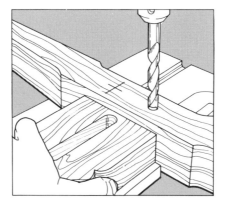

Drilling the 1/2" holes for the pegged joint.

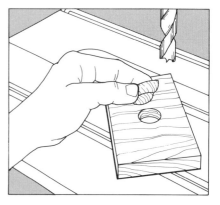

Using a simple jig to hold the caps while drilling.

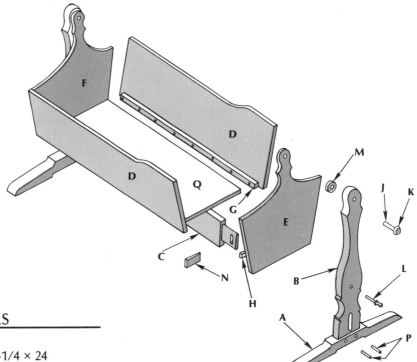

LIST OF MATERIALS

(finished dimensions in inches)

A	Feet (2)	2-1/4 × 2-1/4 × 24
B	Posts (2)	1-1/2 × 4-1/2 × 30
C	Stretcher	1-1/4 × 4-1/2 × 42-3/4
D	Sides (2)	3/4 × 12 × 35
E	Headboard	3/4 × 19-5/8 × 20-1/4
F	Footboard	3/4 × 18-7/8 × 20-1/4
G	Cleat strips (2)	3/4 × 3/4 × 33-1/2
H	Cleat strips (2)	3/4 × 3/4 × 14-3/16
J	Pivot pins (2)	3/4 dia. × 3
K	Pivot pin caps (2)	1-1/2 dia. × 3/4
L	Pivot lock pin	3/4 dia. × 3-3/8
M	Spacers (2)	2 dia. × 3/8
N	Wedges (2)	9/16 × 1-7/8 × 3-3/8
P	Dowels (4)	1/2 dia. × 2-1/4
Q	Bottom	1/4 × 15-11/16 × 33-7/16
	Flathead wood screws	#10 × 1-1/2
	Flathead wood screws	#8 × 1-1/4
	Flathead wood screws	#6 × 1-1/2

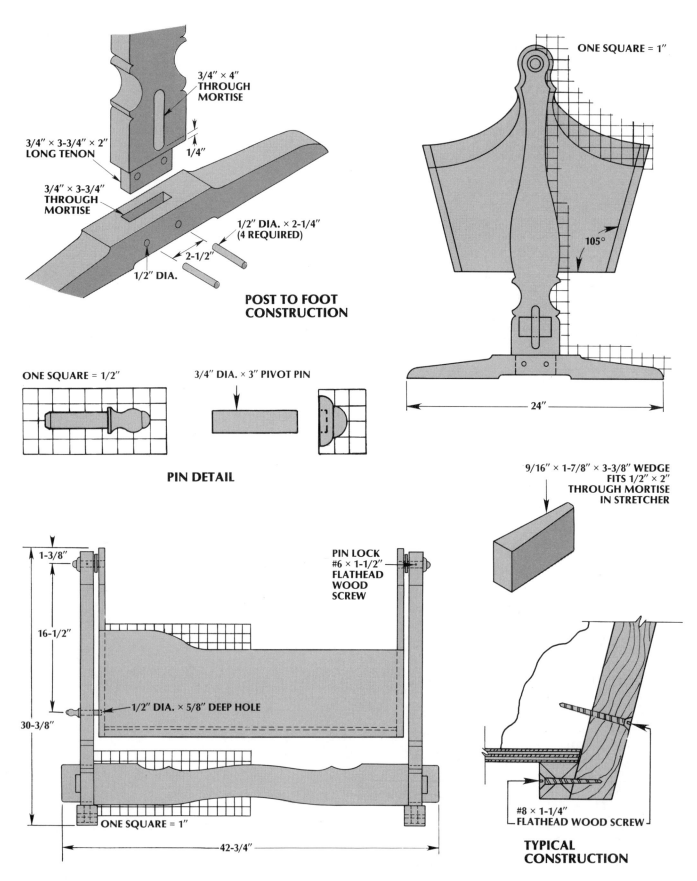

3/4″ × 4″ THROUGH MORTISE

3/4″ × 3-3/4″ × 2″ LONG TENON

3/4″ × 3-3/4″ THROUGH MORTISE

1/4″

1/2″ DIA. × 2-1/4″ (4 REQUIRED)

2-1/2″

1/2″ DIA.

POST TO FOOT CONSTRUCTION

ONE SQUARE = 1″

105°

24″

ONE SQUARE = 1/2″

3/4″ DIA. × 3″ PIVOT PIN

PIN DETAIL

9/16″ × 1-7/8″ × 3-3/8″ WEDGE FITS 1/2″ × 2″ THROUGH MORTISE IN STRETCHER

1-3/8″

PIN LOCK #6 × 1-1/2″ FLATHEAD WOOD SCREW

16-1/2″

1/2″ DIA. × 5/8″ DEEP HOLE

30-3/8″

ONE SQUARE = 1″

42-3/4″

#8 × 1-1/4″ FLATHEAD WOOD SCREW

TYPICAL CONSTRUCTION

STEREO SPEAKER STAND

From *HANDS ON* Sept/Oct 80

A home sound system is a big investment, so why not get maximum performance from your speakers? A tilted speaker stand can greatly enhance the quality of sound, and it's amazingly easy to construct.

1. You'll need three standard-sized dowels to make the speaker stand—1-1/4", 3/4", and 3/8". Cut the dowels to length using a bandsaw.

2. Smooth the ends of the dowels with a disc sander.

3. Take eight of the 1-1/4" dowels and drill 3/8" diameter holes 1-1/16" deep in one end of each dowel.

4. Cradle the dowels on the drill press by tilting the table and rip fence to form a V. Clamp a stop block on the fence to accurately position the stretcher holes.

5. Drill 3/4" diameter stretcher holes 5/8" deep in the 1-1/4" dowels. Make sure the top end of the dowel always faces the same direction.

5. Assemble as shown, using wax on the 3/8" dowels and glue on the 3/4" dowels. Stain and finish according to preference.

7. Small pieces of felt can be glued to the stand to prevent it from scratching the speaker.

Note: By adjusting the length of the dowels, you can accommodate larger or smaller speakers. For example, use 3/8", 1/2", and 1" dowels for smaller speakers.

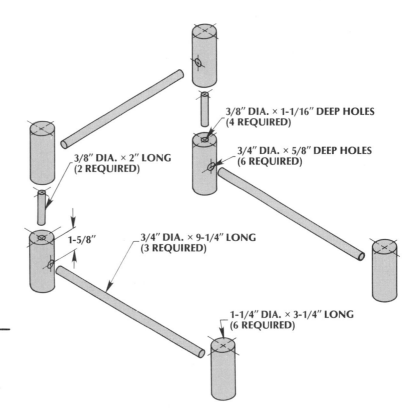

3/8" DIA. × 1-1/16" DEEP HOLES (4 REQUIRED)

3/4" DIA. × 5/8" DEEP HOLES (6 REQUIRED)

3/8" DIA. × 2" LONG (2 REQUIRED)

1-5/8"

3/4" DIA. × 9-1/4" LONG (3 REQUIRED)

1-1/4" DIA. × 3-1/4" LONG (6 REQUIRED)

LIST OF MATERIALS

(finished dimensions in inches)

A	Dowels (4)	2 × 3/8 dia.
B	Dowels (6)	9-1/4 × 3/4 dia.
C	Dowels (12)	3-1/4 × 1-1/4 dia.

LIST OF MATERIALS

(finished dimensions in inches)

A	Sides (2)	3/4 × 11-1/4 × 78
B	Top	3/4 × 11-1/4 × 35-1/4
C	Bottom	3/4 × 11-1/4 × 35-1/4
D	Shelves (as many as you need)	3/4 × 11 × 34-1/2
E	Top face frame	3/4 × 3 × 32-1/2
F	Bottom face frame	3/4 × 2-1/2 × 32-1/2
G	Side face frame pieces (2)	3/4 × 1-3/4 × 78
H	Top front molding	3/4 × 2-1/2 × 40
I	Top side moldings (2)	3/4 × 2-1/2 × 14
J	Base front	3/4 × 5 × 37-1/2
K	Base sides (2)	3/4 × 5 × 12
L	Base cleats (7)	3/4 × 3/4 × 4
M	Back	1/4 × 35-1/4 × 74-3/4
N	Dowels (8)	3/8 dia. × 2

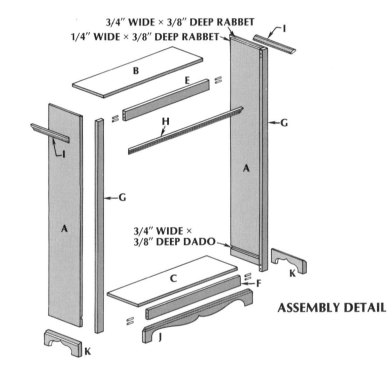

3/4" WIDE × 3/8" DEEP RABBET
1/4" WIDE × 3/8" DEEP RABBET

**3/4" WIDE ×
3/8" DEEP DADO**

ASSEMBLY DETAIL

A simple bookcase—sides, shelves, and a back, held together with nails—is very easy to make. But with just a little extra effort, a simple bookcase can look like one purchased from a quality furniture store. Here are the plans for an elegant simple bookcase that has adjustable shelves.

1. Cut the two sides, the top, and the bottom to the dimensions given in the List of Materials. Cut 1/4" deep by 3/8" wide rabbets in the back edges of all four pieces. Then cut 3/4" wide by 3/8" deep dadoes in the sides to accommodate the top and bottom pieces.

2. This bookcase utilizes a hole-and-peg system to support the adjustable shelves. To mark the location of the holes, use a 6' long stick that is marked at 1-1/2" intervals. Using the marked stick as a guide, indicate the locations of two rows of holes on the inside of each side piece at the 1-1/2" intervals; then drill the 1/4" diameter by 3/8" deep holes.

3. Assemble the top, bottom, and sides, then measure for the back. Cut the back to size, and glue and nail the bookcase together with 6d finish nails. The back will help keep the bookcase square.

4. Cut out the top, bottom, and side face frame pieces. Drill the dowel holes horizontally.

5. Assemble the face frame with dowels and glue, then attach it to the bookcase with glue and countersunk 6d finish nails.

6. Form the molding as indicated on the drawing. Cut it to length and then attach it to the bookcase

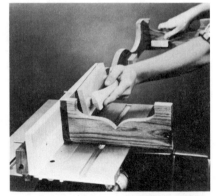

Using the molder to form the contour on the top edge of the assembled base.

with glue and countersunk 6d finish nails.

7. Cut the base pieces to size according to the List of Materials. Transfer the patterns from the drawings to the base front and sides; then use a jigsaw or bandsaw to cut out the base pieces.

8. Sand the contours of the base pieces with a drum sander. Assemble the base pieces, using a molder to form the profile on the top edge.

9. Using glue and #8 × 1-1/4″ flat-head wood screws, attach the cleats to the inside of the base.

10. Rip and crosscut the shelves to size, then use a molder or shaper with a nosing cutter to shape the front edge of each shelf. Install the shelves.

11. Sand the completed bookcase thoroughly, then finish as desired.

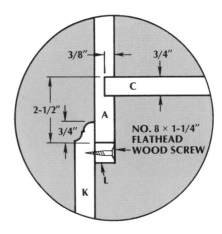

BOTTOM CONSTRUCTION DETAIL

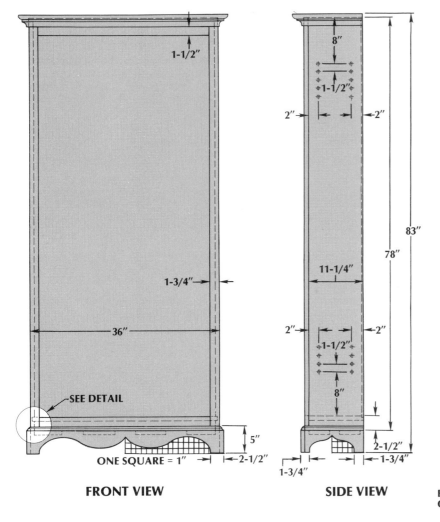

FRONT VIEW

SIDE VIEW

ONE SQUARE = 1″

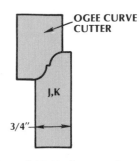

BASE MOLDING DETAIL

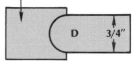

SHELF EDGE DETAIL

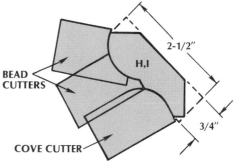

TOP MOLDING DETAIL

POOR MAN'S BUTLER

From *HANDS ON* Nov/Dec 81

predetermined mark. Make several passes, taking a little more stock off with each pass. Square the ends of the stop rabbet with a chisel.

Drill 1" holes for the pegs in the back stiles, then attach the shelf brackets. Assemble the back stiles to the back panel, build the storge box, and attach the seat and lid.

Screw the front stiles to the storage box, then dowel the arms to both sets of stiles. Add the shelf, trim, and rails. Cover the inside edge of the mirror opening with veneer tape. Turn the pegs and glue them into the back stiles.

If you build from fir plywood, apply a light coat of plywood sealer to help it take a stain evenly. Finish with something that won't be affected by wet raincoats—polyurethane or spar varnish.

Attach the mirror to the back with screws and nylon washers. Finally, collect all the clothes off your other furniture and cover the wooden butler with coats and jackets.

Somehow jackets and coats always manage to drape themselves across every available table and chair. If it's getting so you can't see your furniture for the clothes, perhaps you need a 'poor man's butler'.

This particular butler, though traditional in design, is made from contemporary materials. The large panels and shelf are cut from a single piece of 3/4" plywood. Don't try to rip this sheet by yourself—get one or two helpers. We found a carbide-tipped blade worked best; a plywood blade will heat up and begin to wobble in thick stock during a long cut.

Cut the mirror opening in the back panel with a saber saw. We chose to cut a simple oval, 22-1/2" wide × 34-1/2" tall; but you can make the opening any shape or dimension that suits your fancy. The lid can be cut from the seat on a bandsaw—or very carefully on a table saw, finishing up with a handsaw.

The joinery is a snap—most of it consists of simple butt joints and rabbets, all reinforced with glue and countersunk wood screws. The one difficult joint—a stop rabbet in the front stiles—is made by carefully lowering the stock onto the dado blade and rabbeting to a

LIST OF MATERIALS

(finished dimensions in inches)

A	Back stiles (2)	1-1/2 × 1-1/2 × 84
B	Front stiles (2)	1-1/2 × 1-1/2 × 23-1/2
C	Arms (2)	1-1/2 × 1-1/2 × 17-1/4
D	Seat Brace	1-1/2 × 1-1/2 × 27
E	Front and back rails (5)	3/4 × 1-1/2 × 27
F	Side rails (2)	3/4 × 1-1/2 × 15
G	Back panel	3/4 × 28-1/2 × 77
H	Front panel	3/4 × 10-1/4 × 28-1/2
J	Side panels (2)	3/4 × 10-1/4 × 16-1/8
K	Seat and Lid	3/4 × 17 × 29-1/2
L	Bottom	3/4 × 15-3/4 × 27
M	Shelf	3/4 × 7-3/4 × 29-1/2
N	Shelf brackets (2)	3/4 × 7-1/4 × 7-1/4
P	Seat and shelf trim	1/4 × 3/4 × 105
Q	Upper pegs (2)	1 dia. × 6-1/2
R	Lower pegs (2)	1 dia. × 5
S	Dowels	3/4 dia. × 1-1/2
T	Mirror opening trim	3/4 × 93
	Veneer tape	
	Mirror	24″ × 36″
	Flathead wood screws (50)	#10 × 1-1/4
	Roundhead wood screws (8)	#12 × 1
	Nylon washers (8)	1/4″
	Hinges (1 pair)	1 × 2

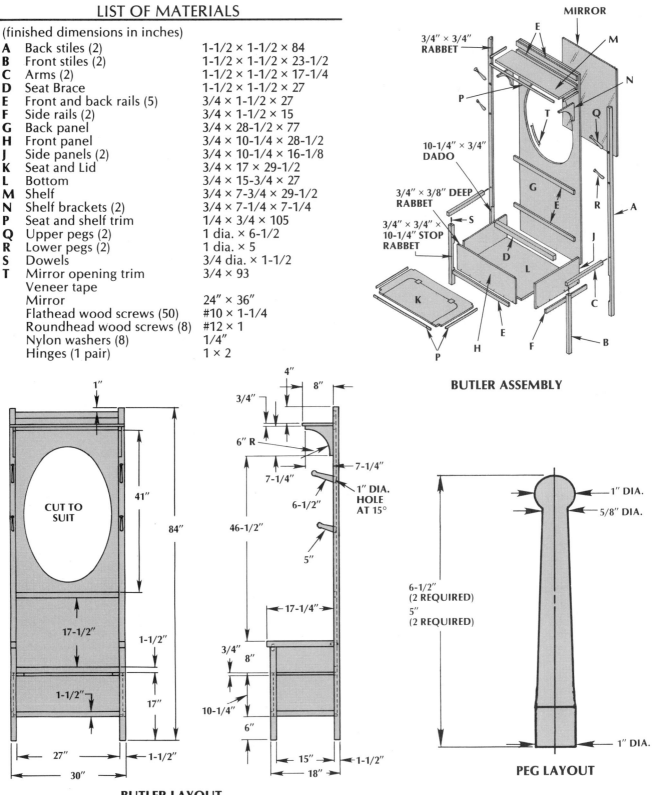

BUTLER ASSEMBLY

BUTLER LAYOUT

PEG LAYOUT

HALL TREE

From *HANDS ON* Jan/Feb 82

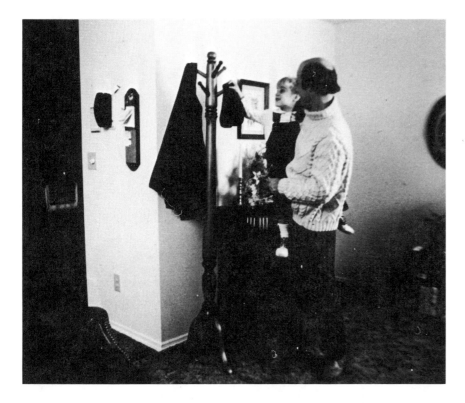

measure the paper and mark it off into three equal sections. Transfer these marks onto the wood. With the worktable at 30° and a V-block to hold your work, drill the peg holes with a brad-point bit or, better, use a Forstner bit.

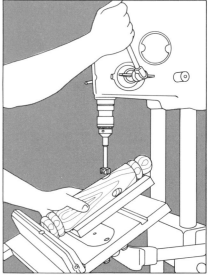

Worktable at 30° with V-block fence forms stop.

This hall tree, made almost entirely with the lathe, is a simple but classically elegant design suitable for almost any decor.

For this project, you'll need a 4″ × 4″ × 8′ and a 2″ × 4″ × 6′ piece of wood. We used redwood for its rich color and ease of turning. Cut the stock to length according to the plans, allowing about 1/2″ extra stock on each end. Turn the three parts that form the main spindle and finish-sand them while they are still on the lathe.

Next, resaw some of the 4 × 4 stock into 1-1/8″ × 1-1/8″ × 12″ and turn the pegs. These can be turned two at a time from a single piece of stock. Finish-sand these pieces.

Now your turning is complete. The next step is to lay out the legs on the 2 × 4 stock. Cut the angle for the tops of the legs and drill them using horizontal boring. Use a stop block to get even spacing. Finish cutting the legs and sand the contours on a drum or belt sander.

Next, with the drill press, drill the holes for the legs in the bottom

Turning two coat pegs from one piece of stock. Use bandsaw to separate after turning.

section of the hall tree. Measure very accurately or use dowel finders for the proper spacing.

The six holes for the pegs in the tapered top are positioned to divide the column in three equal sections. Wrap a piece of paper around the top section and mark the paper for the diameter of the top. Then

For the final assembly, you will need to drill pilot holes into the bottom of the top section, both ends of the middle section and the top of the bottom section. With a 3/16″ bit, drill to a depth of about 1-1/4″. Apply a little soap or paste wax to both ends of the dowel screws and assemble the body of the hall tree with plenty of glue on the end grain.

Glue and dowel the legs into place, then glue the coat and hat pegs in. Apply the finish of your choice. Place it near the door. Then, your final challenge is to get everybody to use it!

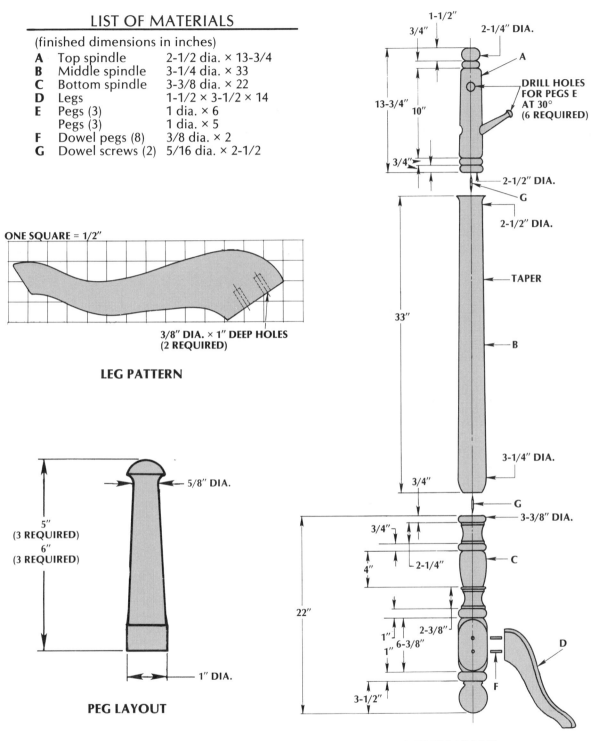

LIST OF MATERIALS

(finished dimensions in inches)

A	Top spindle	2-1/2 dia. × 13-3/4
B	Middle spindle	3-1/4 dia. × 33
C	Bottom spindle	3-3/8 dia. × 22
D	Legs	1-1/2 × 3-1/2 × 14
E	Pegs (3)	1 dia. × 6
	Pegs (3)	1 dia. × 5
F	Dowel pegs (8)	3/8 dia. × 2
G	Dowel screws (2)	5/16 dia. × 2-1/2

ONE SQUARE = 1/2"

3/8" DIA. × 1" DEEP HOLES
(2 REQUIRED)

LEG PATTERN

5/8" DIA.

5"
(3 REQUIRED)
6"
(3 REQUIRED)

1" DIA.

PEG LAYOUT

1-1/2"

3/4"

2-1/4" DIA.

A

DRILL HOLES
FOR PEGS E
AT 30°
(6 REQUIRED)

13-3/4"   10"

3/4"

2-1/2" DIA.

G

2-1/2" DIA.

TAPER

33"

B

3-1/4" DIA.

3/4"

G

3-3/8" DIA.

3/4"

2-1/4"

C

4"

22"

2-3/8"

1"

6-3/8"

1"

F

D

3-1/2"

HALL TREE LAYOUT

133

ELEPHANT BED

From *HANDS ON* May/June 82

To make the bed frame, start by cutting the contour in the tops of the sides and ends on the bandsaw. Sand the contours with a drum sander and mount the cleat strips on the inside of the pieces with screws and glue spaced about 10" apart. Assemble the bed frame with nails or screws and glue, using simple butt joints. Set the plywood bottom into the frame and fasten.

Assemble the legs. Take the leg assemblies one at a time and clamp them into their relative position on the bed frame. Drill 1/4" pilot holes for the hex head bolts and then unclamp the legs. Drill the 5/16" holes for the T-nuts.

Make a desk from the leftover plywood and wood pieces and attach it to the legs.

To make the ladder, it's helpful to mark all waste stock before you start to cut. Cut the hooks to shape on the bandsaw and set aside. Set the miter gauge at 78° and cut the top and bottom ends on the sides. Keep the miter gauge set at 78° and use the dado blades to cut the 3/4" × 3/8" deep dadoes for the steps and the lap joint for the hook on one side. Move the miter gauge to 78° in the other direction and cut the dadoes for the other side. Next, tilt the table to 12° and cut the bevel on the front and backs of the steps.

Round off all exposed edges on the bed. Apply a nontoxic finish of your choice.

Here's a bed that makes use of the vertical space in a small bedroom. Sitting up on high but very stable legs (that's why we call it the "Elephant Bed"), this bed opens up space underneath for a desk and shelves.

This simple structure inspires children to creative activity. Active children, for instance, just might try to climb the shelving! That's why we designed them extra-sturdy.

Also note: *For safety's sake, install a maximum of three shelves with a minimum of 10" between each shelf. Be sure the top shelf is 10" below the bottom of the bed.*

The bed frame is built to handle a twin size mattress with about 7" to spare in width. We recommend using portable tubular guard rails that slip under the mattress to keep children safe from rolling out of the bed. Furniture stores sell a variety of guard rails for this purpose.

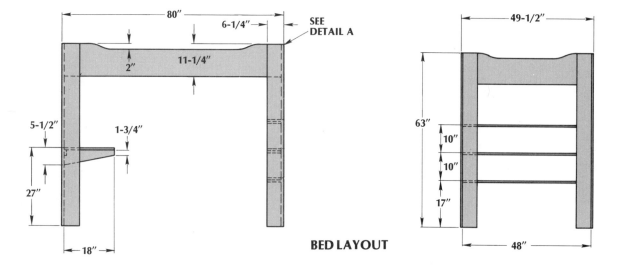

BED LAYOUT

134

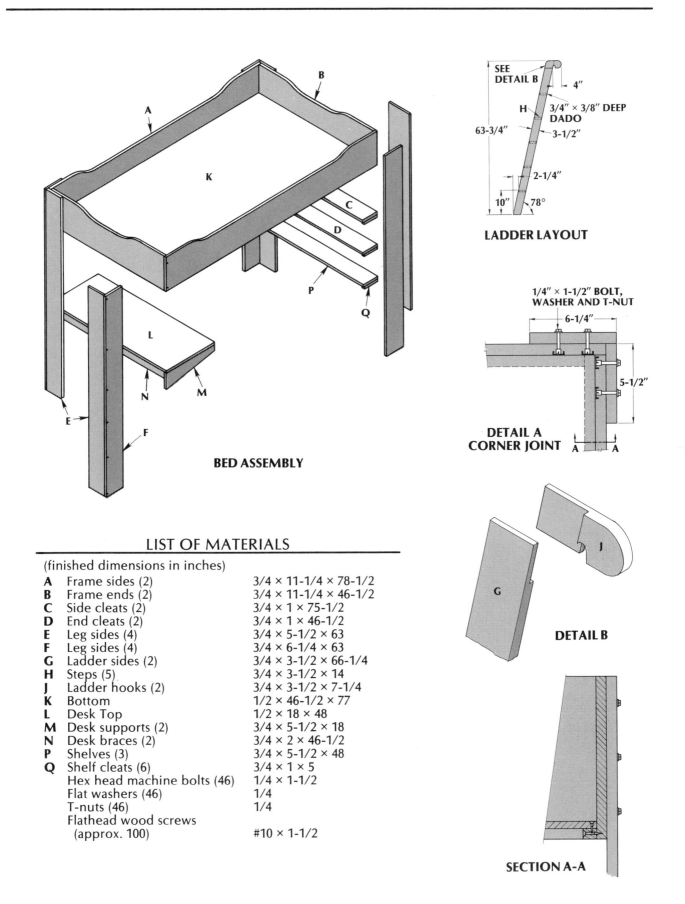

BED ASSEMBLY

LADDER LAYOUT

SEE DETAIL B
4"
H
3/4" × 3/8" DEEP DADO
63-3/4"
3-1/2"
2-1/4"
10"
78°

1/4" × 1-1/2" BOLT, WASHER AND T-NUT
6-1/4"
5-1/2"
DETAIL A CORNER JOINT
A   A

DETAIL B

SECTION A-A

LIST OF MATERIALS

(finished dimensions in inches)

A	Frame sides (2)	3/4 × 11-1/4 × 78-1/2
B	Frame ends (2)	3/4 × 11-1/4 × 46-1/2
C	Side cleats (2)	3/4 × 1 × 75-1/2
D	End cleats (2)	3/4 × 1 × 46-1/2
E	Leg sides (4)	3/4 × 5-1/2 × 63
F	Leg sides (4)	3/4 × 6-1/4 × 63
G	Ladder sides (2)	3/4 × 3-1/2 × 66-1/4
H	Steps (5)	3/4 × 3-1/2 × 14
J	Ladder hooks (2)	3/4 × 3-1/2 × 7-1/4
K	Bottom	1/2 × 46-1/2 × 77
L	Desk Top	1/2 × 18 × 48
M	Desk supports (2)	3/4 × 5-1/2 × 18
N	Desk braces (2)	3/4 × 2 × 46-1/2
P	Shelves (3)	3/4 × 5-1/2 × 48
Q	Shelf cleats (6)	3/4 × 1 × 5
	Hex head machine bolts (46)	1/4 × 1-1/2
	Flat washers (46)	1/4
	T-nuts (46)	1/4
	Flathead wood screws (approx. 100)	#10 × 1-1/2

LUGGAGE STAND

From *HANDS ON* Sept/Oct 84

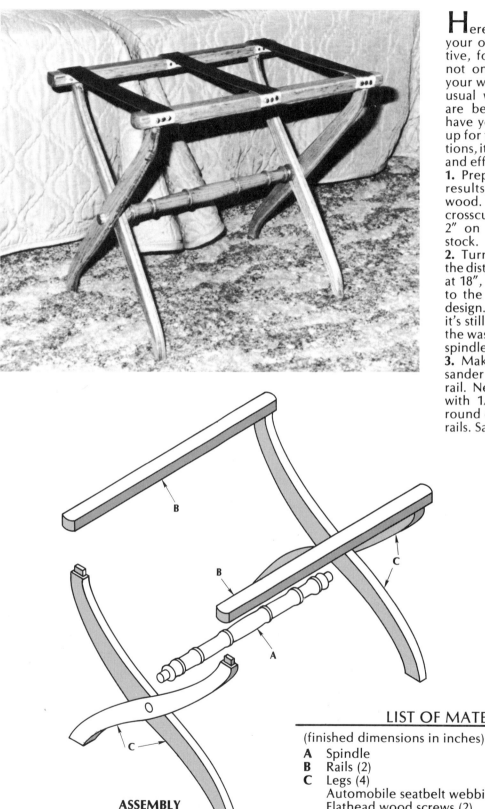

ASSEMBLY

Here's a project that'll please your overnight guests—an attractive, folding luggage stand that's not only practical but shows off your woodworking skills in an unusual way. However, two stands are better than one. Once you have your woodworking tools set up for the various required operations, it takes only a little more time and effort to make a second stand.

1. Prepare the stock. For the best results, use clear straight hardwood. Rip all stock to width then crosscut to length. Leave an extra 2" on the spindle (A) for waste stock.

2. Turn the spindle (A). Keeping the distance between the shoulders at 18", turn the spindle according to the plans or create your own design. Final-sand the spindle while it's still on the lathe. Next, trim off the waste stock after removing the spindle from the lathe.

3. Make the rails (B). Use the disc sander to round both ends of each rail. Next, use a rasp or a router with 1/4" quarter-round bit and round over the sharp edges of the rails. Sand the rails.

LIST OF MATERIALS

(finished dimensions in inches)

A	Spindle	1-5/8 dia. × 22
B	Rails (2)	1 × 1-1/2 × 24
C	Legs (4)	3/4 × 3 × 26
	Automobile seatbelt webbing	6'
	Flathead wood screws (2)	#8 × 1-3/4"
	Carpet or upholstery tacks (18)	#8
	Flat washers (2)	1" I.D.

Mortise the rails. Note the different locations of the mortises for each rail. To allow for excess glue, make the mortises 1/16" deeper than the length of the tenon.

4. Make the legs (C). Use a cardboard template to transfer the pattern to the stock. Using a bandsaw, cut out the legs and use the disc and drum sanders to sand the edges.

Mark each leg for its location on the stand and cut the tenons to fit the mortises.

Stack the legs and tape them together. Pad drill the 15/16" hole in the center. Prevent splintering by backing up the stock with scrap.

Next, use a decorative shaper cutter or router bit to shape the edge.

5. Apply a finish to all parts except the mortises and tenons.

6. Assemble the stand. By building a simple jig, the assembly of the stand will be much easier. Attach two scrap 2 × 4s 15" apart on a 2'

square piece of plywood. Dry-fit the rails, spindle, and legs. Apply glue and place the stand in the jig. Use #8 × 1-3/4" flathead wood screws to secure the spindle to the outside legs.

7. Install the webbing. Cut the webbing into 2' lengths. Fold back 5/8" on each end of each strip and use three #8 carpet or upholstery tacks to attach the webbing to the rails.

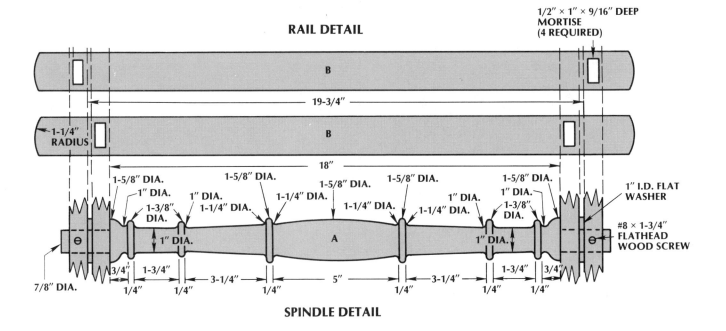

RAIL DETAIL

1/2" × 1" × 9/16" DEEP MORTISE (4 REQUIRED)

B

19-3/4"

1-1/4" RADIUS

B

18"

SPINDLE DETAIL

1-5/8" DIA. 1-5/8" DIA. 1-5/8" DIA. 1-5/8" DIA. 1-5/8" DIA.

1" DIA. 1" DIA. 1-1/4" DIA. 1" DIA. 1" DIA.

1-3/8" DIA. 1-1/4" DIA. 1-1/4" DIA. 1-3/8" DIA.

1" DIA. A 1" DIA.

1" I.D. FLAT WASHER

#8 × 1-3/4" FLATHEAD WOOD SCREW

7/8" DIA. 3/4" 1-3/4" 3-1/4" 5" 3-1/4" 1-3/4" 3/4"

1/4" 1/4" 1/4" 1/4" 1/4" 1/4"

ONE SQUARE = 1"

1/2" × 1" × 1/2" LONG TENON

C 15/16" DIA.

LEG DETAIL

NESTING TABLES

From *HANDS ON* May/June 82

Here's an attractive project that takes less time than it might appear. Many of the setups can be "borrowed" from one nesting table to the next.

You can make these tables from the hardwood of your choice. Stock for the legs should be straight-grained and clear wood due to the tapers you'll form in them.

Glue the wood for the three tabletops, then cut all rails to size according to the List of Materials. Make sure all ends are square.

Cut all the legs to size, but leave them untapered for now.

Locate and drill holes for dowels in the rails. Use the miter gauge and a stop block held with a C-clamp for duplicating hole locations in each set of the three or four rails. Use dowel centerfinders for locating the mating holes in each leg.

Drill the stabilizing dowel holes in the tops of the front legs of the medium and large tables.

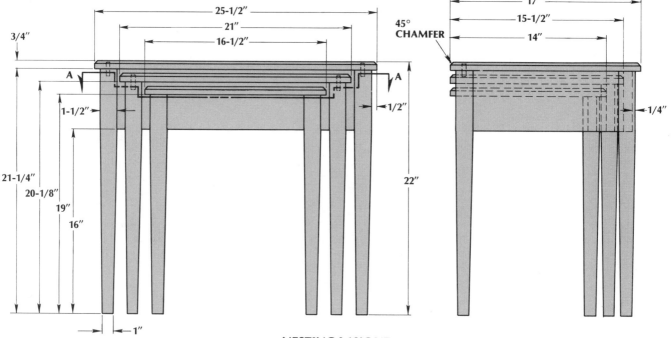

NESTING LAYOUT

Now set the jointer depth to 7/64". Use a stop block at the starting position and make two passes on all four sides of the legs. The taper is the same length on all 12 legs. Then reset the depth of the jointer to 1/32", remove the stop block, and make one final pass over the jointer to clean up the tapered portion.

Use a planer blade to cut the groove on the inside of all ten rails. This groove will accept the retainer clips that will hold the tabletops to the base assemblies.

Cut the tops to size, then set the jointer fence to 45° and cut the chamfer on all the table edges.

Assemble all three bases and finish-sand them. Locate and drill the stabilizing dowel holes in the medium and large tabletops. Apply the finish of your choice. Then attach the tops with the retainer clips and dowels.

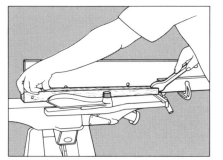

Tapering process for all legs. Note use of stop block and safety push stick.

Forming chamfer on tabletops. Wood extension fence increases accuracy and safety.

LIST OF MATERIALS

(finished dimensions in inches)

Large Table

A	Rails (2)	3/4 × 5-1/4 × 13
B	Rail	3/4 × 5-1/4 × 21-1/2
C	Top	3/4 × 17 × 25-1/2
D	Legs (4)	1-1/2 × 1-1/2 × 21-1/4

Medium Table

A	Rails (2)	3/4 × 4-1/8 × 11-1/2
B	Rail	3/4 × 4-1/8 × 17
C	Top	3/4 × 15-1/2 × 21
D	Legs (4)	1-1/2 × 1-1/2 × 20-1/8

Small Table

A	Rails (2)	3/4 × 3 × 10
B	Rails (2)	3/4 × 3 × 12-1/2
C	Top	3/4 × 14 × 16-1/2
D	Legs (4)	1-1/2 × 1-1/2 × 19

Miscellaneous

Dowels (44)	5/16" dia. × 1-1/2"
Mirror retainer clips (20)	
Roundhead wood screws (20)	#6 × 1/2"

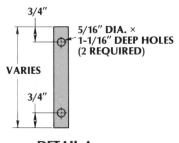

3/4"

5/16" DIA. ×
1-1/16" DEEP HOLES
(2 REQUIRED)

VARIES

3/4"

DETAIL A

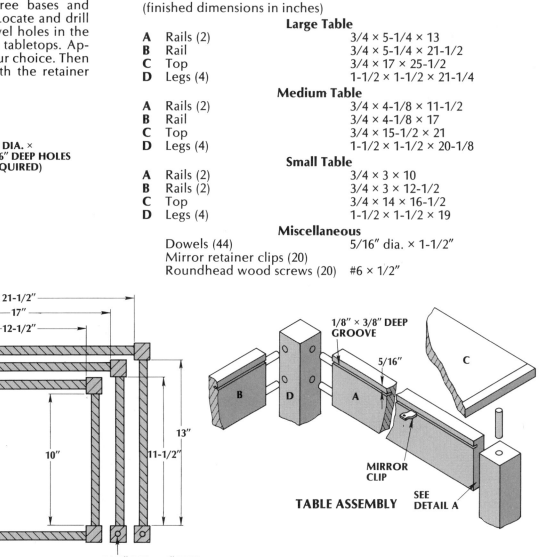

1/8" × 3/8" DEEP GROOVE

5/16"

B

D

A

C

MIRROR CLIP

TABLE ASSEMBLY

SEE DETAIL A

21-1/2"

17"

12-1/2"

13"

11-1/2"

10"

1/4"

SECTION A-A

5/16" DIA. × 1" DEEP HOLE

CHAIR-TABLE

From *HANDS ON* July/Aug 83

The origin of the chair-table design dates back to 16th century England. The chair-table is an excellent example of multipurpose furniture—a chair that provides draft-free seating by the fireside, storage below the seat, and a table when the back is lowered. The idea of the chair-table was popular among furniture-makers on both sides of the Atlantic well into the 19th century. Today, we still have the need for functional furniture, and you can build this versatile chair-table by following these simple steps.

1. Cut out all parts according to the List of Materials. See Step 2 for special instructions on cutting out the top (J). The pins (R,S) can all be turned from a single piece of 1-1/2 × 1-1/2 × 13″ stock (see Step 7).

2. Make the top (J) by first drawing a 42″ diameter circle on your shop floor. Arrange your boards on the circle to maximize the use of your stock. Cut to length and joint the edges. Glue and clamp together the boards for the top. Cut out the top. An option is to use 3/4″ plywood for the top with veneer edge banding to cover the plywood edge. Sand the edge.

3. Drill the dowel holes in parts (A,B,C,D,G). First drill the ends of the sides (C), end (D) and rails (G). Next, locate the dowel positions on the legs (A), and drill these holes. Dry-assemble the sides, ends, rails, and legs. Locate the dowel holes in the tops of the legs for the arms (B). Locate the matching dowel holes for the arms, and then disassemble the chair. Drill the remaining dowel holes.

Round the back end of the arms (B). Locate and drill the 5/8″ holes for the pivot pins (R) in the arms (B), and drill the hole for the locking pin (S) in the front of one arm. Mark the location of the pin holes in the battens (K), and drill. *Note:* One batten has two holes, one for the pivot pin (R) and one for the locking pin (S). Set the battens aside.

4. Assemble the chair. First glue and clamp each of the legs (A) to the sides (C). After these have set up, glue these assemblies to the end (D) and rails (G). Check for squareness as you go. Glue the arms (B) into place.

Attach the drawer runners (F) to the drawer guides (E) with #8 × 1-1/4″ flathead wood screws. Attach these assemblies to the inside of the chair assembly.

Cut out the notches for the legs in the seat (H) and attach the seat with #8 × 1-1/4″ flathead wood screws. Countersink the screws 1/4″ and use dowel plugs to fill the holes.

5. Make the drawer by first checking the size of the drawer opening on the assembled seat. Cut the drawer front (L) and back (N) to allow for 1/8″ total clearance on the width. Cut the front, back, and sides to allow for 1/16″ clearance on the height.

Cut the 1/4″ groove for the bottom with dado blades or with a routing attachment.

Make the 3/4″ wide × 3/8″ deep dado in the sides for the back with the dado attachment. Then, form the locking drawer joint using the dado attachment. Assemble the drawer by gluing and clamping the front, sides, and back together. Check for squareness. Slide in the bottom and secure with 2d wire nails.

6. Contour and drill the battens (K) according to the drawings. Use the bandsaw to cut the angles. Drill screw pockets and pilot holes for the #10 × 1-1/2″ roundhead wood screws. Use an oversized pilot hole to allow for expansion of the top.

Center the chair assembly upside down on the bottom of the tabletop to locate the position of the battens. The battens must run at right angles to the grain of the top boards to provide strength and prevent warping. Mount the battens to the top with the screws. Cap the screw pocket holes with dowel buttons.

7. Turn the pins (R,S) from the 1-1/2″ square stock. Turn all three pins at one time. Note that the locking pin is shorter since it is not a through pin. Next, turn the knob for the drawer. Use the screw center to mount the stock on the lathe.

8. Finishing touches: Final-sand the project and apply the finish of your choice to all surfaces. Cut out felt washers to go between the arms and the battens in order to protect the wood.

ONE SQUARE = 1/4"

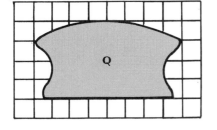

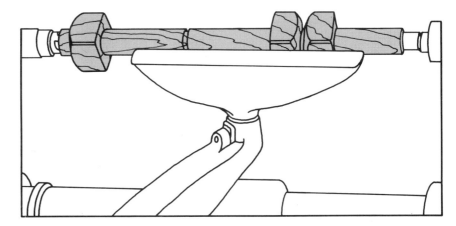

Turning the three pins at one time on the lathe out of a single piece of stock.

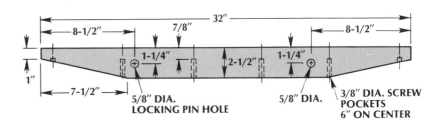

K BATTEN LAYOUT

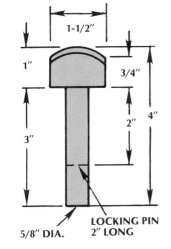

PIN LAYOUT

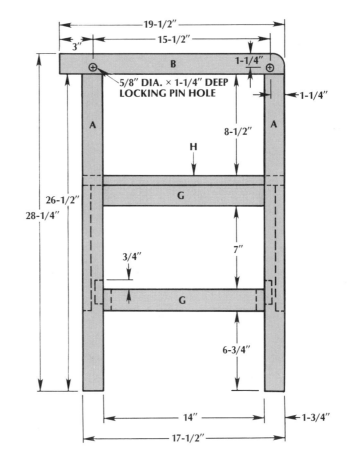

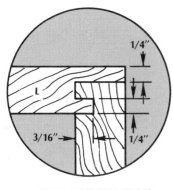

DRAWER JOINT DETAIL

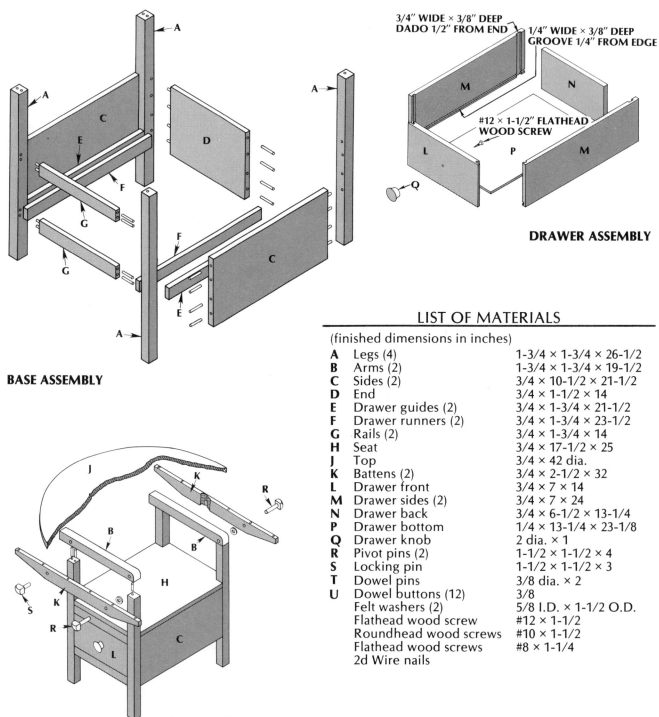

3/4″ WIDE × 3/8″ DEEP DADO 1/2″ FROM END

1/4″ WIDE × 3/8″ DEEP GROOVE 1/4″ FROM EDGE

#12 × 1-1/2″ FLATHEAD WOOD SCREW

DRAWER ASSEMBLY

BASE ASSEMBLY

FINAL ASSEMBLY

LIST OF MATERIALS

(finished dimensions in inches)

A	Legs (4)	1-3/4 × 1-3/4 × 26-1/2
B	Arms (2)	1-3/4 × 1-3/4 × 19-1/2
C	Sides (2)	3/4 × 10-1/2 × 21-1/2
D	End	3/4 × 1-1/2 × 14
E	Drawer guides (2)	3/4 × 1-3/4 × 21-1/2
F	Drawer runners (2)	3/4 × 1-3/4 × 23-1/2
G	Rails (2)	3/4 × 1-3/4 × 14
H	Seat	3/4 × 17-1/2 × 25
J	Top	3/4 × 42 dia.
K	Battens (2)	3/4 × 2-1/2 × 32
L	Drawer front	3/4 × 7 × 14
M	Drawer sides (2)	3/4 × 7 × 24
N	Drawer back	3/4 × 6-1/2 × 13-1/4
P	Drawer bottom	1/4 × 13-1/4 × 23-1/8
Q	Drawer knob	2 dia. × 1
R	Pivot pins (2)	1-1/2 × 1-1/2 × 4
S	Locking pin	1-1/2 × 1-1/2 × 3
T	Dowel pins	3/8 dia. × 2
U	Dowel buttons (12)	3/8
	Felt washers (2)	5/8 I.D. × 1-1/2 O.D.
	Flathead wood screw	#12 × 1-1/2
	Roundhead wood screws	#10 × 1-1/2
	Flathead wood screws	#8 × 1-1/4
	2d Wire nails	

Picnics in the backyard are as American as fireworks on the Fourth of July. And what better base for a picnic than your own home made picnic table.

1. Select the stock. Redwood is the best wood to use for this table. It's attractive, easy to work, and naturally weather resistant. Pressure-treated lumber or cedar is also acceptable.

2. Crosscut parts (A,B,C,F) to length (see the cutout diagram). Set the miter gauge at 90° and use an extension table to support the stock. Use a miter gauge extension for added support and control. Rip a 5' long 2 × 10 in half, then crosscut parts (D,E) to length.

3. Bevel the ends of parts (E,G). Set the miter gauge at 90°.

4. Cut the miters on parts (B,C,F). Adjust the miter gauge to 30°.

5. Assemble parts (B,C,F) with 5/16″ × 3-1/2″ carriage bolts. Use two bolts per joint. Use #12 × 2-1/2″ flat-head wood screws to attach the top and seats (A) to the frame assemblies. The seat and top supports (E,G) are also attached with #12 × 2-1/2″ wood screws.

6. Cut the braces (D) to fit. With the stock on edge, tilt the miter gauge 25° and bevel one end of each brace. Hold the brace in place and mark the lower end for length. Set the miter gauge at 67°, and then cut the bevel.

7. Finish the table to your liking, but consider weathering when making your choice.

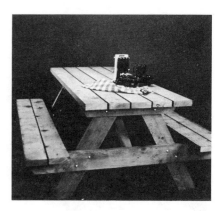

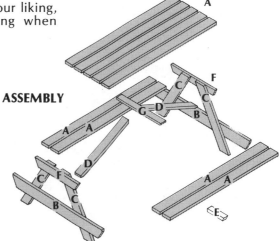

ASSEMBLY

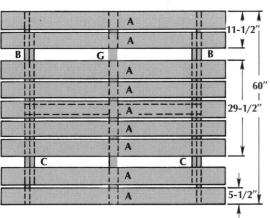

TOP VIEW

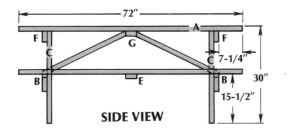

SIDE VIEW

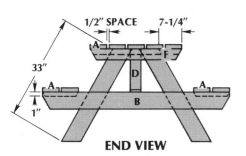

END VIEW

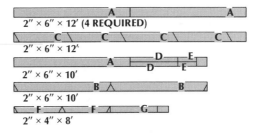

2″ × 6″ × 12′ (4 REQUIRED)

2″ × 6″ × 12′

2″ × 6″ × 10′

2″ × 6″ × 10′

2″ × 4″ × 8′

CUTOUT DIAGRAM

LIST OF MATERIALS

(nominal standard lumberyard dimensions in inches)

A	Top and seats (9 pieces)	2 × 6 × 72
B	Seat supports (2)	2 × 6 × 60
C	Legs (4)	2 × 6 × 36
D	Braces (2)	2 × 3 × 30
E	Center seat supports (2)	2 × 3 × 11-1/2
F	Tabletop supports (2)	2 × 4 × 29-1/2
G	Center top support	2 × 4 × 29-1/2
	Flathead wood screws (60)	#12 × 2-1/2
	Carriage bolts (16)	5/16 dia. × 3-1/2

GARDEN BENCH

From *HANDS ON* June/July/Aug 85

If you've priced sturdy, well-designed, outdoor furniture, chances are you know you're ahead of the game if you can build it yourself. This plan gives you the opportunity to construct a sturdy, easy-to-build garden bench at a fraction of retail prices—and enjoy it for years to come.

Mortise-and-tenon joinery is used extensively on this project and makes for a bench that's long-lasting and durable. Here are the plans for a 6' bench, but don't let our dimensions keep you from building the bench any size you want—this bench plan is easy to adapt to any length.

1. Cut all the stock to size according to the List of Materials. For our bench, we used economical pressure-treated pine, but redwood, oak, cedar, teak, or other weather-resistant wood will also work. Outdoor woods usually require no up-keep and age beautifully over the years.

2. Transfer the pattern of the back legs (B) to 4 × 6 stock and the patterns of the back rail (F) and armrests (E) to 2 × 6 material. Do not cut the contours yet.

3. With a square, accurately mark the locations of the mortises and tenons on all parts.

4. Cut all the mortises in the front and back legs (A,B). Because of the length and bulk of the parts for this bench, be sure to properly support your stock when cutting the mortises.

5. Now cut the tenons on parts (C,D,E,F,G,J) to fit the mortises. Again, because of the length and bulk involved, be sure to support your stock.

Cut the 3/4" wide × 1/2" deep grooves in the upper and lower back rails (F,G).

6. Using a bandsaw, cut out the contours on the upper back rail (F), legs (B), seat supports (C), armrests (E), and brackets (L). Use a drum sander to smooth out the saw marks.

7. Check the armrests (E) for fit with the back legs—the armrests should fit so they'll be parallel to the ground. Use the disc sander to bevel the back end to get a flush fit. Next, drill the armrests and back legs for 1/2" diameter × 3" long dowel pins.

8. Assemble the sides one at a time. Use plastic resin glue and clamps. (Water resistant plastic resin glue is available at home centers and hardware stores.)

9. Attach the splat spacers (I) to the upper and lower back rails with glue; then assemble the back with clamps. Use glue to assemble the back assembly and the seat stretcher (J) to the sides. Using glue and 6d galvanized finish nails, attach the brackets (L).

10. Use 8d galvanized finish nails to attach the seat boards (K). The front board is cut to fit between the two front legs.

11. Reinforce all the joinery with two 10d galvanized finish nails per joint.

12. Round off all the edges with a rasp or coarse sandpaper, and then sand the bench thoroughly to remove any roughness or splinters.

Outdoor woods need no additional finishing beyond sanding. But, if you want to apply a finish, use finishes that are made especially for outdoor use. Oil-based primer is necessary before painting, and spar varnish or an exterior polyurethane are suitable natural finishes.

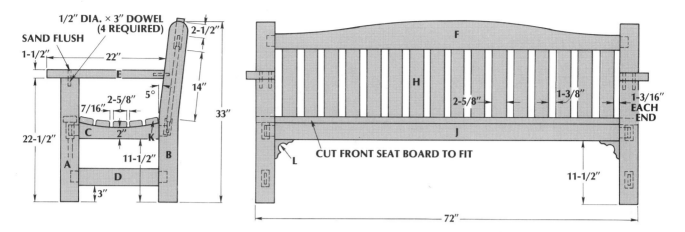

SIDE VIEW

FRONT VIEW

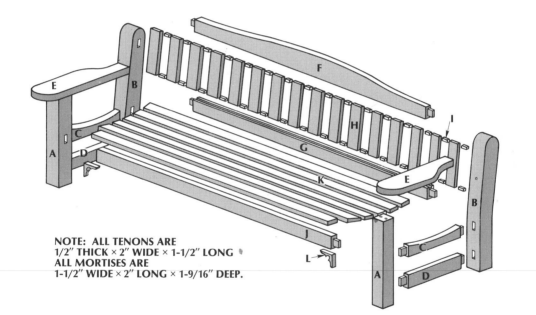

NOTE: ALL TENONS ARE
1/2" THICK × 2" WIDE × 1-1/2" LONG
ALL MORTISES ARE
1-1/2" WIDE × 2" LONG × 1-9/16" DEEP.

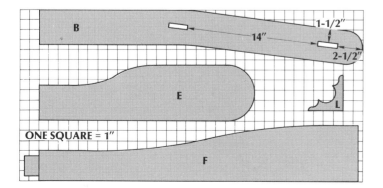

ONE SQUARE = 1"

LIST OF MATERIALS

(finished dimensions in inches)

A	Front legs (2)	3-1/2 × 3-1/2 × 22-1/2
B	Back legs (2)	3-1/2 × 5-1/2 × 33
C	Seat supports (2)	1-1/2 × 3 × 18
D	Leg rails (2)	1-1/2 × 3 × 18
E	Armrests (2)	1-1/2 × 5-1/2 × 22
F	Upper back rail	1-1/2 × 5-1/2 × 68
G	Lower back rail	1-1/2 × 3 × 68
H	Splats (16)	3/4 × 2-5/8 × 14
I	Splat spacers (34)	1/2 × 3/4 × 1-3/8
J	Seat stretcher	1-1/2 × 3 × 68
K	Seat boards (6)	1-1/8 × 2-5/8 × 72
L	Brackets (2)	3/4 × 3-1/2 × 3-1/2
	Dowel pins (8)	1/2 dia. × 3

145

Accessories

Entertainment, kitchen, and accent pieces are among the twenty projects found in this section. These items can add decorative touches as well as serve practical purposes. What makes these projects, as well as those contained in the other two sections, even more valuable is the fact that you can build them yourself.

PENCIL/STAMP HOLDER

From *HANDS ON* Mar/Apr/May 85

Need a project to give as a gift? This pencil/stamp holder is the perfect answer. By using a bandsaw, these hardwood holders are easy to make. They don't involve precision measurements or joinery, and are fun to give.

The following procedure illustrates the necessary steps in making the holders. These steps, however, are the same for any bandsaw box. After practicing the technique, feel free to change the dimensions and design shown in the drawings, and experiment and create your own project.

Here's how to make the holders:

1. Prepare a piece of stock measuring 3″ × 3-1/2″ × 15″—enough for three holders. If you don't have 3″ stock, laminate thinner stock (using one kind, or laminating a variety of contrasting woods) to achieve the required thickness. **Warning:** All stock must be at least 15″ long to allow safe milling later in the project.

2. After squaring the stock, crosscut it into three equal pieces.

3. Next, using a bandsaw with a 1/2″ blade, cut 1/4″ thick sides from each block (see detail A). Keep the pieces together so that the boxes can be reassembled with the wood in the original position.

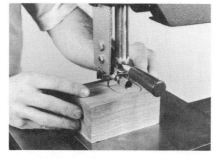

4. Switch to a 3/16″ blade and cut out the drawer block (see detail B). Take the drawer block and cut 1/4″ sides from it by resawing (see detail C).

5. Use a 3/16″ blade to cut out the inside contour of the drawer (see detail D).

6. With a small drum sander, sand the inside of the drawer. Then, using a disc or belt sander, smooth the sides of the drawer body and the surfaces of the drawer sides. Glue and clamp the drawer together.

7. Measure the width of the reassembled drawer and sand the main body to allow 1/16" extra space. Sand the sides smooth, then glue and clamp the main body together.

8. Drill the three holes for the pencils in the top of the main body (see drawings) and drill the knob mounting hole in the drawer.

9. Use a 3/16" blade to cut the top contour (see detail E). Sand the holder and apply the finish of your choice.

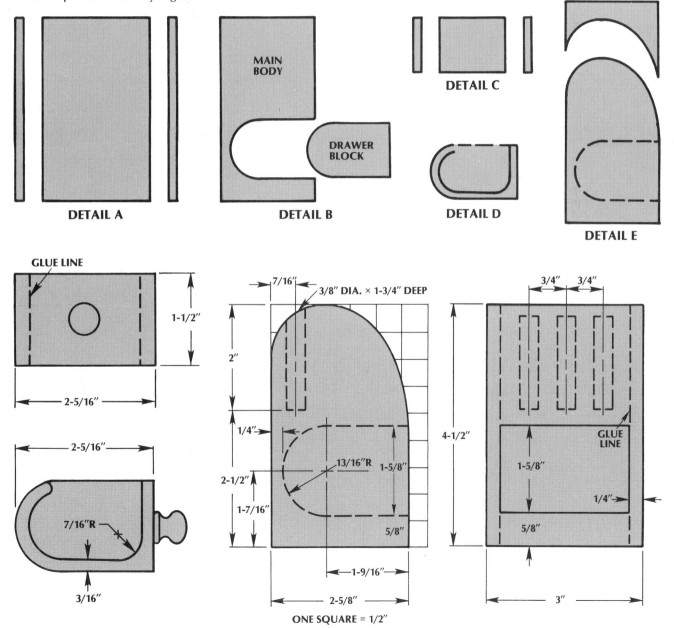

DETAIL A

MAIN BODY

DRAWER BLOCK

DETAIL B

DETAIL C

DETAIL D

DETAIL E

GLUE LINE

1-1/2"

2-5/16"

2-5/16"

7/16"R

3/16"

7/16"

3/8" DIA. × 1-3/4" DEEP

2"

1/4"

2-1/2"

1-7/16"

13/16"R

1-5/8"

1-9/16"

2-5/8"

5/8"

4-1/2"

3/4"   3/4"

GLUE LINE

1-5/8"

1/4"

5/8"

3"

ONE SQUARE = 1/2"

ROLLING PIN

From *HANDS ON* Jan/Feb 82

Compliments of Rude Osolnik

This project is not only very useful, but it's interesting to produce. Cutting laminated hardwood and turning stock diagonally adds tremendous visual appeal and interest. When this utensil is not in use, a holder can be made for displaying it on the kitchen wall.

1. Select the stock. Suggested woods for this project are close-grained hardwoods such as walnut or maple. But you can even use Baltic birch plywood to add a creative flair.

2. Glue up the stock into a 2-1/2″ × 8″ × 18-1/2″ block. Use a waterproof glue such as resorcinol so the rolling pin can be cleaned up in soap and water after it's used. Allow the clamped block to dry for at least 24 hours.

3. Make 2-1/2″ wide slices of the stock at a 10° to 15° angle. The angled cuts reveal more end grain of the wood layers.

4. Square the ends of the diagonally cut laminated stock using a bandsaw or table saw.

5. Mount the stock between centers. Use the gouge to rough it to round, using the calipers to assure uniform diameter. Be careful that the exposed plies don't catch the lathe tool and tear.

6. Mark for the handles and cut using calipers to get the diameter of the middle portion of the knobs. Cut the knob nearest the tailstock first, each knob should be as wide as it is thick.

7. Sand the project while it is still on the lathe. Apply a nontoxic salad bowl finish or mineral oil.

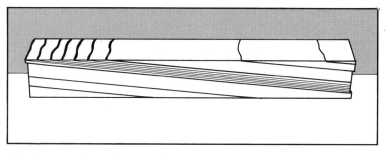

Glued-up stock for laminated rolling pin. Note that stock is cut at an angle on the bandsaw to reveal the laminated plywood and solid wood layers.

ONE SQUARE = 1″

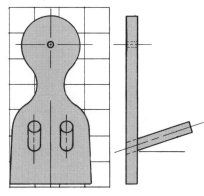

HOLDER

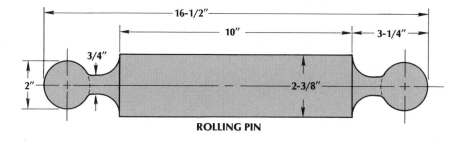

ROLLING PIN

This knife block holder can add a touch of professional charm to your kitchen countertop. It is decorative as well as functional and it's a relatively easy project to put together.

1. Prepare seven 3/4" × 5-1/4" × 10" pieces of stock.

2. Glue up five pieces to form a 3-3/4" × 5-1/4" × 10" block.

3. Follow the plans to form the slots for the knives and knife sharpener.

4. Glue the remaining pieces of stock to the block.

5. Belt sand or disc sand the entire block smooth, then round the edges.

6. Apply the finish of your choice.

7. Attach rubber feet to the base.

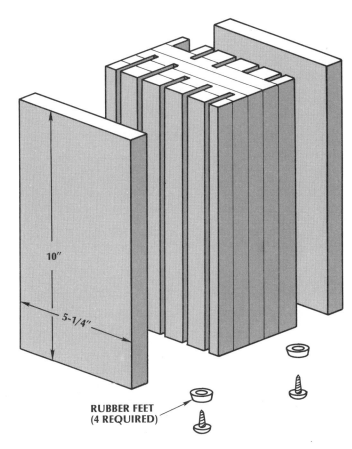

RUBBER FEET (4 REQUIRED)

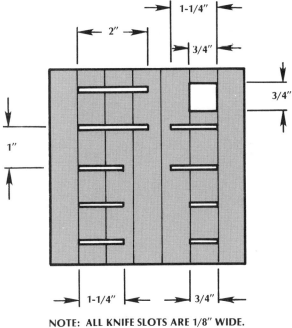

NOTE: ALL KNIFE SLOTS ARE 1/8" WIDE.

SNACK TRAY

From HANDS ON Sept/Oct 80

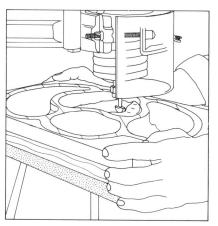

bit and 3/8" pin to clean up the edges of the recesses. Remove the blank from the fixture and cut the outside contour of the tray on a bandsaw.

Round the top edges with a 1/4" round-over bit, and sand with flutter sheets. Finish with salad bowl finish.

Here is an idea for snack trays that can take as many unique forms as the variety of snacks you can create to serve in them.

Cut out a template of a tray with as many compartments as you want. On a router arm, make a routing fixture by attaching this template to the underside of a laminated sink cutout and pin routing recesses in the plastic laminate.

Cut blanks from hardwood stock. (This stock should be 1" to 1-1/2" thick and can be laminated from different colors of hardwood.) Attach the blanks to the fixture with nails or screws. Pin rout the recesses using a 3/4" core box bit and 3/4" table pin. Use a 3/8" straight

ONE SQUARE = 1/2"

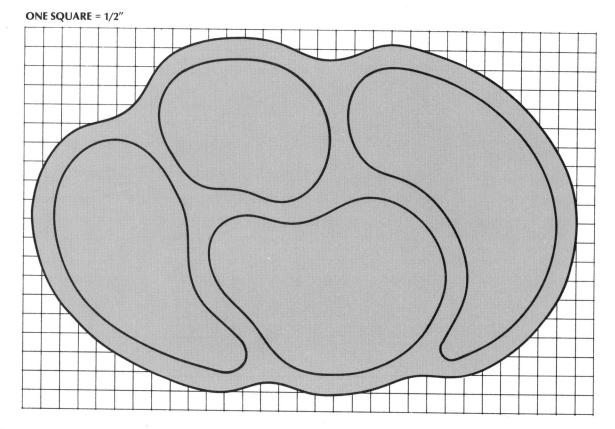

This handy magazine rack not only makes a nice accent piece, but it also serves an important function in keeping your magazines neat and handy. It makes a perfect gift for a friend or for yourself.

1. Prepare a 3/4" × 9-1/2" × 22" piece of stock.

2. Use a jigsaw to cut the base (B) from the top (A).

3. With the shaper, round the inside edge of the top.

4. Cut the outside contour of the top and shape the edge. Shape the outside edge of the bottom.

5. Drill the 3/8" diameter × 1/4" deep holes in the top.

6. Tilt the saw table 10° and drill the 3/8" diameter × 1/2" deep holes in the bottom.

7. Cut the dowels to length and lightly sand.

8. Assemble the rack by first gluing the dowels into the top then glue them into the bottom.

9. Sand the project and apply the finish of your choice.

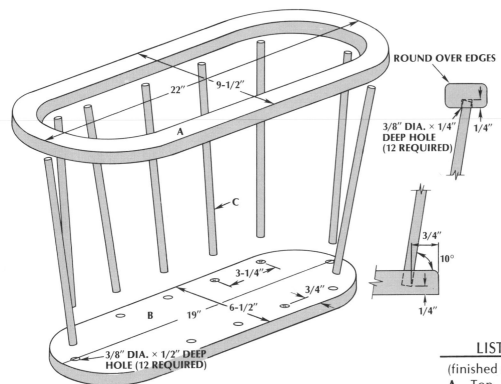

ROUND OVER EDGES

22"   9-1/2"

A

3/8" DIA. × 1/4" DEEP HOLE (12 REQUIRED)   1/4"

C

3/4"

10°

3-1/4"

3/4"

6-1/2"

1/4"

B   19"

3/8" DIA. × 1/2" DEEP HOLE (12 REQUIRED)

LIST OF MATERIALS

(finished dimensions in inches)

A	Top	3/4 × 9-1/2 × 22
B	Bottom	3/4 × 6-1/2 × 19
C	Dowels (12)	3/8 dia. × 12

MIRROR FRAME

From *HANDS ON* Nov/Dec 84

A framed mirror adds depth and warmth to a room. This project will give you a beautiful addition to any room.

1. Glue up and square a 3/4" × 15" × 21" piece of stock.

2. Cut out the 11" × 17" oval center.

3. Shape the inside and outside edge contours using a shaper or router.

4. Form a 5/16" wide × 5/16" deep rabbet on the back of the oval.

5. Sand the frame.

6. Apply the finish of your choice.

7. Paint the inside of the rabbet black so the mirror will not reflect the wood.

8. For mounting the frame to the wall, attach a picture hanger or use a router with a T-slot bit. Install the mirror.

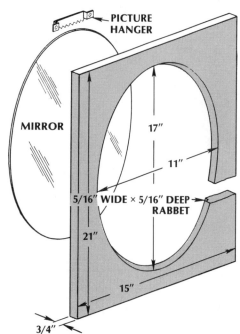

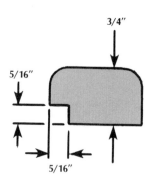

FRAME CROSS SECTION

BUTTERFLY BOXES

From *HANDS ON* May/June 80

The sides of these ingenious boxes can be made from hollow tree limbs. Take a walk through a forest (with permission from the owner) and select a dead, dry branch 6" to 10" in diameter. Cut off a 5" to 8" length, peel off the bark, and sand the hollow with a sanding drum. If you don't want to use a dead branch, you can also cut up an old porch post or turn a hollow cylinder.

Cut out a bottom and assemble it to the base of your box. Then glue up stock for the lid, at least 1-1/2" thick. You may want to use some scraps you have laying around and laminate contrasting woods. These laminations create an intriguing effect when the lid is sculpted.

Cut out a circle for your lid. Then make an S-shaped cut through the center of the circle. Shape the tops of the two lid halves, using the various sander/sculpture techniques. Let your imagination go and make any contours you wish. Smooth out the contours on the 'soft' side of the sander. However, confine most of your sanding to the tops of these pieces, and don't do anything more than remove the mill marks from the sides. When you're done sculpting, the pieces should still fit to-

gether exactly and the lid should fit the top of the box.

Hinge the two lid pieces to the box with metal pins. Be sure to use metal, not wooden dowels—wood will not operate smoothly in humid weather. When you've finished, the lid should close tightly, giving no clue to how it's hinged; then swing apart like two wings.

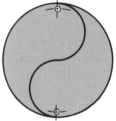

Cut lid apart as shown and drill for hinge pins.

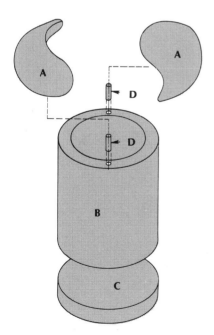

Final shaping of the lid on the 'soft' surface of a belt sander.

Assemble lid halves, Hinge pins, box, and bottom as shown.

PICTURE FRAMES

From *HANDS ON* Sept/Oct 84

Everyone knows how a beautiful frame enhances a painting or photograph. The challenge is getting the right frame, and one of the best ways to do that is by producing your own frame stock.

Here are four designs for picture frames that you can make by using the table saw and the molder attachment. Use these designs as a starting point, then experiment with the settings—table tilt, rip fence, depth-of-cut, etc. You can even change the look of a frame by using different woods, cutting compound miters, combining finishes, and so on.

Safety Tip: Use stock that's 6' to 8' long, then cut to length after all machining is complete. Use fence extensions, feather boards, push sticks and push blocks.

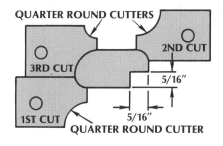

Cut rabbet in back last. Final sand frame after assembly.

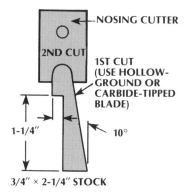

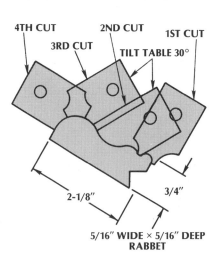

Cut rabbet last. Use dado blades and auxiliary fence. When cutting the miters, use spacer in rabbet so frame will rest flat on miter gauge face.

Tilt table 30° and cut rabbet in back. To cut miters, tilt table 21° and set miter gauge at 49°.

Use proper coving method. Tilt table 30° and cut rabbet in back. To cut miters, tilt table 21°, set miter gauge at 49°.

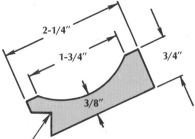

From *HANDS ON* Sept/Oct 83

One way to add a touch of class to your dinner table is with this handy casserole holder. Not only does this holder look great, but it is also very functional.

To make one for your table, use 3/4" hardwood stock for the ends and handles and 1/2" dowel rods for the rack. The ends are 3" high and should be 2" longer than the width of the baking dish. The handles measure 4" shorter than the ends and are 1" wide. On the inside of the ends, drill 1/2" diameter × 1/2" deep holes for six dowel rods (see photo for approximate location). On the outside of the end pieces, drill 1/2" dowel rod holes for the handles. Round off all edges on the ends and handles using the shaper. Cut the dowel rods to the length required and assemble the project with glue and clamps.

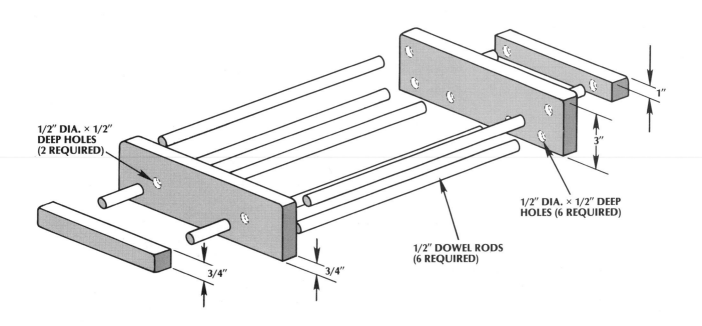

1/2" DIA. × 1/2" DEEP HOLES (2 REQUIRED)

1/2" DIA. × 1/2" DEEP HOLES (6 REQUIRED)

1/2" DOWEL RODS (6 REQUIRED)

1"

3"

3/4"

3/4"

CANDLE BOX

From *HANDS ON* Nov/Dec 84

This candle box not only makes a decorative storage item for your home, but it also makes an excellent gift idea for someone special.

1. Prepare 1/2" stock.

2. Cut all the stock to size according to the List of Materials.

3. Cut out the contours on parts (A,B,C).

4. Assemble parts (A,B,C,D) using glue and 2d finishing nails.

5. Cut the 1/4" wide × 1/4" deep grooves in the three drawer sides (E).

6. Drill the knob mounting hole in the drawer front (F).

7. Glue and nail drawer parts (E,F,G) together.

8. Countersink all the nails and fill the nail holes with wood putty.

9. Use the belt sander to sand the box sides smooth.

10. Attach the base (H) using glue and nails.

11. Apply the finish of your choice.

12. Attach the knob.

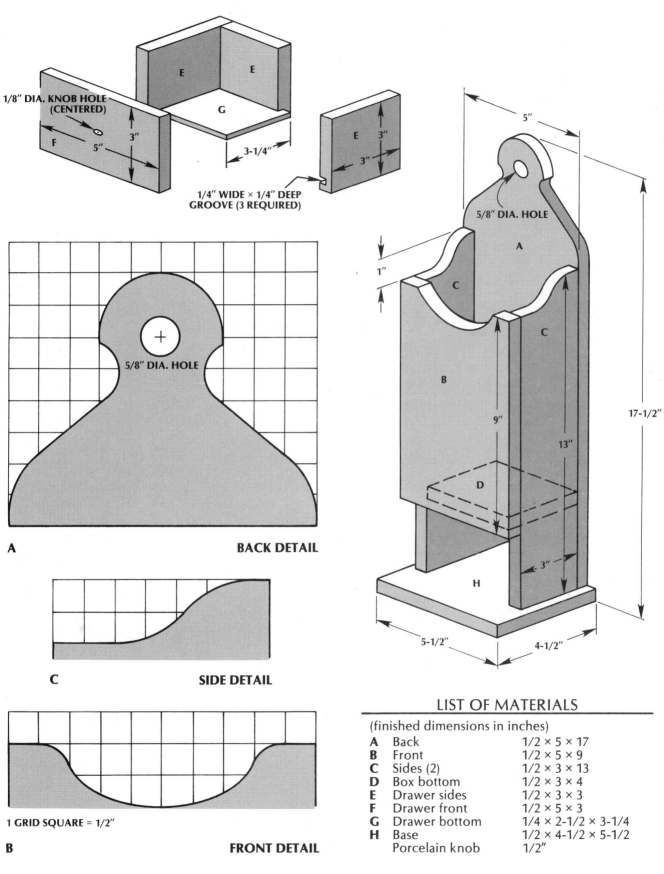

1/8" DIA. KNOB HOLE
(CENTERED)

F

5"

3"

G

3-1/4"

E

E

E

3"

3"

1/4" WIDE × 1/4" DEEP
GROOVE (3 REQUIRED)

5"

5/8" DIA. HOLE

A

C

B

9"

D

13"

3"

H

17-1/2"

5-1/2"

4-1/2"

1"

5/8" DIA. HOLE

A   **BACK DETAIL**

C   **SIDE DETAIL**

1 GRID SQUARE = 1/2"

B   **FRONT DETAIL**

LIST OF MATERIALS
(finished dimensions in inches)

A	Back	1/2 × 5 × 17
B	Front	1/2 × 5 × 9
C	Sides (2)	1/2 × 3 × 13
D	Box bottom	1/2 × 3 × 4
E	Drawer sides	1/2 × 3 × 3
F	Drawer front	1/2 × 5 × 3
G	Drawer bottom	1/4 × 2-1/2 × 3-1/4
H	Base	1/2 × 4-1/2 × 5-1/2
	Porcelain knob	1/2"

WALL DESK

From *HANDS ON* May/June 82

Cut 1/2" wide × 3/8" deep dadoes in sides (A) that will accept the bottom and shelf. Cut the same size groove and rabbet in the back (E) for the bottom and shelf.

Cut 1/2" wide × 1/4" deep dadoes in the bottom (G) and shelf (H) for the drawer partition (J).

Cut a 3/4" wide × 3/8" deep stop rabbet in sides (A) for the back.

Now, cut and sand the bottom profiles of sides (A).

Tilt the table 25° and using the extension table and rip fence to guide the work, cut the angled top edge on the back (E). With the table at the same angle, cut the top strip (C) and front (F).

Assemble and glue the partition (J) to the shelf (H) and bottom (G). Then glue and clamp sides (A) to the shelf and the bottom. Then glue and assemble the back (E) and front (F) and top strip (C). Install the hinges on the top and top strip.

Cut and assemble the stock for the drawer, final sand the entire project and apply the finish of your choice.

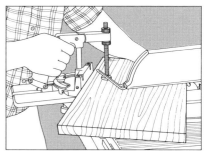

Cutting sides (A). Note use of table extension.

One of the most used "appliances" in the kitchen is the phone. Mounting it on the wall saves space, but leaves no place for the phone book or messages. This wall desk, however, will provide you with such place.

For our wall desk we used maple, but any soft or hardwood will do. You'll need to resaw or plane wood down to the 1/2" thickness required for the shelf, bottom, and drawer parts.

Glue up the wood necessary for the project. Make the two sides (A) from one piece; cut the piece to width, set the miter gauge to 65°, and cut across the middle to make the two sides (A) with a minimum of waste.

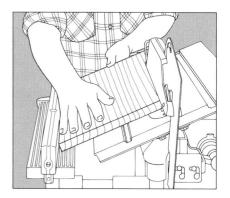

Cutting angled top edge of back (E).

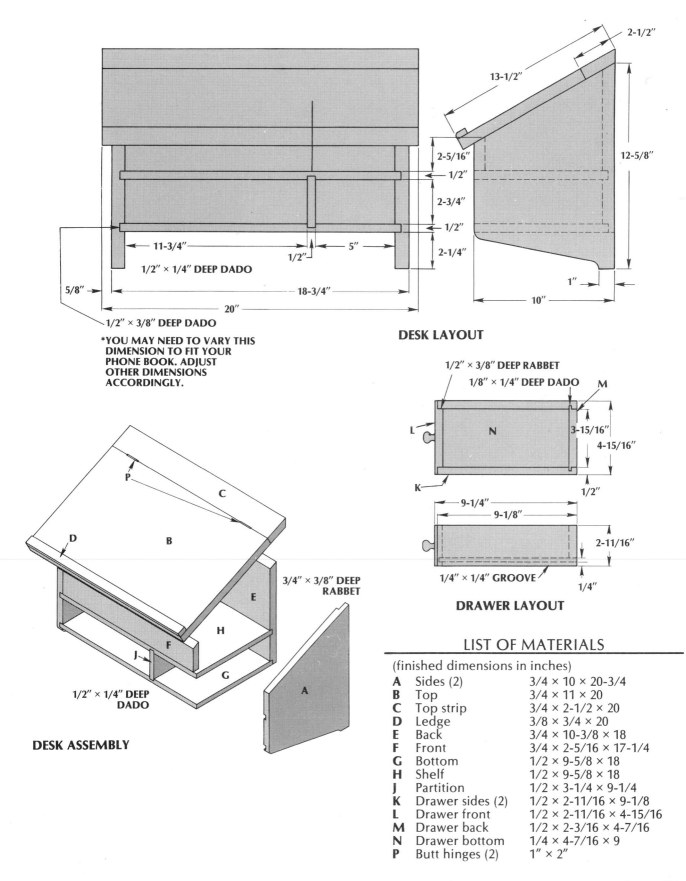

2-1/2"

13-1/2"

2-5/16"

1/2"

2-3/4"

1/2"

2-1/4"

12-5/8"

11-3/4"

5"

1/2"

1/2" × 1/4" DEEP DADO

5/8"

18-3/4"

20"

1"

10"

1/2" × 3/8" DEEP DADO

DESK LAYOUT

*YOU MAY NEED TO VARY THIS
DIMENSION TO FIT YOUR
PHONE BOOK. ADJUST
OTHER DIMENSIONS
ACCORDINGLY.

1/2" × 3/8" DEEP RABBET

1/8" × 1/4" DEEP DADO

M

L

N

3-15/16"

4-15/16"

K

1/2"

9-1/4"

9-1/8"

2-11/16"

1/4" × 1/4" GROOVE

1/4"

DRAWER LAYOUT

P

C

D

B

3/4" × 3/8" DEEP
RABBET

E

H

F

J

G

A

1/2" × 1/4" DEEP
DADO

DESK ASSEMBLY

LIST OF MATERIALS

(finished dimensions in inches)

A	Sides (2)	3/4 × 10 × 20-3/4
B	Top	3/4 × 11 × 20
C	Top strip	3/4 × 2-1/2 × 20
D	Ledge	3/8 × 3/4 × 20
E	Back	3/4 × 10-3/8 × 18
F	Front	3/4 × 2-5/16 × 17-1/4
G	Bottom	1/2 × 9-5/8 × 18
H	Shelf	1/2 × 9-5/8 × 18
J	Partition	1/2 × 3-1/4 × 9-1/4
K	Drawer sides (2)	1/2 × 2-11/16 × 9-1/8
L	Drawer front	1/2 × 2-11/16 × 4-15/16
M	Drawer back	1/2 × 2-3/16 × 4-7/16
N	Drawer bottom	1/4 × 4-7/16 × 9
P	Butt hinges (2)	1" × 2"

BIRD HOUSES

From *HANDS ON* Mar/Apr/May 85

Getting the birds to flock to your home is easy when you provide them with elegant low-cost housing. Here are two houses you can build—one for wrens and one for blue jays. You can make these birdhouses for your yard, and while you're at it, make extras to give as gifts. Easy-to-build, these projects will be a hit with your friends (fine-feathered and otherwise).

WREN HOUSE

Wrens are small songbirds that provide sweet sounding music. And wrens are easy to attract because of their willingness to adapt to both rural and city life.

Constructing this wren house is simple and basic. By starting with an 8' board, you can build four of these houses. Here's how:

1. Cut the ends (A) from a 2' long 1 × 6. Next, use a bandsaw to resaw the remaining stock in half. Plane the resawn boards to 5/16" thick, then cut parts (B,C,D) to size.

2. Tilt the saw table 45° and bevel the roof (B), sides (C), and bottom (D) as indicated in the drawings.

3. Drill the entrance hole no larger than 1" in order to keep out undesirable birds. Next, drill a 1/4" hole for the perch.

4. Use galvanized nails to assemble the ends, roof, and sides.

5. Use a 3/32" bit to drill the pilot holes for the screw eyes in the top of the roof and install them. Tap the perch (E) into place (the fit should be snug), and slide the bottom (D) into position.

6. Apply the finish of your choice (see box). After the finish dries, hang the house from your favorite tree.

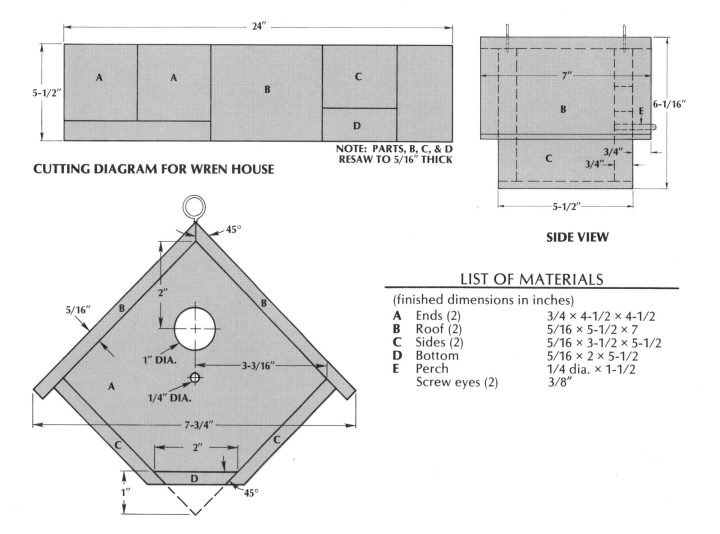

CUTTING DIAGRAM FOR WREN HOUSE

NOTE: PARTS, B, C, & D RESAW TO 5/16" THICK

SIDE VIEW

FRONT VIEW

LIST OF MATERIALS

(finished dimensions in inches)

A	Ends (2)	3/4 × 4-1/2 × 4-1/2
B	Roof (2)	5/16 × 5-1/2 × 7
C	Sides (2)	5/16 × 3-1/2 × 5-1/2
D	Bottom	5/16 × 2 × 5-1/2
E	Perch	1/4 dia. × 1-1/2
	Screw eyes (2)	3/8

BLUE JAY HOUSE

Blue jays, often loud and always protective of their turf, are a beautiful bird to have around. This house provides ample space for blue jays to raise a family. Here's how to make the house:

1. Cut parts (A-D) to length and width from a 3' section of 1 × 6 redwood. Use a bandsaw to resaw part (E) in half to make two 5/16" thick boards, then cut these to length.

2. Tilt the saw table 20° and bevel the tops of the front (A), back (B), and the ends of the roof (D).

3. Return the table to "0." Set the miter gauge at 70° and miter the tops of the sides (E).

4. Drill a 1-1/2" hole in the front (A). Next, drill a 1/4" hole for the perch (F) and a 1/4" diameter mounting hole in the back (B).

5. Use 4d galvanized nails to assemble the house. Mount the roof (D) with hinges; tap the perch (F)

into place; and apply the finish of your choice. Hang the house on a nail or hook about 6' to 10' above the ground.

BIRDHOUSE BUILDING TIPS

Here are a few things you need to know when building birdhouses.

• Use wood that's suitable for the outdoors. Redwood, cedar, and exterior plywood are all good materials. Avoid using pressure-treated lumber—the long-term effects to wildlife are unknown.

• Use only rust-resistant hardware. For nails or screws, use galvanized, stainless, or brass for best results.

• Construct birdhouses so they can be cleaned out at least once a year to control lice. Hinged tops or sliding bottoms are just two constructions that allow for easy cleaning.

• Finish birdhouses with exterior stains or paints. When painting, though, choose light colors in order to prevent heat absorption on hot summer days.

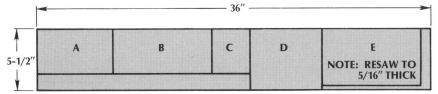

CUTTING DIAGRAM FOR BLUE JAY HOUSE

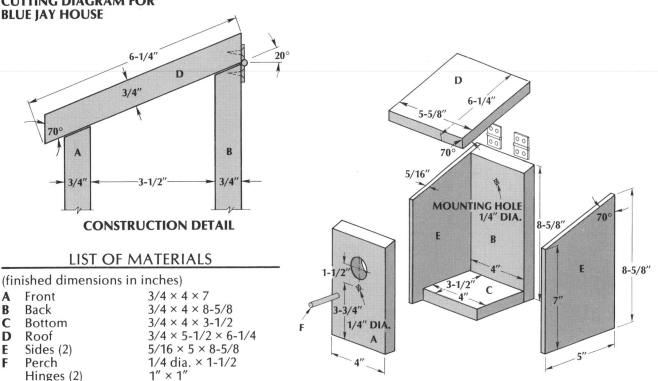

CONSTRUCTION DETAIL

LIST OF MATERIALS

(finished dimensions in inches)

A	Front	3/4 × 4 × 7
B	Back	3/4 × 4 × 8-5/8
C	Bottom	3/4 × 4 × 3-1/2
D	Roof	3/4 × 5-1/2 × 6-1/4
E	Sides (2)	5/16 × 5 × 8-5/8
F	Perch	1/4 dia. × 1-1/2
	Hinges (2)	1" × 1"

JIGSAW PUZZLES

Jigsaw puzzles are popular with children of all ages. The six designs included here are simple to make and are guaranteed to provide hours of safe fun for the kids.

1. Using a belt or hand sander, sand both surfaces of the stock. The stock should be at least 1-1/2" thick plywood or hardwood.

2. Using the plans and carbon paper, trace the full-scale pattern of the puzzle onto the stock.

3. With a jigsaw, cut out the pattern on the bold line. (The dotted lines are intended for detail painting.)

4. Sand the edges of the puzzle pieces, being careful not to distort the interlocking pattern.

5. Beginning with the large areas, paint the design with non-toxic paint or food coloring. A fine-point permanent marker is good for making the finer details.

6. Finish the puzzle with a good polyurethane varnish.

ONE SQUARE = 1"

LIST OF MATERIALS

(unfinished stock dimensions in inches)

A	Duck	1-1/2 × 4-1/2 × 6
B	Bear	1-1/2 × 7 × 8-1/2
C	Apple	1-1/2 × 8 × 8
D	Balloon	1-1/2 × 6 × 8
E	Butterfly	1-1/2 × 7-1/2 × 6
F	Bus	1-1/2 × 7-1/2 × 4-1/2

From *HANDS ON* Nov/Dec 84

It's convenient to have your books close at hand for easy reference. This book rack will not only keep your books reachable and organized, but it will also adjust to accommodate your choice of books.

1. Cut all the stock to size according to the List of Materials.

2. Drill the 1/2" diameter × 1/2" deep holes in the ends (A,B).

3. Tilt the table 5° and drill the 9/16" through-holes in the adjustable end (C).

4. Round over the edges using a shaper or router.

5. Sand all the parts. Do not sand the ends of the dowels (D).

6. Assemble with glue and clamp securely. Be careful not to get any glue on part (C).

7. Apply the finish of your choice.

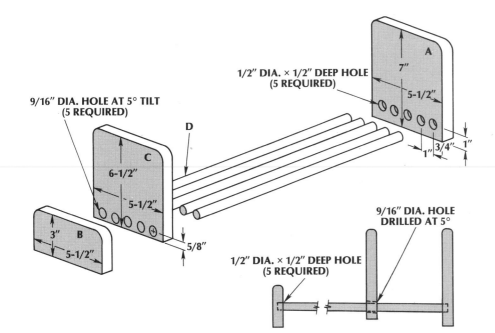

1/2" DIA. × 1/2" DEEP HOLE (5 REQUIRED)

9/16" DIA. HOLE AT 5° TILT (5 REQUIRED)

A — 7"
5-1/2"
3/4" 1"
1"

C — 6-1/2"
5-1/2"
5/8"

B — 3"
5-1/2"

D

9/16" DIA. HOLE DRILLED AT 5°

1/2" DIA. × 1/2" DEEP HOLE (5 REQUIRED)

LIST OF MATERIALS

(finished dimensions in inches)

A	Large end	3/4 × 5-1/2 × 7
B	Small end	3/4 × 5-1/2 × 3
C	Adjustable end	3/4 × 5-1/2 × 6-1/2
D	Dowels (5)	1/2 dia. × 18

GARDEN TOOL BOX

From *HANDS ON* June/July/Aug 84

Here's a really handy carrier for your garden tools that's a cinch to put together. The design for this classic toolbox is based on the tool carriers used years ago by carpenters, and that design can easily serve the gardener of today. Roomy enough for a host of small hand tools, gloves, and seed packets, this carrier is so easy to make that you may want to build several. They're equally useful for the plumber, electrician, or mechanic in your home.

1. Select your stock. Pressure-treated or a suitable outdoor wood such as redwood or cedar is best, but any scrap wood will do. The handle is standard 1-1/4" closet pole stock—or you can use part of an old broomstick.

2. Prepare the stock. Rip the bottom (A), ends (B), and sides (C) to width using the table saw, then crosscut all pieces to length. Cut the contours on the ends (B) with a bandsaw or jigsaw, and sand with the disc sander.

3. Drill the holes for the handle (D). Use a 1-1/4" Forstner bit to drill these 3/8" deep holes. Next, drill pilot holes for the assembly screws.

4. Assemble the toolbox with #9 × 1-1/2" flathead wood screws. Attach the ends (B) to the bottom (A) and insert the handle (D). Attach the sides (C). Round off all sharp edges with a rasp or sandpaper.

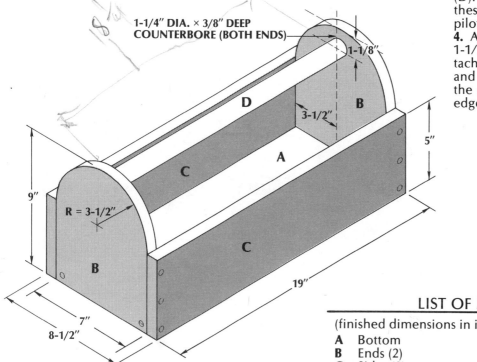

1-1/4" DIA. × 3/8" DEEP COUNTERBORE (BOTH ENDS)

1-1/8"

3-1/2"

5"

9"

R = 3-1/2"

19"

7"

8-1/2"

D

B

C

A

C

B

LIST OF MATERIALS

(finished dimensions in inches)

A	Bottom	1/4 × 7 × 17-1/2
B	Ends (2)	3/4 × 7 × 9
C	Sides (2)	3/4 × 5 × 19
D	Handle	1-1/4 dia. × 18-1/4
	Flathead wood screws (22)	#9 × 1-1/2

MAKING DOMINOS

From *HANDS ON* Jan/Feb 85

To make dominos, carefully resaw and plane a 1-1/4" wide core of either padauk or ash to a thickness of 3/16". Then, build up the domino stock by adding a layer of holly veneer and then a layer of ebony to each side of the core. Once the glue has dried, crosscut the dominos to approximate length and disc sand to final dimensions.

The centerline of each domino is created by using a jigsaw or bandsaw kerf. The dots are revealed by drilling through the outer ebony veneer with a 1/8" twist bit. After the dots are exposed, the disc sander is again used to carefully round all eight edges and four corners of each of the 28 dominos.

The dots on the dominos are revealed by drilling through the top layer of ebony.

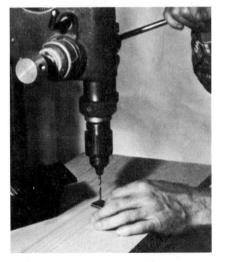

SHAKER PEGBOARD

From *HANDS ON* Apr/May/June 83 and Nov/Dec 84

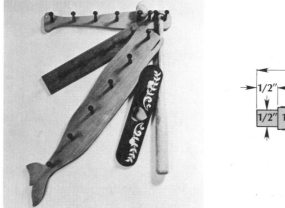

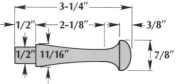

The Shakers had a unique way of storing unused items—they put them on the wall. A pegged board attached to the wall, about 6' up, provided a perfect place for coats, hats, candle sconces, and even chairs. A Shaker pegged board was about the size of a 1 × 4 with either a plain or a beaded edge. Wooden pegs were set into this board every 2" to 8", and the board was attached to the wall.

Even though many of our needs are different from those of the Shakers, there is still the common need for order. And what better place to hang a coat or hat than on a handy peg? Modern production methods have outmoded the old method of turning these pegs one at a time, making such items readily available and inexpensive.

Made out of hardwood, these pegs can fit any room decor in your house. Mount them in a variety of ways: use straight stock and shape the edge; cut out freeform shapes on the bandsaw or jigsaw; or repeat a design on the router arm.

1. Prepare a 3/4" × 3-1/2" × 36" piece of stock.

2. Drill 1/2" diameter × 1/2" deep holes for the pegs.

3. Turn the pegs on the lathe, or purchase ready-made pegs.

4. With the profile of your choice, shape the edge of the board.

5. Sand the board.

6. Glue in the pegs and allow glue to dry thoroughly before applying a finish.

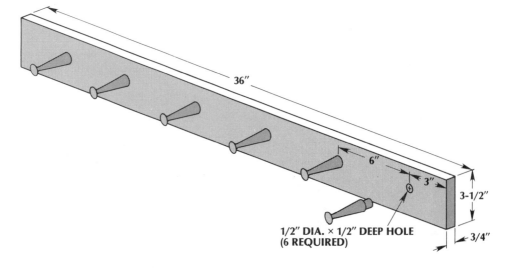

1/2" DIA. × 1/2" DEEP HOLE
(6 REQUIRED)

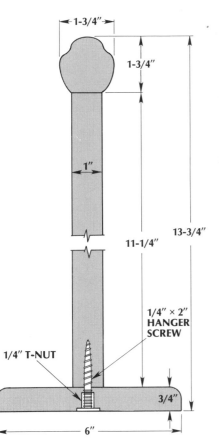

1-3/4″
1-3/4″
1″
13-3/4″
11-1/4″
1/4″ × 2″ **HANGER SCREW**
1/4″ **T-NUT**
3/4″
6″

This project proves that a kitchen item can be functional as well as attractive. This towel holder will add a decorative touch to your countertop as well as have the next paper towel at your fingertips.

1. Prepare a 2″ × 2″ × 14″ piece of stock for the towel bar. If you glue up the stock, use yellow woodworker's glue and allow the stock to remain clamped for 24 hours.

2. Turn the towel bar according to the plans. (The knob design at the top of the bar is optional.)

3. Remove the toolrest and sand the towel bar before removing it from the lathe.

4. Remove the finished bar from the lathe and cut off the waste stock.

5. Use the bandsaw or jigsaw to cut out the round base. Remove the saw marks with the disc sander then shape the edge. (Optional: Turn the base on the lathe.)

6. Drill and counterbore the bottom of the base for a 1/4″ T-nut.

7. Drill a pilot hole in the end of the towel bar for the anchor screw.

8. Assemble the holder and apply the finish of your choice.

COUNTRY CHARM

From *HANDS ON* March/Apr/May 85

These charming folk art animals are easy to make and great as decorating pieces. To make a collection in your own shop, simply transfer the animal patterns to 3/4" stock and cut out with a bandsaw or jigsaw. Paint the pieces with Early American colors or burn in decorations and finish with a stain. Bases are 3" squares of 3/4" stock and the stems are 3/8" dowel.

ONE SQUARE = 1"

One of the most useful items in a kitchen is a cutting board. By following these easy instructions, you can save your countertop from many unnecessary cuts and slices.

1. Glue up nominal 2″ (1-1/2″ actual) stock for the large cutting board and 3/4″ stock for the smaller cheese board.

2. Surface or sand the stock smooth.

3. Make cardboard templates of the designs then transfer the designs to the stock.

4. Use a bandsaw or jigsaw to cut out the boards.

5. Use the disc and drum sanders to sand the edges of the boards, and hand sand the tight spots.

6. Apply a dark stain to the edges for the 'crust,' then apply a nontoxic finish.

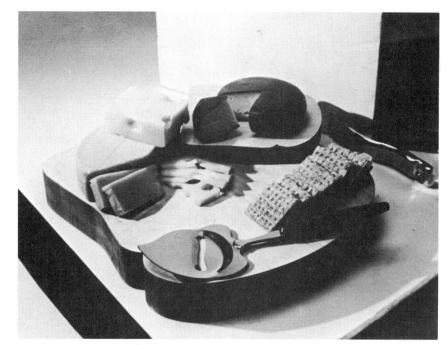

ONE SQUARE = 1/2″

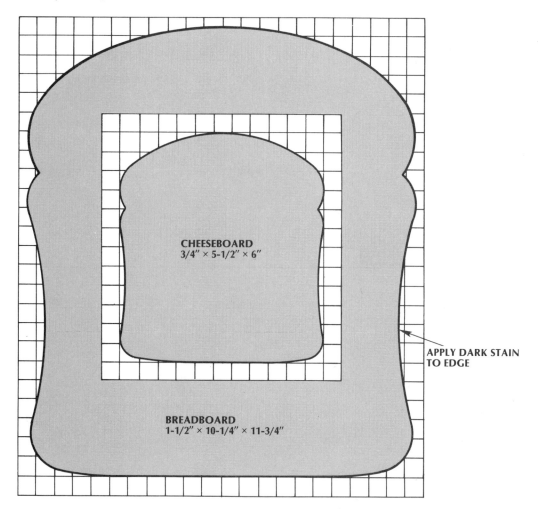

CHEESEBOARD
3/4″ × 5-1/2″ × 6″

APPLY DARK STAIN TO EDGE

BREADBOARD
1-1/2″ × 10-1/4″ × 11-3/4″

TOOL BOX

From *HANDS ON* June/July/Aug 85

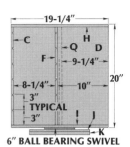

Finding the space to organize all the miscellaneous items in your shop can be a problem. A "lazy susan" storage cabinet could be the solution for you. Using standard storage drawers and less than three square feet of bench space, you can make this handy four-sided storage unit to organize all your small items—even your sandpaper.

Here's how:

1. Start the project by cutting all the parts in the List of Materials to size. Use 1/2" plywood for the main cabinet parts and 1/8" hardboard for the sandpaper shelves.

2. Using a carbide-tipped blade, cut the 1/8" wide × 1/4" deep dadoes for the drawers and trays as indicated on the drawings. Note that the center partition (F) has stopped dadoes with different spacing on each side.

3. Miter the base frame pieces (K) and glue and nail them together. With glue and nails, attach the base (J) to the assembled frame.

4. Assemble the lazy susan by first attaching the parts (E,F,G) together with woodworker's glue and 6d nails. Attach the top (H) and bottom (I) with glue and nails, then attach the sides (A,B,C,D). Attach a ball bearing swivel unit to the base and storage unit.

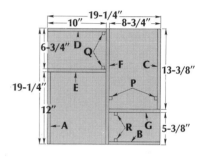

6" BALL BEARING SWIVEL

VIEW D

TOP VIEW

NOTE: ALL GROOVES ARE 1/8" WIDE × 1/4" DEEP

VIEW A

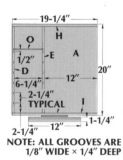

VIEW B

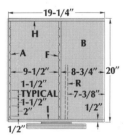

VIEW C

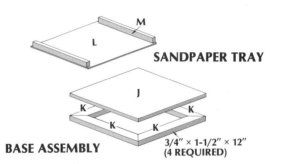

SANDPAPER TRAY

BASE ASSEMBLY

3/4" × 1-1/2" × 12" (4 REQUIRED)

LIST OF MATERIALS

(finished dimensions in inches)

A	Sandpaper side	1/2 × 12 × 19
B	Small drawer side	1/2 × 8-3/4 × 19
C	Large drawer side	1/2 × 13-3/8 × 19
D	Medium drawer side	1/2 × 10 × 19
E	Medium drawer partition	1/2 × 10 × 19
F	Main partition	1/2 × 19-1/4 × 19
G	Small drawer partition	1/2 × 8-3/4 × 19
H	Top	1/2 × 19-1/4 × 19-1/4
I	Bottom	1/2 × 19-1/4 × 19-1/4
J	Base	1/2 × 12 × 12
K	Base frame (4)	3/4 × 1-1/2 × 12
L	Sandpaper trays (12)	1/8 × 10 × 12
M	Sandpaper tray ends (24)	1/2 × 3/4 × 9-1/2
N	Small drawer dust panel	1/8 × 5-3/8 × 8-3/4
O	Medium drawer dust panel	1/8 × 6-3/4 × 10
P	Large drawer stops (2)	1/2 × 1/2 × 19
Q	Medium drawer stops (2)	1/2 × 1/2 × 19
R	Small drawer stops (2)	1/2 × 1/2 × 11
	Ball bearing swivel	6

TABLETOP STORAGE CHEST

From *HANDS ON* Jan/Feb 85

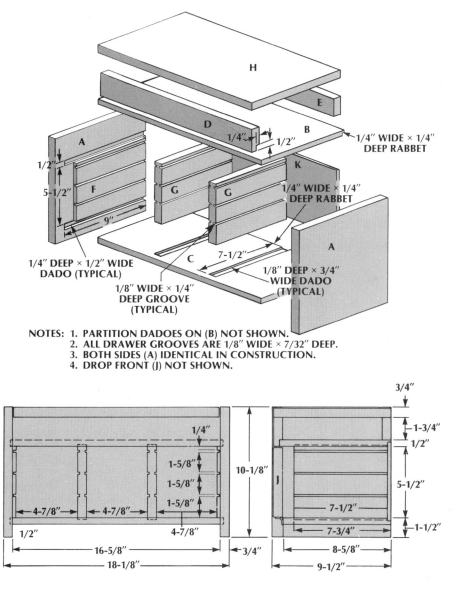

NOTES: 1. PARTITION DADOES ON (B) NOT SHOWN.
2. ALL DRAWER GROOVES ARE 1/8" WIDE × 7/32" DEEP.
3. BOTH SIDES (A) IDENTICAL IN CONSTRUCTION.
4. DROP FRONT (J) NOT SHOWN.

1/4" WIDE × 1/4" DEEP RABBET
1/4" DEEP × 1/2" WIDE DADO (TYPICAL)
1/8" WIDE × 1/4" DEEP GROOVE (TYPICAL)
1/8" DEEP × 3/4" WIDE DADO (TYPICAL)

LIST OF MATERIALS

(finished dimensions in inches)

A	Sides (2)	3/4 × 9-1/2 × 10-1/8
B	Compartment bottom	1/2 × 8-15/16 × 17-1/8
C	Bottom	1/2 × 8-11/16 × 17-1/8
D	Front rail	3/4 × 2-1/4 × 16-5/8
E	Back rail	3/4 × 1-3/4 × 16-5/8
F	Drawer supports (2)	1/4 × 5-1/2 × 7-1/2
G	Drawer partitions (2)	3/4 × 7-1/2 × 5-3/4
H	Lid	3/4 × 9-1/2 × 16-5/8
J	Drop front	3/4 × 6 × 16-5/8
K	Back	1/4 × 6 × 16-5/8
	Butt hinges (4)	1-1/2 × 1
	Brass knob	5/8
	Friction lid support	
	Wide hasp	3/4
	Small organizer drawers (9)	1-5/8 × 4-7/8 × 7-1/2

Ample storage space is a necessity for any craftsperson or do-it-yourselfer. Here's a very versatile storage box plan that is suitable for shop or home, depending upon the material used.

One particular benefit of the cabinet is the use of readily available drawers. Because of the seamless drawer construction, this chest is ideal for sewing supplies, art supplies...even a rock collection!

1. Cut parts (A,B,C,D,E,F,G) to size according to the List of Materials.

2. Lay out and cut the 1/2" wide stop dadoes in the sides (A) for parts (B,C). Next form the 3/4" wide stop dadoes in parts (B,C) for the partitions (G). Square all dadoes with a chisel.

3. Cut the 1/4" × 1/4" rabbets in parts (B,C) for the back (K).

4. Attach drawer supports (F) to the sides with glue and clamp. Set the supports (F) 1/4" in from the back edges of sides (A).

5. Lay out the drawer grooves on the partitions (G) and supports (F), then cut these with a carbide-tipped saw blade set at a 7/32" cutting depth. Check drawers for fit.

6. Glue and clamp parts (A,B,C) together. Check for squareness as you apply clamping pressure. Reinforce the joints with countersunk #8 × 1-1/2" flathead wood screws.

7. Cut parts (D,E) to final length and glue and clamp these into place.

8. Attach the back (K) with 2d nails.

9. Cut the lid (H) and drop front (J) to finished dimensions, and attach to the chest with the hinges.

10. Apply the finish of your choice.

173

ODDS AND ENDS STORAGE CHEST

From *HANDS ON* Nov/Dec 83

rabbet in the back edges of the sides (A) for the back (J).

4. Attach the drawer guides (E) to the partitions (C) with 4d finish nails and glue. Mount the guides flush with back edges of the partitions and with a 6-1/16" spacing between each. Attach the 3/4" × 3/4" filler strip (D) to the top partition.

5. Assemble sides (A) and partitions (C) with glue and 8d finish nails. Double-check your spacing to make sure that there is a 6-1/16" vertical space between each partition. Glue the drawer dividers (F) into place.

6. Shape the edges of the top (B) and the drawer fronts (K) with a 1/4" quarter round shaper cutter, or use a hand-held router with a rounding-over bit. Shape just the sides and front edge of the top.

7. Attach the top (B) to the case with 8d finish nails and attach the back (J) with 2d common nails.

8. Miter the corners of the base pieces (G,H). Cut the scrollwork using bandsaw or jigsaw and sand the parts on a drum sander. Attach the base pieces with 4d finish nails and glue.

9. Drawer construction. With 16 drawers, you'll need to use a few production techniques. Rip all drawer stock to proper widths, and then crosscut the pieces to equal lengths (use a miter gauge stop rod or a stop block clamped to the rip fence for this operation). Use a dado assembly or a saw blade with a 1/8" kerf to form the grooves in the drawer sides (L). Glue and nail the drawers together, and glue and clamp the fronts (K) into the ends (M). Flush-sand the drawer bottoms and sides using a disc or belt sander. Slide the bottoms (N) in and tack in place with 2d nails.

10. Finishing touches: Final-sand the chest and remove all dust with a tack rag. Finish as desired and attach the knobs.

Here's a great piece of furniture that solves a big storage problem— where to put those decks of cards, cassette tapes, scissors, needlepoint supplies, and dozens of other odds and ends. Designed to look like the kind of chest used in old-time drugstores, this apothecary chest has sixteen drawers to accommodate lots of things.

This apothecary chest is built out of #2 common pine throughout, except for the hardboard back and the drawer bottoms. You can save money by using particleboard for the partitions and plywood for the drawers.

1. Cut out the top (B), sides (A), drawer fronts (K), and base pieces (G,H) first. This allows you to select the best wood for visible parts. Cut the drawer fronts (K) about 1/8" oversize since the finished drawer sides and bottoms are sanded flush after final assembly.

2. Cut the remaining stock to size according to the List of Materials. We glued up the 14" wide partitions (C) using solid pine. You can also make these partitions out of 13-1/4" wide particleboard, then glue and nail a 3/4" × 3/4" strip of pine facing to the exposed edge.

3. Form the 1/4" deep × 3/8" wide

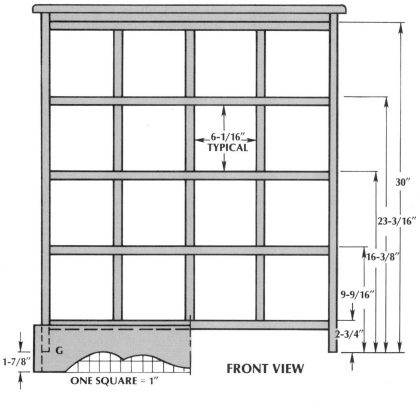

6-1/16"
TYPICAL

30"

23-3/16"

16-3/8"

9-9/16"

2-3/4"

1-7/8"

G

ONE SQUARE = 1"

FRONT VIEW

D

F

E

33-3/8"

H

15"

SIDE VIEW

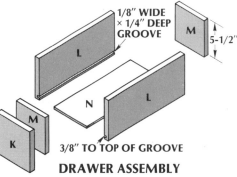

1/8" WIDE
× 1/4" DEEP
GROOVE

M

5-1/2"

L

L

M

N

K

3/8" TO TOP OF GROOVE

DRAWER ASSEMBLY

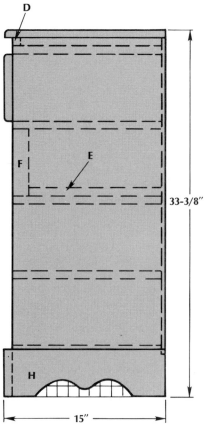

D

J

C

C

C

C

C

3/8" WIDE
× 1/4" DEEP
RABBET

G

A

E

F

H

CASE ASSEMBLY

LIST OF MATERIALS

(finished dimensions in inches)

A	Sides (2)	3/4 × 14-1/4 × 30-3/4
B	Top	3/4 × 15 × 31
C	Partitions (5)	3/4 × 14 × 26-1/2
D	Filler strip	3/4 × 3/4 × 26-1/2
E	Drawer guides (12)	3/4 × 3/4 × 12-1/2
F	Drawer dividers (12)	3/4 × 1-1/2 × 6-1/16
G	Base front	3/4 × 4-1/4 × 29-1/2
H	Base sides (2)	3/4 × 4-1/4 × 15
J	Back	1/4 × 28-3/4 × 27-1/4
K	Drawer fronts (16)	3/4 × 6 × 6
L	Drawer sides (32)	1/2 × 5-7/8 × 13-3/4
M	Drawer ends (32)	1/2 × 5-1/2 × 5
N	Drawer bottoms (16)	1/8 × 5-3/8 × 13-3/4
	White porcelain knobs (16)	

Home Improvement

Many people work very hard at making their home cozy and inviting as well as functional. Oftentimes, this involves adding the right finishing touches. The twelve projects here contain many options and suggestions for you to obtain the best utilization of space and convey the mood you wish to create. These projects can be applied as facelifts for an older home or incorporated when building a new home.

Windows and doors are like pictures on the wall. As such, the same considerations that go into picture frames should also go into the moldings around these doors and windows. Dress them up with some fancy or unusual moldings, but don't stop with the selection available from the local lumberyard. Select the design and wood you want by creating your own moldings. Here's how:

1. Plan your trim. Decide what kind of trim you want. Window trim that meets with the stool is called conventional framing. Choose between mitered corners at the top or use corner blocks. Corner blocks allow you to butt-join the trim. This is an easy way to add a decorative treatment to the framing. Around the doors the trim goes to the floor or joins with a block of wood (plinth) at the baseboard. The method of treating windows with no stools is called picture framing. Remember: When measuring for mitered framing, add twice the width of the stock to the length of each frame member.

2. Design the contours. Use molding knives from the molding attachment as templates to draw the contours you want. Then, move knives into various positions to get different contours. Keep in mind that the contours on the knives are slightly longer than the actual cut. Remember that the table saw can be used for bevels and chamfers, and the lathe can be used for turning the corner blocks on screw centers. Plan on making extra trim to avoid duplicating machine set-ups.

3. Prepare stock. First, rip all stock to width. Use only straight, true and clear stock for your moldings. Ponderosa pine, fir, poplar, walnut, oak, cherry, mahogany, and butternut have all been used extensively in finish carpentry work.

After ripping the stock to width, cut the 1/8" deep relief in the back using the 1" blank knife set of the molding attachment or use the dado attachment. This relief will allow you to adjust to inconsistencies between the wall and the door or window jamb.

4. Mold the trim. Use scrap stock to locate the proper settings for your table and fence. Use a molding jig to make this operation easier and safer. For narrow trim, mold the edge of a wide board, and then saw-off the part that you want. Be sure to use push stick, push blocks, and feather boards at all times on these operations.

5. Install the trim. Use a miter saw. Use finish nails to attach the molding and use a nail set to countersink the nails. Fill the nail holes with wood putty and apply the finish of your choice.

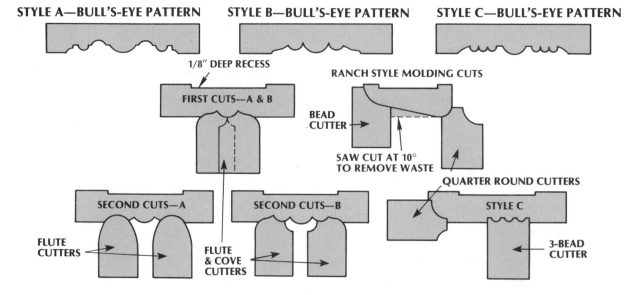

From *HANDS ON* Sept/Oct 83

Baseboard moldings play several important roles in any room. Applied where the floor meets the wall, they form a visual foundation for the eye while covering the unsightly floor and wall seam. And they also protect the walls from kicks, bumps, furniture, and cleaning tools.

Baseboard molding has to be installed after the door trim is in place since the length of the baseboard is determined by the width of the door trim.

Here's how you can create baseboard molding for your room.

1. Plan your molding. Baseboard moldings consist usually of either one, two, or three parts. The *base molding* is the wide piece that protects the wall. It can carry a decorative molding itself. *Base shoe*, a trim piece of molding that looks like (but is *not* the same as) quarter-round molding, hides any unevenness between the bottom of the base and the floor. Base shoe is an optional trim with wall-to-wall carpet. A *base cap* is added to the top of an unmolded base to hide gaps between the wall and the base top.

Make a full-scale design of the molding you want using your selection of molding knives as templates, then measure the walls. Be sure to add 20% to the total length for mitering, errors in cutting, and other waste.

2. Make the molding. One of the advantages of making your own molding is that you can select the type of wood you want. In order to make the job of molding and installation easier, select stock that's straight and free of defects.

For the base molding, cut a 1/8" deep relief in the back side with the 1" blank molding knives. This relief allows the molding to fit the wall without gaps.

Make the base shoe and base cap moldings efficiently and safely by cutting the profiles on the edge of a wide board, then sawing off the profiled edge. This method allows the stock to be supported while it's being molded.

3. Installation: The first step to installation is to mark the locations of the wall studs. Use a magnetic or electronic stud finder; or tap lightly along the wall with your hammer

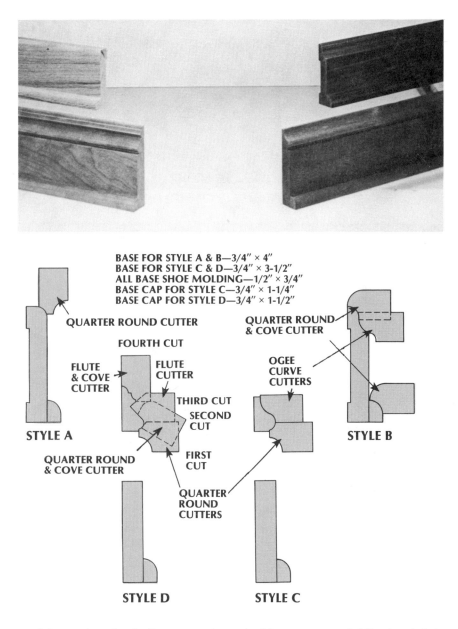

BASE FOR STYLE A & B—3/4" × 4"
BASE FOR STYLE C & D—3/4" × 3-1/2"
ALL BASE SHOE MOLDING—1/2" × 3/4"
BASE CAP FOR STYLE C—3/4" × 1-1/4"
BASE CAP FOR STYLE D—3/4" × 1-1/2"

QUARTER ROUND CUTTER

FOURTH CUT

FLUTE & COVE CUTTER

FLUTE CUTTER

THIRD CUT

SECOND CUT

FIRST CUT

QUARTER ROUND & COVE CUTTER

QUARTER ROUND CUTTERS

STYLE A

QUARTER ROUND & COVE CUTTER

OGEE CURVE CUTTERS

STYLE B

STYLE D

STYLE C

and listen for the hollow sounds between the studs; or measure from any known stud locations.

Start by installing the base on the longest walls first. Sink two 8d finish nails at each stud—drilling pilot holes first with a 7/64" twist drill. It helps to cut the base just a trifle long so that it can be "sprung" into place. Too long, though, and you'll punch holes in the wall or cause cracks in the corners. If your molding is not long enough, use a miter lap joint to join two shorter pieces at a stud and nail through the joint.

Next, install the base to the remaining walls with butt joints at the inside corners and 45° miter joints at the outside corners. If the base is molded, you will need to miter or cope the inside corners. After installing the base, follow the same procedure for the base shoe and base cap.

4. Finishing touches: Countersink the nail holes and apply a clear finish such as polyurethane varnish. Fill the nail holes with a wood filler that matches the color of your stock. If you paint the molding, countersink and fill the nail holes before applying the paint.

CEILING MOLDINGS

From *HANDS ON* July/Aug 83

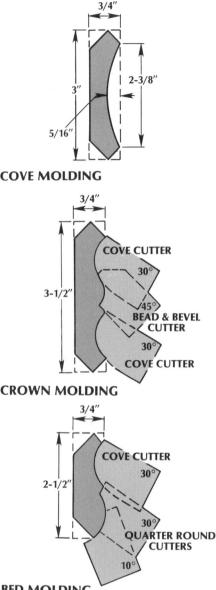

COVE MOLDING

3/4"

3"

2-3/8"

5/16"

CROWN MOLDING

3/4"

3-1/2"

COVE CUTTER

30°

45°

BEAD & BEVEL CUTTER

30°

COVE CUTTER

BED MOLDING

3/4"

2-1/2"

COVE CUTTER

30°

30°

QUARTER ROUND CUTTERS

10°

Doing your own room remodeling offers tremendous satisfaction for several reasons. Most importantly, you know you're doing it yourself, and you can take pride in seeing the fruits of your labor—a room that's fresh and different. Another cause for satisfaction is saving money by doing it yourself, using your own time and resources. But, the real pleasure of room remodeling discussed in this series is knowing that what you have done is unique—that you have made woodwork that's simply not available to the average homeowner.

Designed to cover the seams where the ceiling meets the walls, ceiling moldings do double duty by also providing an eye-pleasing transition from one surface to another. Again, as with other moldings, the design and type of wood allow you to add personality to your room.

Here's how to create ceiling moldings for your room:

1. Plan your molding. There are three kinds of ceiling moldings you can make—*crown, bed,* and *cove.* An example of each is illustrated below. Crown and cove moldings are always "sprung," meaning that

they have beveled edges that rest on the ceiling and wall, thereby spanning the ceiling wall joint. This spanning allows the molding to readily adjust to minor irregularities and provide a clean line where it meets the ceiling or wall. Bed molding can be either sprung or plain—the latter type fitting snug into the joint.

Use one of the designs illustrated at left, or create the profile you want by applying the molding cutters in various positions.

2. Prepare stock. It is necessary to use straight, true, and clear stock for your molding. For our examples we used walnut, cherry, and oak. Rip stock to required widths. Prepare extra stock to allow for cutting errors.

3. Cut the profiles. As you can see by the crown and bed moldings we feature, using just a few cutters can yield many attractive profiles. The cove molding, on the other hand, requires no shaper work; rather, it's done entirely on the table saw. Always be sure to use push blocks, push sticks, feather boards, and a roller stand for safety.

4. Bevel the molding. After you have completed the profiles, bevel the edges of the molding on the table saw. Tilt the table 45°, mount the rip fence below the blade, and use a feather board to help guide the stock.

5. Install the molding. Start installing the ceiling molding on the longest wall first. Drill 7/64" pilot holes for 8d finish nails and nail the molding through the plaster or drywall into the upper wall plate. For large moldings, nail through to the ceiling joist. Cut the molding just a trifle long so it can be lightly sprung into place. If the molding isn't long enough, use a miter lap joint to join two shorter pieces. Install the remaining molding by mitering the outside corners and coping or mitering the inside corners.

6. Add finishing touches. Countersink the nails and apply the finish of your choice. Fill the nail holes with wood putty that matches the color of your finished molding.

From *HANDS ON* May/June 80

This window greenhouse is perfect for growing house plants, garden seedlings, flowers, or even a miniature vegetable garden. It's easy to build and can be attached directly to a window frame with screws, or installed in the window cavity like an air conditioner. The window greenhouse should be 12" to 18" deep, depending on its overall size; the larger it is, the deeper it should be. The dimensions may be lengthened or shortened to fit the windows in your home.

NOTE: If the greenhouse will be mounted permanently, its inside rear dimensions, where it meets the window frame, should be the same as the inside dimensions of the window frame. If, on the other hand, the greenhouse will simply rest in the window cavity, the outside dimensions of the greenhouse, where it will enter the window cavity, should be 1/8" smaller than the inside dimensions of the window cavity.

1. Cut all pieces to size according to the List of Materials.

2. To make the top portion of the greenhouse, first cut grooves in both ends of the horizontal pieces. To do this, bolt a large scrap of wood to the miter gauge; this extension should reach to within 1/8" of the rip fence and be perfectly square with the fence and table. Hold the pieces firmly against the extension in order to cut the grooves accurately.

3. Because the top rests on the greenhouse at a 25° angle, cut the upper horizontal piece at 25°. Machine 1/4" off the top of the lower horizontal piece to allow rain to run off the greenhouse without soaking into the wood.

4. To make the front of the greenhouse, cut the upper edge at 25°. Cut a 1/4" wide × 3/8" deep groove on the inside of the lower horizontal piece, and a 1/4" wide × 1/4" deep groove in the edges of the vertical pieces.

5. To make the sides, cut the upper edge at 25°. Cut a 1/4" wide × 3/8" deep groove in the lower horizontal pieces. In addition, cut a 1/4" wide × 1/4" deep groove in the inside of the front vertical pieces. The upper pieces are right triangles with their longest sides slanted at 25° to the horizontal.

6. To make the bottom of the greenhouse, cut a 3/8" wide × 1/4" thick tongue in the right, left and front edges of the redwood boards. To do this, use a dado blade and stack the knives to cut a 3/8" kerf. Set the table and rip fence so that the dado cuts a 1/4" deep × 3/8" wide rabbet. With the fence and table properly adjusted, cut a rabbet in one edge of the boards, then turn the boards over, end for end, and cut more rabbets in the same edges from the opposite side.

Fit the bottom pieces together with tongues and grooves, making sure that their combined width, when joined, matches the length of the front and back pieces.

7. Attach the front to the side with a 1/2" × 1/4" spline in the grooves of the vertical pieces. Slide the bottom into the grooves of the lower front and side pieces.

8. Attach a board of the same width as the back vertical side pieces to the tops of the back vertical side pieces with wood screws. Hinge the top to this board.

9. Using 3/4" × 3/4" redwood strips, make a lip around the front and side edges of the top. Drill a small hole through the greenhouse frame from the inside and partially through the lip. Insert a nail in the hole to lock the top closed; the nail can be removed and the top propped open when ventilation is needed.

10. Install another lip around the back of the greenhouse to help mount it or fit it to the window.

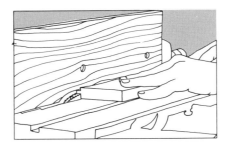

Making a tongue with a dado blade.

11. Cut or purchase glass panes of correct dimensions, to fit the top, sides, and front. Hold the glass in place with glazier's points while you apply glazing compound around the edges.

12. Insert two or three brass screws in the lower edge of the top piece to keep the pane of glass from sliding off. Extrude a bead of silicone caulk along the lower edge of the top, then position the glass on the bead. The silicone will prevent the entry of moisture along the lower edge.

NOTE: If the greenhouse will be permanently mounted, wait until it has been attached to the window frame before installing the panes.

13. To mount the greenhouse permanently, use the back lip to screw it to the window frame, then apply a durable adhesive caulk around the joint to keep out moisture and cold air. To set the greenhouse in an open window, remove the top and slide it in until the back lip butts up against the sash, then reattach the top. Put weatherstripping around any cracks.

14. Finally, attach a strip of flashing to the greenhouse or window so that the hinges are covered. This material will help to prevent leaks.

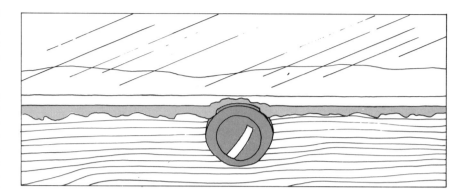

Brass screws and washers keep glass from sliding off top; silicone seal keeps moisture from seeping underneath.

LIST OF MATERIALS

(finished dimensions in inches)

A	Top horizontal pieces (2)	3/4 × 1-1/2 × 18
B	Top vertical pieces (2)	3/4 × 1-1/2 × 12
C	Front horizontal pieces (2)	3/4 × 1-1/2 × 18
D	Front vertical pieces (2)	3/4 × 3/4 × 10
E	Side horizontal pieces (2)	3/4 × 1-1/2 × 8
F	Triangular side board (2)	3/4 × 6 × 8 × 10
G	Side vertical pieces (2)	3/4 × 1-1/2 × 10
H	Side vertical pieces (2)	3/4 × 1-1/2 × 12
J	Bottom pieces (2)	3/4 × 8 × 10 redwood boards
K	Lips (2)	3/4 × 3/4 × 18 redwood strips
L	Lips (2)	3/4 × 3/4 × 12 redwood strips
M	Hinge board	3/4 × 3/4 × 18

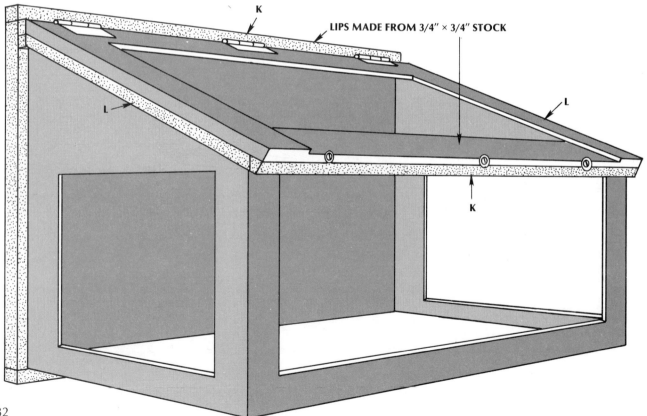

LIPS MADE FROM 3/4″ × 3/4″ STOCK

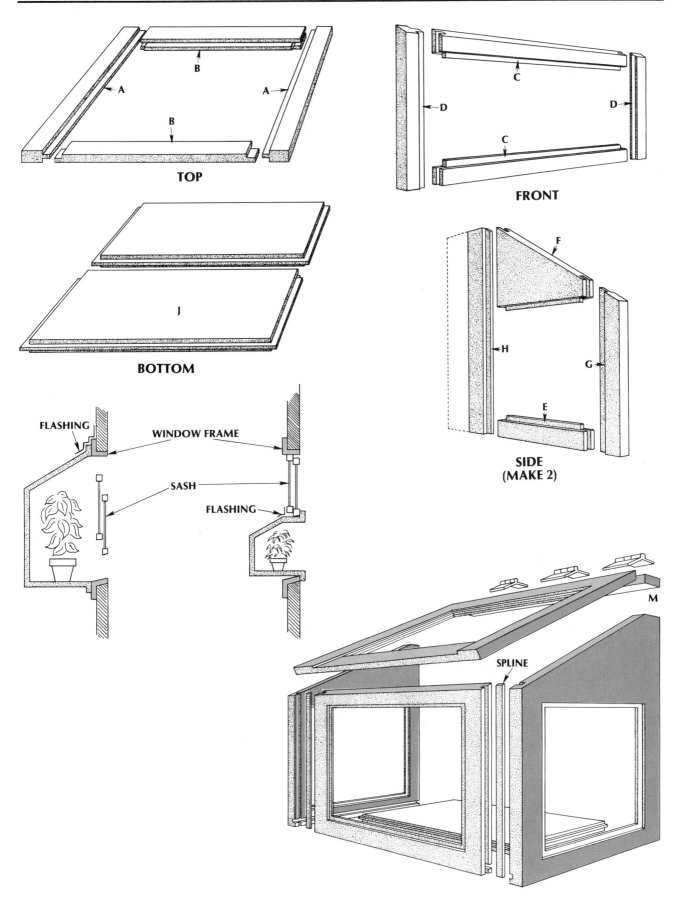

TOP

FRONT

BOTTOM

SIDE
(MAKE 2)

FLASHING

WINDOW FRAME

SASH

FLASHING

SPLINE

POT AND PAN ORGANIZER

From *HANDS ON* Nov/Dec 80

There must be a law somewhere that decrees that no matter which pot or pan you want to use, it will *always* be at the bottom of the stack. How many times have you had to get down on your hands and knees, reach into the darkest recesses of your cabinets, and move half your cooking utensils just to find the one you wanted?

There is a way around this dilemma. Instead of stacking your pans vertically on a shelf, one on top of the other, file them horizontally in a drawer! A deep drawer with moveable dividers will organize your utensils. And it gives you the versatility to add new items and discard old ones. Just rearrange the dividers to accommodate new pots and pans.

But you don't want to do away with shelves completely. Some items, like small appliances, are most efficiently stored on shelves. But you can convert some of your shelves so they pull out like drawers, eliminating the need to get down on all fours and rummage around. Drawers and sliding shelves put the utensils you need within convenient reach.

MEASURING AND MATERIALS

Most under-the-counter cabinets have room for one deep drawer and one pull-out shelf. The depth of the drawer is determined by the diameter of your largest

pans—usually 10" to 11".

The length of the drawer and shelf should be 1/8" to 1/4" less than the depth of your cabinet. This will give you room to close the cabinet doors when the drawers and shelves are retracted. The width should be a hair less than the width of the door opening.

For the most part, these drawers can be built from inexpensive materials—we used #2 pine and 1/4" masonite. But make the runners and guides from hardwood.

MAKING THE DRAWERS

The drawers are made from seven pieces—front, back, bottom, two sides, and two runners. Most of the pieces are joined to each other using simple dadoes except for the joinery between the sides and the front. This joint has to stand the strain each time you open and close the drawer. One of the strongest joints you can use at stress points like this is a sliding dovetail.

Using a router accessory and 9/16" dovetail cutter, rout two vertical slots in the drawer front. The center of these slots should be 7/8" from either side.

To make the mating dovetails in the sides, use a horizontal router. Adjust the table height so that the dovetail cutter bites into the wood just enough to cut half the dovetail, 3/8" in from the end. Using a miter gauge and safety grip, pass the sides under the router, against

the rotation of the cutter. Flip the board and repeat the operation to cut the other half of the dovetail.

The other joinery is cut using either straight router bits or dado blades.

Cut additional 1/4" wide × 3/8" deep dadoes in the insides of the sides, perpendicular to the length and spaced every 2". These will accommodate the spacers you'll need to organize your utensils.

Rout a handle in the front of the drawer 5" long, 1-1/2" wide, and 1-1/2" below the top edge.

Assemble the front, sides, back, and bottom with glue and wood screws. With a sander, slightly crown the bottom edge of the runners—this will help reduce the friction, making the drawer easier to pull in and out. Attach the runners to the drawer with glue and screws.

MAKING THE SHELF

Cut four boards, 3/4" thick × 3" wide to make a shelf frame. Cut a 1/4" wide, 3/8" deep dado down the middle of the inside edges of the frame members, using either a 1/4" straight bit or dado blades. Then cut a 1/4" thick × 3/8" long tenon in the ends of the front and back frame members. On the bottom side of the front frame member, rout or dado a groove 3/4" wide, 1/2" deep, and 5" long. This groove will serve as a pull for the sliding shelf.

Cut a piece of 1/4" masonite to fit inside the frame and assemble the pieces with glue.

INSTALLATION

To install a drawer and a shelf in your cabinets, make two simple guides out of a piece of 1-1/4" thick × 5" wide hardwood. Cut two dadoes 1/2" deep down the length of the board. The dado for the shelf should be 13/16" wide, for the drawer, 1-1/2", spaced as shown. Cut the board in half to make your two guides. (*Note:* As described, these guides can be used to mount a shelf above a drawer, as our pictures show. If you want to mount the shelf below the drawer or mount several shelves or drawers, you'll have to make more than one set of guides.)

Using brad point bits, drill two 1" holes, 3/4" deep in each of the guides and centered 5/16" below the dado for the drawer. These holes should be positioned 3" back from the front edge of the guides and 3" back from the center. They will form a recess in which you can mount shower stall rollers. These rollers make excellent glides for heavy drawers.

Purchase four rollers 3/4" in diameter. Mount them with #8 × 1-1/4" roundhead screws in the recesses you've just drilled. (You may have to ream the centers of the rollers out a bit if the #8 screws won't pass through.) Use the pilot hole left by the brad point bit to center the rollers in the recesses. When mounted, they should protrude into the dado slot 1/16".

Mount the finished guides to your cabinet frame. Just tack or clamp them in at first, to make sure you've got them level and that your drawers and shelves slide easily. (There should be about 1/16" of play for both the drawer and the shelf, if you use the measurements we've given you. If you want a tighter fit, adjust these measurements accordingly.) Once the guides are properly placed, mark them for position and attach them to the cabinet frame with glue and wood screws.

Slide the drawers and shelves into place. Cut as many spacers as you need (2 to 4 per drawer) from 1/4" masonite and put them in place.

And that's it, except for putting away your pots and pans; then standing back and admiring how organized they look.

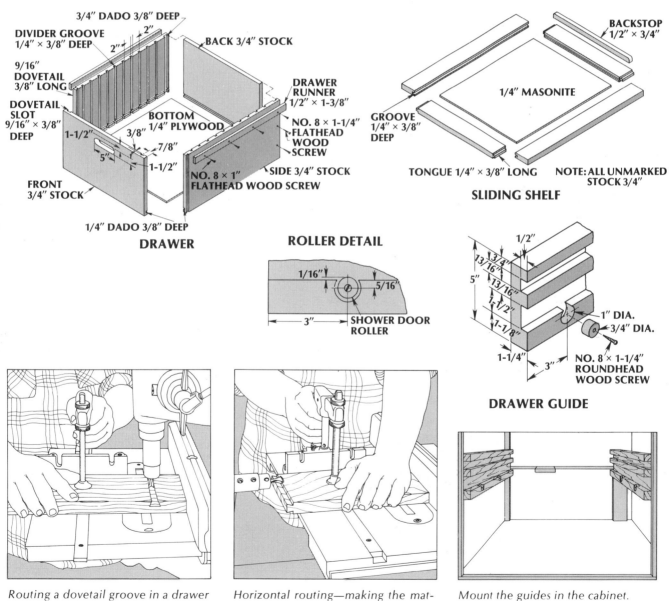

Routing a dovetail groove in a drawer front.

Horizontal routing—making the mating dovetail.

Mount the guides in the cabinet.

WORKBENCH-ON-THE-WALL

From *HANDS ON* Jan/Feb 84

Working with wood is a hobby that can consume a lot of space in a home. A woodcarver who carves miniatures may need only a kitchen tabletop, but other woodworkers seem to need an entire basement and a two-car garage. For the average woodworker, space must be shared—next to the laundry room or side-by-side with the family car. Here's a compact workbench-on-the-wall that serves the needs of the space-conscious woodworker as well as the needs of the rest of the family.

This workbench-on-the-wall is easy to build and quite versatile. When not in use, it folds up and out of the way to permit dust-free storage of tools and easy access to the floor for cleaning. And, because of the compact size and low cost, it's feasible to build several—one for each of your D-I-Y activities.

For instance: three benches in a row would give you over 12′ of workbench surface, plus individual space for your tools. But don't stop there. Consider this handy bench for a...

- sewing center
- potting/garden bench
- electronics bench
- finishing bench
- mechanic's bench
- child's desk

To build this bench you will need to:

1. Cut all stock to size according to the cutting diagram and the List of Materials. Remember: Measure twice, cut once.

2. Cut the dadoes in the legs (M) for the stretcher (K) using the dado attachment. Attach the stretcher to the legs using glue and screws.

3. Make the bench top (A) by first laminating the plywood with glue and screws. Apply the facing pieces (E,F) with glue and 6d finish nails.

4. Assemble the case by first attaching the shelves (C) and bottom (P) to the sides (B) with glue and screws. Check for squareness as you progress. Next, attach the upper and lower cleat strips (G) with glue and screws (the lower cleat strip is fastened with longer screws). These strips need to be secure since they will be used for mounting the bench to the wall. The side cleat strips (H) are attached with glue and nails. Attach the pegboard (R) with screws, and

then glue and nail the stop (L) into place.

5. Attach the gusset (D) with glue and screws to the case and then attach a 5″ strap hinge to the gusset.

6. Form the mortises with a chisel in the bench top (A) and the bottom (P) for the hinges.

7. Attach the bench top assembly to the case with the butt hinges. Then attach the leg assembly with the strap hinges.

8. Leg brace. Cut a 45° bevel on the end of the leg brace (J) and glue and clamp the back-up block (N) to the beveled end. With the bench propped open, locate the position of the leg brace and attach it to the gusset strap hinge.

Clamp the brace to the stretcher (K) and drill the 3/8″ bolt hole through the stretcher, brace and block.

9. Attach the screw hook and eye to the lower shelf, and to the back-up block.

10. Mount the workbench on steel shelf brackets that are fastened to wall studs. Steel shelf brackets are available at hardware stores and home centers. Fasten the case to the wall with 3-1/2″ lag screws through the upper and lower cleats. After the workbench is attached to the wall, tack the hardboard top (Q) in place with 4d nails.

This workbench folds up and out of the way when not in use.

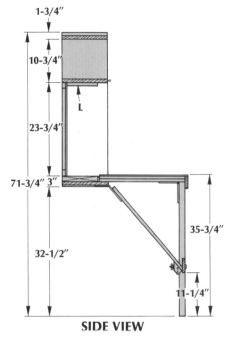

SIDE VIEW

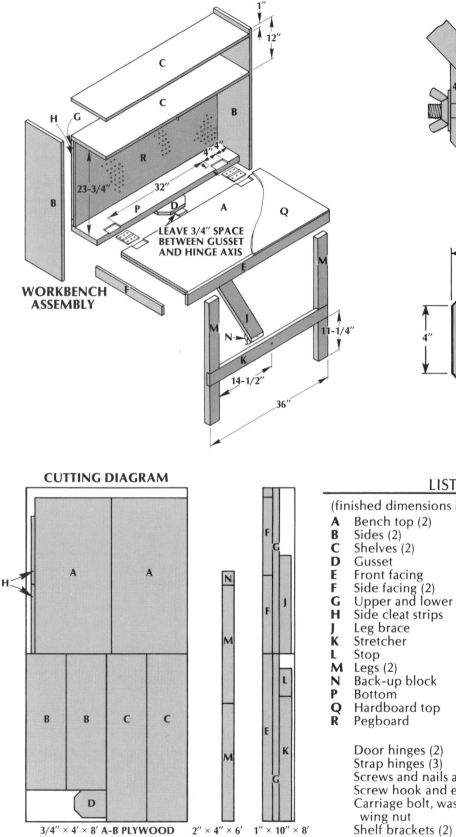

1″

12″

C

C

B

H G

B

R

23-3/4″

32″

4″ 4″

P

D

A

Q

LEAVE 3/4″ SPACE BETWEEN GUSSET AND HINGE AXIS

E

F

M

M

N

J

K

11-1/4″

14-1/2″

36″

WORKBENCH ASSEMBLY

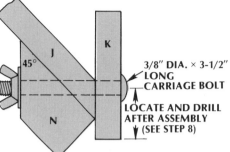

J K

45°

N

3/8″ DIA. × 3-1/2″ LONG CARRIAGE BOLT

LOCATE AND DRILL AFTER ASSEMBLY (SEE STEP 8)

BRACE AND LEG DETAIL

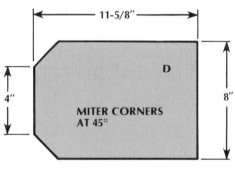

11-5/8″

D

4″

8″

MITER CORNERS AT 45°

GUSSET DETAIL

CUTTING DIAGRAM

H

A A

B B C C

D

N

M

M

F

G

F

J

L

E

K

G

3/4″ × 4′ × 8′ A-B PLYWOOD   2″ × 4″ × 6′   1″ × 10″ × 8′

LIST OF MATERIALS

(finished dimensions in inches)

A	Bench top (2)	3/4 × 22-3/4 × 46-1/4
B	Sides (2)	3/4 × 12 × 39-1/4
C	Shelves (2)	3/4 × 12 × 48
D	Gusset	3/4 × 8 × 11-5/8
E	Front facing	3/4 × 3 × 47-3/4
F	Side facing (2)	3/4 × 3 × 22-3/4
G	Upper and lower cleat strips (2)	3/4 × 2 × 48
H	Side cleat strips	3/4 × 3/4 × 19-3/4
J	Leg brace	3/4 × 3-1/2 × 27-3/4
K	Stretcher	3/4 × 3-1/2 × 36
L	Stop	3/4 × 3-1/2 × 7-5/8
M	Legs (2)	1-1/2 × 3-1/2 × 34
N	Back-up block	1-1/2 × 3-1/2 × 3
P	Bottom	1-1/2 × 8-5/8 × 48
Q	Hardboard top	1/4 × 23-1/2 × 47-3/4
R	Pegboard	1/4 × 23-3/4 × 48

Hardware

Door hinges (2)	4 × 4
Strap hinges (3)	5 × 5
Screws and nails as required	
Screw hook and eye	
Carriage bolt, washer, and wing nut	3/8 × 4
Shelf brackets (2)	

SHELTERED SWING

From *HANDS ON* July/Aug 82

On those lazy summer afternoons, you can't beat the simple enjoyment you get from this sheltered swing. With its own built-in "mini-porch," it offers protection from the sun's rays while letting in all the fresh air.

1. First, cut all parts to size according to the List of Materials.

2. Use your bandsaw or jigsaw to form the contours on the seat supports and arm rests, as well as the angle in the bottom of the back supports.

3. Assemble the five seat supports and the front and rear rails to form the rectangular base of the swing.

4. Attach seven slats, spaced at 1/4" intervals, to the rectangular base. Secure the slats with 3d galvanized nails, drilling pilot holes for each of them.

5. Secure the arm rest supports with carriage bolts, nuts, and washers. The bolts and washers also act as anchors for the swing chain.

6. Drill holes in the arm rests for the chain to pass through. Attach the arm rests to the arm rest supports with 6d galvanized nails.

7. Assemble the back of the swing and attach five slats, spaced at 2" intervals, to it. Place the final slat on the top of the back assembly to cap it.

8. Using 6d galvanized nails, attach the back assembly to the rear seat rail; drive the nails through the bottom of the back supports. Insert carriage bolts through each of the armrests at the spot where they adjoin the back supports.

9. Sand the entire swing thoroughly. Finish (if desired) with polyurethane or spar varnish.

10. The shelter assembly is made from the pressure-treated posts and beam. Bolt the rectangular frame of the roof assembly to the posts.

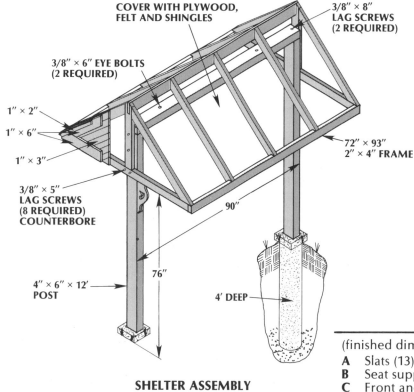

COVER WITH PLYWOOD, FELT AND SHINGLES

3/8" × 8" LAG SCREWS (2 REQUIRED)

3/8" × 6" EYE BOLTS (2 REQUIRED)

1" × 2"
1" × 6"
1" × 3"

3/8" × 5" LAG SCREWS (8 REQUIRED) COUNTERBORE

72" × 93" 2" × 4" FRAME

90"

4" × 6" × 12' POST

76"

4' DEEP

SHELTER ASSEMBLY

LIST OF MATERIALS

(finished dimensions in inches)

A	Slats (13)	1/4 × 1-3/4 × 55-1/2
B	Seat supports (5)	3/4 × 2-1/4 × 14-1/2
C	Front and rear rails (2)	3/4 × 2-1/4 × 60
D	Armrests (2)	3/4 × 2-1/4 × 17-3/4
E	Armrest supports (4)	3/4 × 2 × 8-3/4
F	Back supports (5)	3/4 × 1-1/2 × 22

11. Use a slotted 2 × 4 to extend the ridge board; this will allow the roof rafters to clear the crossbeam.
12. For roof decking, use two full sheets of exterior plywood covered with 15 lb. felt. Three-tab shingles are recommended.
13. Cover the gable ends with 3″ strips of cedar. The fascia boards should be made from 1 × 6 cedar; 1 × 2 cedar furring strips are then attached to the fascia boards to support the metal drip edge.
14. Use an 18′ length of chain to attach the swing to the shelter.

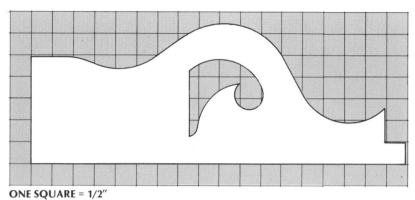

ONE SQUARE = 1/2″

DECORATIVE SCALLOP LAYOUT

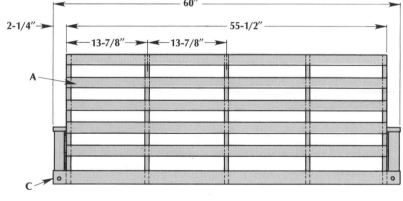

MIDDLE RAFTER LAYOUT

END RAFTER LAYOUT

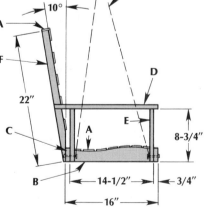

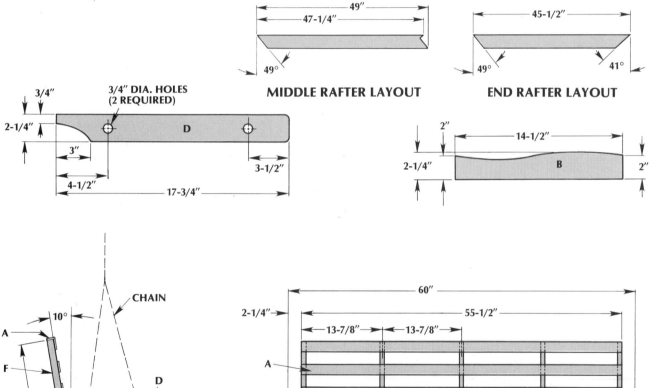

SWING LAYOUT

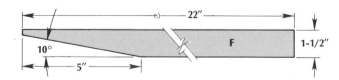

Index for Book I

Index for Book II